More Views from North Lochs

Aimsir Eachainn

More Views from North Lochs

Aimsir Eachainn

Hector Macdonald

BIRLINN

First published in 2009 by
Birlinn Limited
West Newington House
10 Newington Road
Edinburgh
EH9 1QS

www.birlinn.co.uk

ISBN: 978 1 84158 805 6

British Library Cataloguing-in-Publication Data
A catalogue record for this book is available from the British Library

Typeset by Hewer Text UK Ltd, Edinburgh
Printed and bound by CPI Cox & Wyman, Reading

CONTENTS

FOREWORD

This book contains the final selection of the columns of Aimsir Eachainn which appeared in the *West Highland Free Press*, covering the period from 1989 to 1995.

When the first instalment of 'A View From North Lochs' was published in 2007, my family found it touching that so many people bought the book, and the feedback we received was so positive that it justified printing this second book.

My sister, Fiona, and I have selected 140 columns which are set out in chronological order, and we hope readers will agree that they are well worth a second read and that the quality of my father's writing has passed the test of time.

My father always talked about 'the book', and so I know he would be very proud to have two books published now, albeit posthumously.

I am also pleased to report that we did not receive any libel suits following the first selection, and I am hopeful that this book will be equally well received.

My father was an optimistic man and I would like to open this book with an article he wrote about golf. His outlook to life was much like his outlook to this sport, and I think this article sums him up nicely.

The final Aimsir Eachainn was finished by Archie Macdonald. Hector and Archie were long-time friends and had just returned from a sailing trip together. My father loved nothing more than being out in the boat, so it was fitting that he experienced one final voyage before he died.

Iain Macdonald
July 2009

BIOGRAPHY

Hector Macdonald was born in Ranish, on the Isle of Lewis, in the winter of 1945. He shared a black-house with his parents, a brother and some cattle. His early years in this most scenic of villages were a time for forming lifelong friendships with boys like Coinneach Iain, Roddy John, Wee Alex and Johnny Walker.

In 1956 the family upgraded to Leurbost, where he found new friends such as Roddy and Calum Iain Smith. And when Hector went to school in Stornoway he met Dodo and John D., who would later become the Garrabost Historian and the Barvas Navigator.

On leaving school he boarded the good ship Weather and studied meteorology, learning his trade on the high seas of the Atlantic, where he served under men who taught him the fine art of being a civil servant. Men such as Leslie and Archie Macdonald, who, despite the general consensus, were not brothers. Other lifelong friends he made in the Met Office were Norrie Munro and Alex Macdonald.

The Seventies brought marriage to Maggie, two children and adventures in Africa with the Jacksons and the Macarthurs.

After enjoying the best parts the world had to offer, Hector returned to Leurbost and built a house on the croft with the help of tradesmen such as Karachi, Kenny the Plumber, Roddy Danny and Angus Beattie. He was glad to be back home, where he enjoyed battling wits with the likes of Murdie Siarach and the West End Tory, John Allan. If Hector needed a mechanic, he had Aonghas Beag, and when he needed a strong back, he had Angie Hogg.

He settled down and began to write for the *Stornoway Gazette* in 1979. This was the first outlet for his weekly columns before he was poached by the *West Highland Free Press*, and under the tutelage of Brian Wilson found a true home for a style of writing that could be described as thought-provoking, sometimes irreverent but nearly always funny.

A prolific reader, he enjoyed many styles of writing, from the poetry of Dylan Thomas to the adventures of Nevil Shute. But I would say he admired most the comic talents of mainstream authors such as James Thurber and Flann O'Brien and the less well known but brilliant Jaroslav Hasek and John Kennedy Toole.

He made the most of his time on earth. As well as working at the Met Office and writing, he started a business in the early Eighties: Western Isles Salmon, which he founded with Calum Macdonald. They were the first small-time independent salmon farmers in the country, and although the business was fraught, they enjoyed the highs and suffered the lows without regret. This was also a time for learning new tricks from visionaries such as Donald Taylor and Neil MacPherson.

Hector lived life to the full and he always made time for his family. Trips abroad with his wife were always an experience to remember.

Stornoway Golf Club, the Criterion Bar and Donnie Campbell Bookies were some of the many local haunts that provided many hours of entertainment and inspiration. Mention must also be made of Comhairle nan Eilean Siar, who are an unfailing source for satire.

Hector died in 1995, which was of course sad for many reasons, one of which was because he had so much more to offer us as a writer.

Iain Macdonald
July 2009

TRIUMPH OF HOPE

If there is one quality, above all others, that is essential in the golfer, it is the quality to forget. The average hacker can wipe disasters from the slate while his stockings are still wet. On the other hand, a rare good shot lodges in the memory like the imagined sunny summers of youth. The fact that I write this on the morning after the 1989 Western Isles Open illustrates this wonderful capacity to forget. Not only have yesterday's humiliations been forgotten, I fancy I can win next Saturday's competition or maybe even this coming Wednesday's. This peculiar brand of unrealistic expectation must not be confused with mere optimism. A growing boy can be optimistic about some day being 6 foot 2 with broad shoulders. This is a reasonable hope because the boy hasn't tried growing before. The average club golfer has no such excuse for his wishful thinking: he has tried before many times, perhaps as recently as the night before the 'big one', and failed miserably. Very likely on the night before, he hit 96 bad shots and 3 good ones. This irrational mind expects to recapture the good ones on the day and repeat them consistently. In his fevered brain it is not impossible that he'll come close in the best gross score despite the dismal statistic on Galloway's computer showing that he hasn't broken 80 since 1969.

On the morning of the great event he is up at the crack of dawn cleaning clubs, removing hard skin from his own heels, and has very likely eaten an extra black pudding for strength. Possibly he has treated himself to a new glove or even a new truss and a can of insect repellent so that his journey through 36 holes might be smooth and free of pain. At 08.00 our hero, having done innumerable practice swings and thus having wasted several of his good shots, presents himself on the first tee. Already he is sweating freely and breathless with anxiety. At 08.01 he is deep in the Castle jungle.

He has possibly lost his ball and is heading for at least an 8. But no, his ball is found and he spots an 18 inch wide, 120 yard tunnel to the green. Jack Nicklaus in his prime would not attempt it. Even Ballesteros would play back and settle for a possible 6, but not your 20-handicapper. Somewhere in the dim recess of his skull a voice whispers that the ball is only 1.68 inches in diameter. He squares his shoulders and lunges at the ball. When the leaves settle the gleaming new 65i is still in the same spot, only now it has settled deeper in the undergrowth. Our hero tries to smile at his partners, who have come to gloat but can only manage a sickly grin. Anxiety has momentarily given way to embarrassment. He makes what he imagines is a nonchalant swing and rattles the ball off 6 trees. The ball is now lost and your man's torment is at an end. A dreadful 12 is recorded with 35 holes to go, but there is always next year.

In the meantime something much worse has befallen the last of the threesome to tee off. He almost made the gap at the Castle. He cannot quite see the green but he still manages to cut a 5 iron round the corner and sinks a long lucky putt for a miraculous birdie three. He is no longer one of us. He is out there on his own. This could really be his day. With only one major hazard behind him, he is already indecent in his haste to reach his drive and has to be reminded from time to time that 'we' are still playing and to please mind his manners.

Round about the turn there is the customary pause and a little arithmetic is done. Our first hero has continued in the groove he found on the first and has now become a bit of a comedian. He always just comes out for the laugh. The other fellow, the guy with the birdie on the first, sits staring at his card in disbelief. His luck has continued and he sees no reason why it should not last all day. He starts to mutter quietly. 'If I can get past the Dardanelles in 6 or even 7 . . .' This is not addressed to his partners or to anyone else, for by this time no one else exists. He always knew he could do it and now, at last, this moment has come. He scrambles a 4 at the Whins with a long single putt, yet somehow thinks he was unlucky.

On the Dardanelles tee he delivers a long lecture about people who leave bunkers in a mess and he pulls his drive short and tight to the trees on the left. He is not unduly worried: he has a lot of strokes to spare. All he needs now is a longish hook. Although he has sliced incurably for 20 years, as his 22 handicap certifies, he is at this stage convinced he can make a par. (Remember 7 would have been fine.) Twenty minutes and 2 balls later this distracted and disorientated individual can be heard wondering if it was a 13 or 14. His marker is marching slowly ahead like a mourner at a funeral who realises the exact age of the deceased is not important. The man who fell at the first has now become a philosopher and makes some observation on the quality of life and how it is better to go quickly than to suffer a prolonged and painful demise.

There is at this stage only the comfort of the 19th ward to look forward to. In the space of 2 pints a remarkable transformation takes place. Beaten, broken men are quickly mended and deep despair gives way to renewed hope. Whispered, isolated snatches of conversation merge to form a general hum. Pretty soon a distinctly audible 'if only' can be heard on all sides. The healing process is now under way and although this day is lost it is already forgotten.

The day is certainly lost as the rules stand at present, but this need not always be the case. The Macleod brothers, John Neil and Ian, have long lobbied for reform in Golf Club tradition. Perhaps influenced by a boat-building father, they feel the shape and beauty of the shot is of primary importance. Many good shots are lost balls and a million ugly hacks get better results than they deserve. With this in mind they propose a trial by jury at the end of each round. The best hard luck story wins the day.

My only fear is that the present membership includes too many silver-tongued rascals like Dixie and Bronco who could more than make up for their physical disabilities with unbelievably true stories. Yet there are so many in that age group whose only hope of ever winning anything had to be through the 'jury system', for THEY have lived too long for hope to triumph over experience.

1989

FRIDAY, 27 JANUARY 1989

UNNATURAL OCCURRENCES

I try never to talk about the weather unless a fat fee is agreed in advance. What is more, I refuse to 'listen' to any talk about the weather. Weather and people's recent medical operations are two subjects I declared taboo as long ago as 1958 when I realised that my neighbours in Sleepy Hollow spoke of nothing else. Yet there are times when the strictest rule must be broken, and this is one of them.

Have you noticed the sort of weather we've been having this year? Hurricanes we've been used to since birth, but daffodils at New Year are far from natural. I told you in December the old Caithness fellow was planting some early carrots and you all laughed at him. Who's laughing now? He has them thinned and is already sorting out the Kerrs Pink seed. What is more, I can reveal that my old friend Daniel in the East End tends his sheep wearing only boxer shorts under the oilskins. But don't get excited, Alice; you're both too old now.

I'm sorry, I have no explanation for these unnaturally high temperatures, but I know a man who has. Last Sunday I ventured into the Castle Grounds for a brisk run to ease the guilt and shed the flab of seasonal self-indulgence, and who should I meet on his daily 20-mile walk but Big Dan from Shawbost. For a guy who not long ago had all four valves and the gasket replaced in his chest, he sets a lively pace (I'm pleased to say I was able to assist with the operation, but we won't talk about that). Like most men who are forced to spend their lives outdoors, he notices things we don't. You and I probably take it for granted that the shortest day of the year is the 21st of December. Well, that is no longer the case. Dan has been studying form.

He says the shortest day last year was a week earlier. Furthermore, he says, the evenings are getting noticeably brighter but the mornings are not. What do you make of that as a scientist, *ars esan*? There can be only one explanation. We've been hit and they're not telling us. It could possibly be something Reagan did before the end or it could have been a stray meteorite. I have no wish to alarm the man in the street, but we have obviously been tilted. As yet the effect has been beneficial, but how long for we can only guess. In the meantime we must take advantage and pretend it's May.

The big-time sheepmen are rubbing their subsidy forms in gleeful anticipation. Bumper crops and triplets all round are guaranteed. And the best news of all is that from now on towrists are going to do the work. The HIDB's grand plan to promote the native to tourist-attraction status (leaked to this paper two months ago) has now been officially launched. Cowan probably broke a bottle over Dr Hunter's head. My friend Big Carloway had intended to buy an expensive electric shearer, but this is no longer necessary. Although tourists cannot be expected to be fast with the shears, what does it matter as long as there are enough of them. Calum Reilly is only too willing to dress in a kilt and try to look ethnic for the Kodak Instamatics.

The Board's intention is to charge adventurous tourists about £15 per day for the privilege of being a temporary crofter. This seems to me to be far too cheap. Have you seen what the Kenyan Tourist Board charge for a look at *their* tame natives? I would think for a glimpse of our U.W.O.L. 25 quid a day would still be a snip; and if they want to cut peat with Angie Hogg, £30 and free insurance is still a bargain. As an added incentive we could offer money prizes for anyone who would last 10 minutes with him.

The scope of this scheme is limited only by our leaders' imagination. We will have no need for expensive tractors because I foresee a thousand city dwellers desperate to carry our peats home in creels while at the same time knitting a bobbin stocking. Hoteliers in Majorca are worried, and no wonder.

Do you have ten acres with which you can take advantage of our better weather and free labour? If you have and were planning to plant asparagus or something equally exotic, well, forget it. I have a much better idea. Forget the tourists and get in touch with the Ministry of Agriculture. From them you will get several hundred pounds an acre for taking it out of production. For doing nothing, do you hear? What do you think of that? Not a lot, I hear you grumble, because only half of it is arable and the other half is a bog. Don't worry, because this is where you really score. At this stage you approach Nature Conservancy and say you had planned to plant some trees when you saw three lapwings and a corncrake nest.

What this patch might be worth is anybody's guess. I've been trying to get a figure out of Stewart Angus but he's a firm's man. Still, we have Lord Thurso's case as a precedent. Don't settle for anything less than ten grand.

It wouldn't be right to say goodbye after a week of unnatural occurrences without mention of British Airways and their recent excellent timekeeping. Yet some lout had the audacity to complain to me that they only arrive on time because they had to leave the papers in Glasgow. This seems to me the best idea they ever had. If that is what it takes to be punctual, long may they leave their cargo of lies and obscene pictures of bathing royalty behind. Better still, let them drop their vanload of *Sunday Times* and *News of the World* in the Minch. I have already seen my colleague Leslie's mind deteriorate beyond repair through reading Murdoch's lewd and libidinous parcels of filth. More strength to your turbo, BA; but surely you could delay two minutes for the *Observer* so we can learn from Ascherson what might be happening on the outside.

FRIDAY, 17 FEBRUARY 1989

Bhiodh iad ag ràdha uaireigin gun robh am facal faisg air balaich an Taobh Deas. Tha a h-uile duine tha thall an sin a' smaoineachadh g' eil iad càirdeach do dh'Ailean Sheonaidh. Ach chan eil balaich an Taobh

Tuath cho slac. Thachair mi ri fear òg a bhuineas dhomh anns a' Chrit an latha roimhe – mac Mhurdinag Dhòmhnaill Fhionnlaigh. 'Càil a' dol thall?' ars esan. (Tha e a' fuireach an Steòrnabhagh, 's cha bhi e a' fàgail a' mhetropolis tric.)

'Cha chuala mi dad,' arsa mise, a' feuchainn ri bhith smart. 'Cha chreid mi gun bhàsaich duine a bhuineas dhuinn.'

''S math sin,' ars esan, ''s mo chòt' aig na cleaners.' Fuirich thusa, tà.

Cò thachair rium an uair sin ach 'Chuck', agus gu nàdarrach thuig mi gun bhàsaich duine a bhuineadh dhomh agus a bha a' coimhead an ìre mhath sunndach fhathast, ach abair call. Ma bha aon duine eile ann an Alba a bu chòir a bhith air feum a dhèanamh, 's e siud e. Bha e cruaidh, bha e luath 's bha e làidir, 's bha cic aige mar doncaidh, ach chaidh an tàlant sìos pìoban an taigh-mhùin anns na Highlander's. Cha chan mise a' chòrr.

Cha robh mi ann nuair a thàinig Mairead Ros timcheall còrnair Chromwell Street. Cnap mòr airgid aice na dòrn, a' faighneachd an dèanainn film còmh' rithe. Cha bhi cus pàighidh ann, ars ise, ach expenses gu leòr. Thèid sinn dhan àite as fheàrr leat air aghaidh na talmhainn agus dèan beagan còmhraidh ris a' chamara. Well, sure, no bother, arsa mise, dè mu dheidhinn nan Seychelles? Tha eagal orm nach ruigeadh an sporan aic' air an Equator, agus mar sin thàinig oirnn seatlaigeadh air Ràthairnis.

Tha mi a' dol a shealltainn dhi na creig air am biodh mo sheanmhair Prabag, aig an robh a' bhuisneachd, a' creagach airson nam bodach ruadha air an robh sinn beò. Bha mi gu math òg aig an àm, is chan eil mo chuimhne ach meadhanach, ach bha an Geaman ag innse dhomh gum biodh Prabag a' cur na dàrna cois tarsainn air an tèile ceithir turais agus a' tilgeadh còig smugaidean mus leigeadh i dubhan dhan an t-sàl. Chan eil fhios am bu chòir dhomh tobair na buisneachd a shealltainn do Mhairead ('s am pàigheadh cho bochd), ach, what the hell, tha mi faighinn plug airson na Nobhail. 'S ann an Sloc nam Marbh a tha an epic a' fosgladh. Balach beag, gun fhios aige cò athair. Tha Ràthairnis agus làithean m' òige air m' inntinn bho chionn ghoirid agus tha e a' dèanamh dragh dhomh. Chen eil càil a chuimhn' agam dè dh'ith mi anns a' mhadainn, ach tha cuimhn' agam de thuirt Bolaidh ri Iain

Mhurchaidh air feasgar Dimàirt ann an 1949. Chuala mi mu dheidhinn nan 'lucid moments' a tha seo faisg air an deireadh, agus 's fheàrr dhomh sgrìobhadh mus ring am bell.

Bha Coinneach ag innse dhomh a-raoir gun robh athair, aig 'eil cuimhn' air Prabag, a-staigh aige bho chionn ghoirid. Chan eil aig a' bhodach ach black and white agus cha robh e air mòran colour fhaicinn. Cò a nochd ach M Thatcher an aodach dubh. 'O, Dhia, ' ars esan, 'cuin a bhàsaich an duin aice?'

I'm sorry, Malky, there are some things that have to be said in English. Our children's Higher Art teacher, Mr Paterson, says they have a communication problem. Personally, I though Melissa and Fiona's problem was stopping the flow of nonsense, but your man is right. He says that island girls, and presumably boys, are too reticent. They do not push themselves and they are generally too quiet. Whatever they shout in Keose and Leurbost they tend to whisper when they reach Glasgow or Edinburgh. This is nothing new but we should be thankful for people like Mr Paterson who dare to say what must be said. I wouldn't mind betting that even Coinneach Mòr himself didn't say much during his first year at university.

When I came down from Fidigarry meself, a full six months passed before I spoke to anyone in Leurbost – and even then it was the girl next door, Alice. I didn't actually speak: I sent her a love note. Unfortunately I spelled *gaol* (love) *goal* and she thought I was talking about the night Bayble beat us 22-nil. Because of this lamentable breakdown in communication Ewen was able to step in and steal her from me.

At the age of 17 I went to London, and, by God, could they communicate. For two weeks I gazed the rustic gaze and wondered at their wonderfulness but in the third week I twigged. It was all gob. Unluckily, for people who have a low bullshit tolerance, gob makes the world go round, so your man Paterson is right. OK, Mairi, Melissa and Fiona, pay attention and listen to your teachers.

Did I ever tell you that Màiri Sìne from South Dell has the sweetest voice in the Highlands? After years of being in love with the Barvas

Navigator's wife I fell out of it the other night when Màiri sang. Nobody now figures in my fantasies except Màiri Thormoid. The psychoanalysts I consulted at great cost will remember that Alice's Aunt was called Màiri Thormoid. The great clarity we talked about earlier was perhaps not so clear after all. Did I love Alice or Màiri's scones? I guess we will only discover these things in The Novel, a ghràidh.

FRIDAY, 24 FEBRUARY 1989

Captain Dewar of Caledonian MacBrayne seems a modest man. He probably doesn't seek gongs or awards; nevertheless, I have put his name forward for some form of recognition. Perhaps a humble MBE or the Freedom of Loch Broom would be acceptable to him.

When the *Suilven* sailed from Stornoway on the afternoon of Monday 13th February I knew we were in the eye of the storm (even harder to sail through than the eye of a needle). There was an uneasy quiet on the waters and you could sense the tall trees that shelter the harbour bracing themselves for a north-westerly. Perhaps one or two old hands noticed the strange behaviour of seals and fulmars in the outer harbour but the majority were ignorant of the signs, and optimistic. They naturally thought the worst was over and they couldn't be expected to know better: most of them were fish farmers on their way to the Mod in Edinburgh and there is hardly anyone who knows less about sea and weather than a fish farmer, unless perhaps a pig farmer.

Several of the passengers (Harris types) had been aboard the *Hebridean Isles* when she made an abortive attempt to cross the Minch earlier in the day. They were clearly shaken but trying to hide it behind nervous laughter. Gordon MacKay looked very white and had lost his hair. Chris Bayly had a distant gleam in his eye that betrayed a longing for his old croft in Tasmania, and he had gone ominously quiet. Murdo MacKay, as you would expect from a man with an Achmore background, was totally oblivious to the power and danger of the ocean. Lewis MacLeod is nowadays so taken up with parenthood and nappy changing that he doesn't notice anything much. Jerry Luty flew as always.

With this motley crew aboard I was naturally uneasy. All too obvious, although I tried not to alarm the wife, there was not one soul on the ship I could rely on in an emergency – not even Calum Russell. Cromarty was helping the cook make 'soup of the day' (I can recommend it – very easy to bring up).

Fortunately the Barvas Navigator happened to be at home and I was able to check the previous evening that this temporary relief skipper, Dewar, was seaworthy. 'He's OK,' said the Navigator, a man of few words. And, sure enough, he was OK. Maggie discreetly inspected the man and declared herself satisfied. 'He has a calm, mature West Highland look about him,' she said. 'I don't think you will need to go up on the bridge this time.' Although some cynics will misunderstand her advice, I trust her judgement, so I went and lay down in a lifeboat.

We made good time to the Summer Isles, in the lull, but unluckily the depression was travelling faster than the ferry. This, I hasten to add, was not Captain Dewar's fault: it was the fault of CalMac's hierarchy who think we still aren't over the '74 fuel crisis. The storm caught up with us halfway down Loch Broom. At that moment I was daydreaming . . . looking at the back end of Tanera Mor and wondering how 11 people could be worth three million pounds. Just as we got in among the Bulgarian klondykers, the storm became a hurricane. There is a little dip in towards the pier which in normal circumstances (under 70 knots) affords a bit of shelter. But by the time we drew level, as the Ullapool lights went out, the only thing left standing on the pier was the sturdy figure of Sandy Boots.

I have no doubt, as someone remarked, that under the command of certain skippers you and I know well we would have disembarked at the Garve Hotel. Yet this man Dewar somehow manoeuvered his way round several sheltering pursers and came to rest in the normal position against the pier. Perhaps an MBE is not enough.

*　　*　　*

If you think the Minch is dangerous, it is nothing compared to the mainland where the foolish habit of planting trees that grow to 80ft is permitted. Thank goodness 'we' are not allowed to plant trees that grow taller than a landlord. Two hours after docking I stopped to fill the radiator at Aultguish Inn, and I feel I can safely say that were it not for an adequate ballast in the form of one's wife, one wouldn't be here today.

But the danger of the Highlands is nothing compared to the risks you have to run in Edinburgh if you drive that devilish contraption, the motor car. The people of Edinburgh drive normally until they come to a roundabout, then they go mad. It reminded me a little of old Singapore before they had rules and regulations. Try to avoid Edinburgh. It is quite clearly suitable only for Edinburgowegians or whatever you call them.

Whoever chose Edinburgh for the Mod (perhaps the Commissioners?) should be shot. Fish farmers, or at least those who know anything about the actual practice, are Hebrideans, Orcadians, Shetlanders and even Skyemen. These people don't want to go to Edinburgh because Edinburgh is not ready for them. Edinburgh folk are fine in their own way, but they seem to think it is normal to go to bed around midnight. At midnight the men of Harris hadn't even shaved for their night out. And at one o'clock in the morning they hadn't found the main body of delegates. 'We came across some kind of cultural barrier,' said Gordon. 'Just as well,' said Maggie. 'I saw only two men, two gentlemen, I wouldn't be ashamed to be seen with after 11pm – Angus Graham and David Windmill of McConnells.'

Another disadvantage with such spaced out hotels is that travelling time gives rumours time to grow faster and wilder than they do in the Highlands. On Tuesday morning in Leith tremendous damage had been done to all farms in the north-west. By the time you reached Corstorphine Road every cage in Lewis was adrift in the Minch. 'Perhaps we'd better go home,' *arsa mise*. 'What could you do anyway?' says Calum. Quite right, too. But let's get the show back to Inverness.

*   *   *

Now on the way back . . . Let's just say we wouldn't have got back at all but for Captain Angus 'Texi' MacLeod. But that is another story.

FRIDAY, 24 MARCH 1989

Every so often, when men like the Barvas Navigator come home with tales from Arabia, I get the urge to travel. Unfortunately, as so often happens after Cheltenham, my personal circumstances are what the gentler classes call reduced. Nevertheless, I resolved that by hook or by crook I would take some time off to broaden my horizons (and, who knows, maybe my mind as well).

In one day I travelled to Harris and Ness. How about that? To Harris first, to scrutinise a wee company called Hebrides Harvest in which I have a modest stake. Although I was far from ready for such a journey, with my back, the rewards more than compensated for my discomfort.

My first reward was to be greeted in a most friendly and courteous manner when I had expected hostility. You see, we in Lewis have been taught to be wary when crossing the Clisham. To add to my fears, half the members attending the meeting were from the Southern Isles. You wouldn't believe how they've come on since we saved them from Inverness and the Dochfours.

I think now I begin to understand why our councillors like to attend so many meetings in the South, and why they're determined to prolong them till the end.

Although money was discussed and other matters of serious and distasteful nature, the atmosphere was one of enthusiasm and jocularity. An old colleague of mine had long ago observed that our neighbours down South laughed more than we did; but then, I thought, what else can they do. Until recently I had only ever attended meetings in Lewis where these tend to be of a prayerful nature. Hence our surprise when we land in a gathering with an air of merriment.

By the way, I've noticed in recent months that all business in Lewis is approached prayerfully. The word is everywhere, and I'm not sure this is right. There is something inherently selfish about a 'prayerful group'. When the Supreme Architect of the Universe is busy elsewhere with major catastrophes, is there not something narrow in your approaching your AGM – whether you're a butcher or a multinational – prayerfully? Why should He have time for your greedy little demands. I'm not sure it's not blasphemous.

But to get back to Harris, where so many interesting things are happening. I am now convinced that more organisations should make their headquarters there (quite apart from that rare and precious phenomenon, David Cameron). If I have any complaint with David, it is that he is over-friendly with the hired help. But I cannot help that, being of the old school.

Anyway, to my astonishment I discovered we were doing very well, and I was due a huge dividend that more than makes up for Cheltenham. In addition to this bonanza, just when you thought you couldn't take much more, we were led to a table that creaked under the weight of the finest fare, including smoked salmon from Carloway. This was followed by cormorant casserole – although, naturally, John Murdo cannot advertise it as such on the menu, ever-mindful of 'Maggie's Greening'.

I pocketed the swag and headed for the Clisham and, do you know what I'm going to tell you, my back felt fine. My only fear is that I will pay dearly for all this good fortune on the other side. Already, on this side, I feel I am being punished, with applications from Skyemen to join HH. Personally, I will use my vote to exclude the rascals. I would much rather have the Mull company in with us than 'them ones'. Wouldn't be surprised if Tommy Mackenzie and Somhairle Hallaig are involved. Dreamers we can do without when we're trying to make money.

Somewhat elated and brim-full of fine feeling for my fellow man, I rounded up what I could of Seumas Cleite and headed for Ness (Captain Kelso was having a short break in Inverness). It was proposed, seconded and passed unanimously that Raymond the Deliberator should drive. RJ Smith did the navigating. We figured if Roddy got the choir to Killarney and back he could get us to Ness.

We started from the Golf Club, and we were making good progress for the first stretch of the journey. Confidence in Raymond was high until we got to the Roundabout at Manor. On the way through Laxdale all the evening traffic overtook us, including Calum Crotchy on his bicycle. Directions from our navigator were few and confusing, possibly because of his position crouched down on the floor. I have no doubts about Chris Corden, in that way, but I still have the marks of his fingers just above my left knee.

We reached Eoropie and unluckily passed it, which meant we had to turn the car around. Chris had asked out at South Dell so he could stretch his legs, and by the time we found the Social Club he had dealt the first hand.

Now if you need your horizons broadened Eoropie is the place. Even in the dark you can almost see America. The result of our match with Rona is, of course, of no interest to readers of this paper, but it could have been better for us. Chris and I thought we were doing well (remember, we were sitting in the back of the car), but the journey must have taken too much out of the driver and navigator. Still, the venue was much more civilised than Stornoway, with ladies bringing delicacies to table at regular intervals. The guga vol-au-vent was superb. I suppose we had no chance with a very noisy home support, up in the rafters, cheered no doubt by the Rev. Angus. Remind me to have second thoughts about that earlier 'by the way'.

Chris drove home, and I must admit it was remarkably stress-free. These Callanish Primrose Pills have a wonderfully soothing effect on the nerves. With a pocketful of those I would enter a Harris car rally with Raymond the Deliberator.

FRIDAY, 31 MARCH 1989

Who should drop in on me unannounced yesterday but Cunninghame North and his Lady. Like all couples who are blessed with issue late in life, they are totally obsessed with the bairn. Wee Highland Mary herself seems fine and healthy, considering – although, as you would expect, a little hyperactive. I had hoped to learn a bit about what is happening in Parliament but all I got was 'Who do you think she's like?', never mind the dumping of nuclear waste.

By sheer coincidence who should roll through my door at the same time but DHM MacIver, who looks as if he too is expecting something. My goodness, *arsa mise*, I'd heard you were dead. Far from it, *ars esan*, I'm firing well on three cylinders. My medical men have given me another few years without as much as a rebore, he said; will you vote for me?

And I thought he'd arrived to spread manure as he used to, in the old days, at this time of year. Well, why not, as he is the only man who has bothered to ask so far. He quickly outlined his plans for the education department and the so-called legal department, and I believe he's got some good ideas. DHM knows that if you ask for two hundred thousand you've no chance but if you ask for ten million you are taken seriously. The dilapidated Nicolson Institute is probably now beyond repair, so it is maybe best to bulldoze it and extend some of the rural schools.

DHM had started canvassing in Ranish, Crossbost and Grimshader before he descended on Leurbost. This leaving of the important places till last is probably a good plan of attack – collar the boys with the money first and then use the loot to campaign in the main centre of population. I would have guessed he'd been to Ranish because when I visited some folk there on Saturday night they were talking all sorts of nationalistic nonsense. Men who used to have some sense, like Coinneach Iain and William McIlvanney, have succumbed to sentimentality and wishful thinking. Either that or they've been brainwashed by DHM, unless it's the drink. The dangers of nationalism are too many to do a 'by the way' here, but the most obvious one – the building of barriers when we should be trying to knock them down – should be enough.

Still, at local government level perhaps they cannot do too much damage (what does a little war between Leurbost and Shawbost matter?). So I think I'll take a chance on your man for North Lochs Councillor.

Can we, I wonder, sue the council as a parish and distribute the certain winnings among the poor in the congregation? That is only one of the many schemes DHM has in mind.

By the way, there is a new kind of nationalism developing in Scotland that is almost understandable. It is a kind of defensive philosophy to counteract a vicious South-East of England Nazism. But this is not a disease we can contain within any traditional border. It is more of a state of mind that doesn't belong to any one region although it tends to be associated with the South-East at this moment (in time). Man, they say, is naturally greedy, so we should build a social system that caters for greed and encourages it. Of course we are greedy – and woman, too – which is why we must oppose their system against natural inclination. Our grand scheme will always be less efficient economically, but that doesn't matter; it is better than slavery. Our radicalism will never descend to anarchy. We in the Lodge will make sure of that.

I am often asked by curious non-members why I, as a medical man, felt the need to join. 'You are already,' they say, 'wealthy beyond the dreams of avarice. Why do you feel you must belong to a gang of grown-up Boy Scouts?' To be perfectly honest, I was very young at the time. The Craft, in Scotland, smacked of socialism and was practised largely by the working man. I had sentimental notions of his nobility then.

Some *are* noble, of course. So are some of the nobility. The Duke of Kent, the Metropolitan Police Chief, greasers in the James Watt Dock and myself. What a laugh! But there I was in the noose when I was too young and innocent to realise what they were up to. Still, it does seem to work. Better to be under the control of the ancient stupid nobility than modern Thatcherites.

So many invitations these days! The strangest of all is the one from the Director of Education and Dòmhnall Lìsidh to attend the next meeting of their committee. Why it? Are they planning to discuss something so important that they need an observer? Could it possibly be the meeting at which they hope to appoint some missionary as Rector? Or are they planning to hang me from a bridge and tear my tongue out? Who knows.

But to get back to this election . . . I hear rumours of Aonghas Beag, Briggs and someone called Russell being prepared to take the big man on, but so far these are only rumours. My only fear for DHM is that he may have been seen in the company of Cunninghame North last Saturday. Will they now believe DHM is a dangerous leftist?

Of much more interest than the contest for a seat on the Council is the battle for the Scottish Cup. I happened to overhear a gang of Leurbost youths planning a trip to the final. They think it is certain to be a Celtic-Rangers affair again. But they don't know what I know.

It grieves me, but Celtic will probably beat the Hibs, who are now sailing under the Panamanian flag in order to save money. But the outcome of the Rangers v St Johnstone clash is far from certain. Remember this match is being played on the Pope's own ground. Not only do I know of plans to plough the field a little, I also hear that a bunch of wealthy businessmen – including Souness's ex-father in law – have plans to take the entire St Johnstone team to Lourdes.

FRIDAY, 14 APRIL 1989

I've often envied Romans, Anglicans and Russian Orthodox Christians their Lent. Muslims have their Ramadan and Jews do so much fasting and feasting one cannot keep track. But see us, we have nothing. For 365 days we gorge ourselves with food and drink until you wonder why we don't burst.

What I should have said was 'why more of us don't burst'. As only we doctors know, a lot of us do burst, in one way or another, and it's all down to our continuous guzzling of all that is rich and poisonous. Now, if we observed that healthy and civilised period of restraint and penitence called Lent, if nothing else it would bring New Year celebrations to an end. Forty days of fasting at this time would set the liver up nicely for the Glasgow Fair. The benefits of Lent could even last until October and the Mod. Not us, though. Man, that John Knox was one strict fella.

The odd thing is that, although we have no Ash Wednesday, no

Ramadan and no Easter, we've taken a great liking to Christmas. Johnny Knox wouldn't like that, but we don't care. We wouldn't care if Johnny and Mr Calvin himself were alive right now and preaching against Christmas, and I'll tell you why. At Christmas we have yet another opportunity to slacken the belt and worship at the trough. That is the sort of religious holiday we like.

And the result of our strange form of worship? Go on, tell me. Yes, what else but pressure – hypertension, as we call it in the surgery and the electronic workshop. If I could explain so my patients in Aignish will understand . . .

Imagine the front tyre of your bicycle has a bald patch and the inner tube is threatening to bulge through. The last thing you want to do is pump more air into the tyre. Well, the same thing applies to tubes that carry the blood through your corp, only instead of air think of duff and Guinness. As for marag, whisky and Golden Virginia, I can only compare that lethal mixture with giving the big girl next door a crossbar with the bad tyre – out comes the inner tube, and 'bang', you're dead.

I could show you letters from some old boys and some not so old who are too far gone to walk to the surgery (but I won't, of course, because that would be unethical). What they want basically is a drug to reduce the pressure so they can carry on with the pleasures of the table. Far better, I tell them, to cut down on the black pudding for breakfast and make do with three or four spuds with the salt mackerel. But what's the use. Look at this one from Crossbost:

> *Dear Dr Eachainn,*
>
> *I noticed recently when I try to bend down to tie my bootlaces I get black spots in front of my eyes and sometimes everything goes black. I find this problem is even worse when I get up for a snack in the middle of the night. Can you do anything? Sincerely, DMH (address withheld for the wife's sake)*

Dear DMH,

Yes, I certainly can (*you see, I never liked this fellow*). Either get your wife to tie your bootlaces or take some bread and cheese to bed with you.

Your caring doctor, E.

And another one from a concerned wife:

Dear Dr E,

I don't like the colour of my husband, especially late on Saturday night. I can see his face from here when he comes off the bus, even when there is no moon. Do you think this has anything to do with all the salt mutton he eats?

Mrs X.

Dear Mrs X,

You could be right. The salt mutton would make him very thirsty. Has he ever tried drinking water on its own? If he finds he cannot stomach neat water, perhaps you should cut out the salt mutton. Either that or apply a thick coat of make-up to his face so he doesn't glow in the dark.

Your compassionate doctor.

Excuse me, there's the phone ... Sorry about that. I thought it was another patient, but it was only Malky. He tells me the Arts Council have offered him so much money he cannot see how he can spend it all this year.

He says he has an application from Donald John MacSween for a Gaelic elephant for his Gaelic Circus and he wants my opinion. Well, *arsa mise*, what a fine idea. Not only would the brute be a great boost for the circus (and certainly a lot safer than a one-wheeled cycle), think what he could do for the crofts in Point. All that Gaelic manure might even attract an additional grant from our own and the Irish DAFS.

But never mind your problems, what about mine and the lack of Lent. He promises he'll see what he can do about having a special Gaelic Lent that is not quite so strict or so long to begin with. Amazing man. and he's not even a doctor.

FRIDAY, 12 MAY 1989

Somehow I feel I've been sold a retriever in a poke. The last owner saw me coming and obviously sussed at once that here was a man more at home among sheep and sheepdogs than with pedigree gun dogs. Aye, right enaff, we were in Inverness – the Capital of the Highlands, the Venice of the North, where they speak the best Italian in the Warrld. But we're a long way from home, so I'd better begin at the beginning (where else).

For some time now I've felt kind of left out of things when my colleagues talk about their dogs. JR has his Shetland Collie, Gordon naturally sports a Corgi and others have flirted briefly with 'Labs'. The Ranish crowd made a pile out of breeding Labs a few years ago but IDP refused grant aid, so that was that. Anyway, as I said, I couldn't join in their conversations, which is disconcerting for someone who usually not only has an opinion but also likes to have the final word.

So, in the guise of one concerned for the welfare of elderly hospitalised in-laws, I accompanied herself to Inverness to see what specimens of canine nobility were for sale in the *Courier*.

I need hardly remind any of you, except those doing O-Level Geography in a couple of days' time, that to get from here to there – unless you've won the pools and can afford British Airways – there is no getting out of my *Suilven*. Unless you're my wife, who luckily happens to look a bit like Ossian's wife, and her husband has more power than the original Celtic hero (although he's still scared to meet me and the West End Tory on the Grimshader Moor for a couple of rounds).

Co-dhiù, the new *Suilven* was fine but for this bearded vandal who appeared at 6am, masquerading as one of the ship's officers, and switched on the television. We wouldn't have minded the news, although some of us were trying to sleep, but a violent American video nasty at full volume is another matter. The horde of holidaying primary children loved it, but I'm sure it didn't help poor Norrie Macgregor on his way to represent Stornoway in a sporting event in Elgin.

Please don't misunderstand, I hate to complain. The food is now excellent and I understand Roddy the Cook intends to serve, to the passengers, some of the delicious small summer salmon hitherto reserved for the crew. I cannot remember now if it was coming or going the Editor of the Greysheet nearly bought me a drink or if it was the other way about, or, indeed . . . *(Stop that at once – Ed.)*

OK, sure, you know how easily I am influenced and get carried away. Back to the dogs. But it wasn't just the dogs. The old Da-in-Law was recovering from surgery in Raigmore, and you know how these old fellows don't trust strange doctors. They like to have familiar medicinemen about them, especially medicinemen who know a bit about the law. *I* was not the one who brought up the distasteful subject of 'the will' (although it cheered him up) – it was he. We laughed a little, though, reminiscing about the old guy in Loch a' Ghainmhich, Pegleg, who came in very handy for planting potatoes. *He* laughed even more when I told him I was taking home with me an English Springer Spaniel. If my new puppy can make a man laugh, straight out of the theatre, then it must be worth something. I didn't confess I'd actually *paid* for a dog that wasn't a Collie: he might have fallen out of bed.

Now, I am not a man who rushes into a business deal before I've spoken to a consultant, and the best consultant is always the one who has been bruised and scarred by early mistakes and yet has survived. Naturally I called on the Garrabost Historian. He himself is the proud owner of a fine Labrador. He is also, now, the hoarder of one of the best malt libraries in the North. Like most men, he gets meaner and more conservative with each passing spring. He keeps a bottle of Crawfords for people like me, but when he produces the malts he has a special glass not much bigger than a Drambuie glass, and it has a lid – like a mini-teapot – to prevent evaporation. Yet by the time we had broached the peaty Islay clay jars he had identified some Collie in his Labrador. Should dogs keep men in towns, *arsa cuideigin*.

This obsession with Collies, if analysed, is essentially Calvinist and Tory. Dogs must pay their way, earn their keep, make a profit for their masters or be starved. This message is so ingrained in our souls that urbanised prisoners like my friend the Historian are so tormented by the guilt of owning something useless that after a sniff of Laphroaig they could see a Collie in a half-sheared Poodle.

In Ullapool I met, once again, Sandy Boots, an authority on dogs. He assures me that the best instinct in the Springer Spaniel is his fierce determination to drag the kill home with him, be it pheasant or sheep. I hope he's kidding about the sheep part.

Many years ago I had a Lassie-type Collie in the bush. I don't know who trained her originally because I inherited her fully grown, but he was either a Boer or a Scottish Colonial. Her idea of exercise, and Collies need 'work', was a distant African with a bag of maize on her head. A drop of blood cost little but each bag of maize cost a quid. Very quickly they learned that the profitable route home was in sight of Lassie, and was well worth a scratch: the spilt bag was not all lost.

A sheep at the going rate is not worth a lot, and certainly not as much as a bag of mealies, but no one can convince the shepherd of this. This is why I hope Sandy was pulling my leg. A retriever, a gun dog, is what a Springer Spaniel is supposed to be, for goodness's sake. 'Go get one of Dolly's hens,' I shouted. But he just started playing a game with one of them – who could pull out the daffodils – and he won. But he's only 10 weeks old.

To set my mind at rest I took the beast down for Daniel's inspection, and only Calum Iain in Oban can fully appreciate how high I had climbed the consultancy ladder in this case. Daniel took one look at the poor dog; he coughed and I think he spat, but I don't think he deigned to pass comment. My own old fellow just laughed and said something about funny ears, but you wait till I bring home the prizes from the Carloway Show.

FRIDAY, 26 MAY 1989

Where were you and what were you doing on the Sunday the Ferry sailed, we will be asking each other in years to come. And of course nobody, or very few, will remember; because, as a news item, it falls some way short of the day Kennedy was gunned down.

Somewhere on the serious pages of this paper Torcuil has what he thinks is the quote of the week, from a *Sun* reporter (who else). I tried to buy it off him but the zip on my purse is jammed. Never mind, I have a good wan from Rusty, my man in Aberdeen. He has the happy knack of being 'on the spot'. Remember, he discovered Le Comte, and he is invariably within earshot when some yaw-yaw is ga fhosgladh fhèin a-mach in the Highlands. Had Rusty not wasted his time writing nonsense and acting he would have been a top investigative journalist or a minister. But there you go.

Anyway, he just happened to come on the scene when a certain cameraman was getting the bum's rush from Balmoral. At the same moment a big Grampian polis was bearing down on the unfortunate Cameraperson. 'What the ****ing ****! do you think you're doing?' demanded Her Majesty's guardian. 'Just taking some shots for Sky Television, sir.' 'Well, get your arse into that car and head back for Portree this meenit.'

We'll get back to thugs in uniform in a minute, but first pause to consider why the arch-republican Murdoch should want some footage of Her Serene Highness's summer bothy. It wouldn't surprise me in the least to learn he has plans for the first woman President of England.

Talking of England and the English, why should we, in Scotland, be subjected to Scottish football on television when we could watch the English Cup Final without the aid of satellites? Answer me that one, Jimmy. For two pins I would buy one of these dishes they're talking about but I'm afraid, instead of football, I might see an even more sophisticated and sadistic expression of violence. Listen, if I want to see blood I'll go to the actual football ground.

Our young fellow went to Hampden for his first experience of war and the Ma was naturally worried. I reminded her that many of his ancestors rushed back from Argentina in 1915, at the age of 16, to fight in the French trenches. 'But they were fighting Germans,' says she, 'no' Huns.' Her Partick upbringing, you see. 'This is a valuable experience for the lad,' I said, with the calm detachment of one who had seen experience in the old Mac's Bar on a Saturday night.

I suppose, secretly, I had expected Rangers to win, and that their animal following might be somewhat appeased. Yet once again, and I say this as one who is totally impartial, flair and adventurous play overcame brutality. This was unfortunate for the handful of Celtic fans who made the long journey from Stornoway.

The police made a fine job of bus routing on the way to Hampden but after the game some of them had lost enthusiasm for the task, or perhaps, if we give them the benefit of the doubt, they made some mistakes.

After a brief argument with the law, the Stornoway Celtic Bus driver reluctantly agreed to veer through Bridgeton, where a horde of Rangers supporters had been tidying the streets – you know, gathering bricks and stones. There is no way of knowing if these supporters are to be numbered in the recently-formed branch of the Rangers Young Conservatives, but it wouldn't surprise me, following recent trends among wealthy English lager-louts. What I do know for certain is that their retarded behaviour has little to do with football, religion or conservation of ancient modes.

So began our young fellow's most important 'O'-Grade to date. He'll take some time to forget the fanatical face of the hooligan who stared at him mindlessly before flinging the bottle at the bus window. Luckily there were no serious injuries, maybe because the driver sensibly decided to ignore red lights.

Ironically, by the time the bus came under fire, there were only Celtic colours on board. On the way down some Rangers supporters had hitched a lift. This strange mixture of passengers must have caused some consternation in the ranks of the Glasgow Polis, who are, or were, in the main, not long on imagination – although I'll bet they've heard of Sky(e) Television.

Our ambassadors were, naturally, segregated on arrival because each tribe has its own territory on the terracing. This seems a big mistake. They will naturally form gangs (here we go again), and the bigger the better. I would force them to mix, even at the risk of a little fisticuffs. If the guy on each side of you is a 'Hun' and the guy on each side of them is a 'Gael', you might feel a little vulnerable, and you could learn some new songs – quietly. This is where the Lewis busload could have done its bit to bring enlightenment to the unfortunate denizens of the tenements. Perhaps it is too late. Our earlier missionaries who went down there to stay quickly adapted to the jungle, learned city tribalism and often exceeded the indigenous population in bigotry.

So, what is new? Who is to blame? Have we not been here one hundred times before? The Celtic/Rangers divide was inspired and fuelled by religious and political leaders. Some political influence remains, but since the demise of old-fashioned religion it is merely a peg to hang the jacket on when a man needs a fight. Ban the game and they'll only start in the golf clubs where they have access to lethal weapons. What I cannot understand ... Well, not entirely ... I can see ... How shall I put it. I appreciate how *they* might behave like psychopaths, for they know not better; but we, for goodness's sake ... we are *Protestants*.

FRIDAY, 23 JUNE 1989

FOOTBALL AGUS GOLF AGUS CAJUN MUSIC

Football is really my game. I only play golf because Lochs don't use a left-half any more and I cannot cope with this modern nonsense about sweepers and strikers. Difficult enough to keep your one good eye on the ball (in both games) without having to think about high-tech stuff like tactics. But tactical psychology is the stuff of modern sport, so I guess we have to adapt or die. Look at Dixie there.

The main weapon in his psychological destruction of opponents has for years now been his wife's washing machine. We all know the machine should have been scrapped in the Sixties. It destroys his starched collars and cummerbunds and it has chewed half of Mattie's whalebone corsets, yet your man will not part with it. It serves his devious purpose.

Every Saturday Robbie Macrae and I – both of us highly-trained athletes – peak in the early afternoon. We are coiled and ready to spring about one o'clock or thereabouts. Thereabouts is when Dixie phones to say he has to fix the washing machine. We know it's a con, *he* knows we know it's a con and Mattie has probably already done the washing in Loch Crunnabhat to save money, but still we fall for it. He keeps us waiting every time until he's certain our mental preparation is ruined. When he finally appears at a brisk trot he often says: 'Hurry up, there is not a moment to be lost; I have to be back before the machine breaks down.' He has us destroyed before we reach the halfway house.

Robbie had the notion that we should take a collection in the village for a new washing machine, but it probably wouldn't meet the other fellow's specification. Anyway, he has a new ploy. If things are not going his way – i.e. if he misses a 20-foot putt – he has 'the ferry to meet'. This 'ferry chant' can start as early as 5 o'clock, because his resources don't stretch to a watch. It is not beneath him to ask for the time as you draw your weapon back – provided his own car is safely parked – on the dangerous last avenue where many a windscreen has been lost to an anxious hook. If I had my way, and I know others agree, I would have him banned until he starts going to church.

After an early summer season of Dixie's immoral golf I was pleased to accept a challenge from the visiting Cunninghame North. You probably know the type – 'Mum's politics wouldn't allow her to send me to a public school, so she spent the money on my golf pro. I haven't played since I was a deprived child in Dunoon. Anyway, golf is a working man's game in Ayshire.'

The bet was not extravagant – a bottle of House of Commons malt against a salmon. The guy was obviously on a high after the Euro results and, although I wasn't entirely displeased with my own Green Party's performance, he had me three down after three. His drastic hook has now become a gentle draw to the left, and it goes a long way.

The third party in our threesome was Malcolm – the son of the aforementioned Robbie – fresh back from his first year at Glasgow University. I hasten to add, lest his father be concerned, that the young fellow was not involved in the betting, if for no other reason than the fact that Cunninghame North and I know our limitations. My only worry about Malcolm is the length and strength of his long irons. Was he studying seriously or practising on Glasgow's Corporation courses?

About the same time as I started pulling a few back, rumour filtered through to the course about a non-EEC Scandinavian country dumping salmon on the European market.

Now, this is what makes me think the new breed of Labourite may be fit to govern: in less time than it takes to assess the FT index Cunninghame North had worked out that, given inflation of eight per cent and the falling price of salmon, he had struck a bum deal. By the time he got back to Westminster he thought a bottle of House of Commons firewater could be worth two salmon.

Personally I don't think their poison is worth a smoked haddock, and if they had more men of discerning palate in power they would drink nothing but peaty Islay malts. The only trouble with the latter is the way they encourage the growth of heather. Did you ever notice Denis Healey's eyebrows?

But to get back to the game, in which I thrashed your man severely, I was still two down at the turn. 'Think,' *arsa mise*, 'of how you will gloat tomorrow when you get back to The House. There is no jibe too cheap nor one jeer too shallow.' Dixie's philosophy.

He couldn't keep his head down after that for the conjuring up of devastating one-liners to bunker the Tories. I look forward to my bottle of paraffin.

*   *   *

As I sit here at my lonely loom I hear the strains of Cajun music from the wife's boudoir. Even through two walls and my cloth ears it seems they are fond of the tune we knew as 'Kennag Mòr'. Did we send some very dark men from Harris to Louisiana in the days of the Clearances, or did some Breton landlord settle in Balallan? If anyone can shed a little light on this puzzle, there could be a bottle of House of Commons malt in it.

Earlier in the same day, while driving home from my charitable hobby as psychiatrist to Air Traffic Control, I tuned in to Radio Inverness. Maggie herself was reading the blood sports news. Her report of a fierce football confrontation between Struan and Glenelg was brilliantly understated – 'Plenty of fun in my house last night, two men killed' was never in it.

What struck me as odd was the way the two teams got on so well while the referee was away looking for the polis. I wonder, did he take the ball?

Friday, 4 August 1989

Now that winter is upon us we must, for old times' sake, welcome the 'English Crowd' – men and women like Munro of Melbost and Libby of Seaforth Road who, although strictly speaking they cannot be classed as English, are nevertheless a wee bit tainted. After 20 years in exile who can blame them for having acquired some of the less desirable traits of the Anglo-Saxon race.

Libby, after umpteen years in Bracknell and a few in Liverpool, has assimilated some strange vowel sounds but retains her generosity. Norman still sounds the same, a maw to his Branahuie back teeth, yet he carries his Golden Virginia *spliùchan* in a locked purse. He doesn't, of course, carry any money at all. I remember only too well when he didn't carry cash for the simple reason he didn't have any. But nowadays be forgets.

This forgetting the wallet, or the purse, is one of the least publicised aspects of English 'eccentricity'. So accomplished is their propaganda machine that they have succeeded in persuading the rest of the world that the French and the Scots, especially the Scots, suffer when they suffer not from that disease with which they, the English, are so sore afflicted – tightfistedness. With similar success they put it about in the 17th century that syphilis was the 'French Disease'. Now that I come to think of it, perhaps they were right. But as we have learned, in the last three hundred years, to understand English cunning, it was probably the 'English Disease'. Be that as it may, there is no doubt that the great modern 'English Disease' is obsession with penny-pinching, and please don't quote me exceptions. I could show you boys in Carloway who wouldn't play poker with deuces wild: remember, we are generalising.

The strange thing is that these exiles should choose to come back to Lewis for their holidays, year after year, when they could easily afford to go to Bali or beyond. Now that the children are more or less off their hands, I suppose they'll slip into the habit of a fortnight on the old sod and another in the sun, if for no other reason than that no amount of money or meteorological ken can ever make the same two weeks coincide.

Wee Alick – for whom I worked as a houseboy in Grosvenor Crescent, Hillhead, for many a year – has also made it his custom to call back in August. In the old days he picked the Glasgow Fair but now he works for Rupert Murdoch and could, I'm sure, spend every second weekend in Los Angeles if he wished. Yet he prefers to spend his August with Mairi Alexander in the damp Ranish *seileastair*.

We can understand why people like the Barvas Navigator should come back occasionally. Apart from conventional obligation to say hullo to the wife once in a while, *they* are tropical birds and look as if they need relief from the sun. Those who come from dampest England to spend their free-days in Lewis are not so easily explained. Living for their houses, as they do, I suppose they need a good feed. There are probably deeper-seated reasons for their annual migration, and perhaps we'll find time to examine these when they go away.

There is one who won't go away, for I understand he intends to remain in God's own land for the rest of his days. For reasons which will soon be apparent he must remain anonymous.

To escape some other old friends who have retained that olde Stornoway hobby, the demon drink, we set out to play golf – a new vice for your man. Up on the cold, exposed, notorious Gunsite, he produced (to my astonishment and delight) his hot water bottle. 'I thought,' *arsa mise* . . . 'Never mind,' says he. 'Man cannot live by bread alone.' When I reached the sanctuary of the 19th I was unable to read my bingo card. I must break with my habit of naming names, for your man has his heart set on The Ministry. Which ministry, I don't know; but don't worry, P. I won't let dab.

By the way, I hear the most interesting and scandalous stories about another old friend, Maclennan of Kenneth St, a potential chauvinistic firebrand. But until I get the facts confirmed by the Millionaire Cobbler I cannot risk censure by the Press Council, far less a writ. Let us just say, for the moment, he has let the side down badly.

By another way, and this is ever more worrying, who should I find playing bingo with one's wife but one's dentist. I may have drawn some comfort from P's hot water bottle but not to such an extent that *all* goes unnoticed. I mean to say, one doesn't expect to find one's dentist playing bingo. Good grief, one's dentist!! How can I ever again let a man loose in my gob whose attention is on sixty-six clickety-click, or whatever Bronco calls it – never mind on 'on its own, number twelve' – when I've only six green tusks left. OK, sorry, one guy you don't antagonise is your dentist. Times are hard in the NHS and we all have to make a few bucks where we can, which brings me back to the beginning.

These are difficult times for all of us. Eighteen years you labour to feed the brats, then they come home with Higher results that you should be proud of, and maybe secretly you are, but at the same time all they mean is that you are condemned to a further period of degrading poverty.

I tell a lie. In 25 years I have never had to worry about the groceries, until now. I would see the point for boys, who should obviously seek further education, but girls? Why don't they find a rich husband? What do they need with booklarnin?

Thank goodness for the Royal Bank. Come and join us, they say to potential young students, and you can have an immediate overdraft of

250 quid. If I had known then what I know now, I would have voted for Thatcher in 1962. It took me 10 years to get an overdraft of 250 notes. Perhaps I should have listened to my English friends and put a little aside every morning and every afternoon and every . . .

FRIDAY, 15 SEPTEMBER 1989

There was a time, and a very happy time it was, when this paper used to lash out. But we were young then. Lashing out was fun. Now it seems a long time since any lord of the land attempted to sue us.

I blame the proprietor. Creeping middle age, fatherhood, election to Parliament and the dreadful prospect of being the next anti-poaching minister have blunted his sword. Our unanimous decision to sack him and replace him with Allan Whiteford, who has miraculously escaped menopausal withering of the felt tip, was not taken a day too soon, if you ask me.

Were it not for young Torc, they say, we would be indistinguishable from the Stornoway Greysheet. And even Torcuil, being of ultra-respectable Lewis stock, doesn't lash out so far and wide as a young idealist should. Our dear Editor is not blameless. Forgive me for saying this, but I'm only saying it because it must be said, and if I don't say it there are plenty who will . . . *(Enough of that, Ed.)*

Well, it's only what the young bucks of South Lochs are saying. You cannot edit a radical paper with one eye on the sky for falling writs. Let them sue and be dashed, is what the boys are saying. Some of these fiery youngsters tell me that they've had enough. With the Mod just round the corner they have decided to form a resistance movement. They are going underground (a territory with which the boys in South Lochs are all too familiar) to produce their *own paper*. I'm only sorry they consider me too old and conservative to contribute.

They intend to bring forth their first issue on Friday 22nd. It should be available in all the best newsagents at the very reasonable price of ten pee. Any money raised will go to a local charity, which if the truth be known, is the main reason I cannot write for them (get the money in your fist is one thing I learned from Coinneach).

I suppose we must get used to collections for the cost of essential care for the elderly and infirm. The economic state of the nation being what it is, I'm sure it is only a matter of time until they come round begging for pennies for nuclear weapons.

Winter must be very close. I base that profound statement not just on the recent warm weather in the North-West while the rest of Europe shivered and dripped, but on the urgent messages I receive from Captain Chris telling me that the Golf Winter League and the Bridge Season is about to start. You can now stop buying the local papers, Mrs Burns, because they will, as you say, be clogged with bridge and golf, especially now that Whiteford has access to two sheets. Boring, Barbara, I agree; so let us be grateful for the new paper, *Smudge*, where you will find no old fogey rambling. In a desperate attempt to join in the spirit of things I hosted a bridge foursome for the whole of Friday evening and most of Saturday until the cock crowed (crew) at least four times. I'm afraid Kelso is getting too bad-tempered to partner this season. He threw his cards down and almost swore at me just because I couldn't tell the red cards from the black at 0300 GMT (that dashed peat smoke). Is this man fit to be a leader of men? Come back, Bruce Knight.

Dr Taylor and his wife Silvia take it extremely serious. Had old man Taylor not been present I think she would have hit young Donald, and who could blame her. I would have smacked him myself had I not remembered he played rugby for Glasgow University. Not that I know much about rugby, but I guess that playing for Glasgow University is like making the second eleven for Carloway FC.

To cheer Sylvia up, after a mad response from the *doctor*, I remind her of the day we nearly lost Donald. But for Aristotle Mackay's eagle eye Dr Taylor and Mac Choinnich would not be with us today.

Aristotle Jack spotted them first. Although visibility was so poor due to peat smoke you could hardly see the man in Gairloch Lighthouse going home for his tea, AJ said: 'I think that boat in Broad Bay is in trouble.'

'What,' arsa mise. 'Is it sinking?'

'Much worse,' ars Aristotle. 'It's being driven towards Point.'

There wasn't much wind in it. We watched for a while, secure in the knowledge that Big Carloway was in the other end and could always be called upon to swim out and pull them in with his teeth.

While Thompson held her with the oars Dr Taylor pulled furiously at the outboard. It was easy to tell Thompson from Taylor at a distance because there is a shape of head on both of them you could tell on a damh in the drove. In no time at all it was obvious to Thompson that Taylor's mechanical knowledge was even less than his chemical. But these old Seagulls are tough to start.

Every time Thompson moved aft to have a go at the machine several yards were lost, and when Taylor (who played rugby for Glasgow University) struggled with the oars they drew one hundred yards nearer to Portnaguran (agus abair guirean).

Every time Thompson went aft he threw Taylor for'ard and, every time, he had to regain the nautical half-mile Taylor had lost. I could have spent the day on the roof, because there were no tornados in these days, but Aristotle, who has been cursed with a soul, felt he should alert the Shore Section.

I don't know till this day if was it Bathais, Gordon or Uilleam a' Bhob-saidh who was in charge but the resulting fiasco, not unlike the mock Icelandic Cod War, was a tale of narrow misses. For half an hour they shot across each other's bows throwing ropes until Thompson finally had enough and threw Taylor into the rescue boat.

At four on Saturday morning Silvia said: 'I'll never forgive Aristotle.'

FRIDAY, 6 OCTOBER 1989

IF LIE FROM, ME LIE TO ME

It is worse the one beside me is growing. I was going down the A9 the other day full stoor with the wind behind me and the big road open before me thinking it would be myself that would be there when I reached. The one beside me was also thinking it would be myself that would be there when I reached. The one beside me was also thinking who would be there but her too destroying money in the big stores before they closed. And no voice on how hard every penny is earned or even would we reach at all.

But there was no doubt on her because didn't Alec Murdo himself come aboard before we sailed and gave us all, every son and daughter of mother, the full blessing. He blessed me and the one beside me, he blessed 40 children who were leaving the island for the first time one by one and he blessed in the going past two or three salt mackerel I was taking out for the Historian. Say the things you'll say about the one that is there, he will not leave anyone out or outside. I was taking fear that if the end would come on affairs it would come on us to put him ashore at the Light.

Ah, but little does all that count at the end of the day. For at the end of the day what is going to happen is going to happen. 'There is a wee case at me here,' said Liz Macaulay, 'I'm taking with me to Glasgow, if there is a chambre in the car.' Now it wasn't lack of accommodation but lack of strong springs on myself and the car that almost beat the two of us. Declining to the backbone of the boat with Liz's case full of compressed herring and Kerr's Pinks, I went as near my demise as I want to be the first time.

Look at them now going south with nothing on their minds but how good the big town is going to be. Who will be there but them.

Down by Pitlochry the one beside me said something about Bus a' Leadaidh coming from Gravir and was that as fast as he would go (I'm only doing this, Liz and Fiona, because you'll be joining the Oceanic Society, as Leslie calls it).

To show them that it wasn't on *Panorama* I saw the world I opened her out at every thing she would do, but at the same time a huge vessel at the front of me pulled out to starboard to pass a bigger one in front of him. They did battle for five minutes or maybe six and the second one wouldn't give an inch to the other. And the one beside me, all the time, without one thought on how near we were to eternity, but that the shops would be closed.

About the end over, pulled one in. Away that I went but about that time weren't they coming at me like the red bullet of their life from ahead. And, this is as true as you're alive, there wasn't one there who had a word of what lies await for him at the end.

'This is not a dual carriageway, you fool,' said the one beside me in her own language. Now this is the difference, long and wide, between them and us. They cannot convey the contents of their little minds to the listener of small understanding. And it was the Lord that did for me that the shell of my understanding was not spread on Tayside tarmacadam. I wouldn't care but for wasted Mod practice.

But we weren't there when an alteration dramatic came on the face of the situation. Before you could say God bless me nobody was making forward progress at all.

Happened it was a day when everyone who is in Glasgow escapes for one hour for to go to the Highlands in their Japanese cars full of dogs. Between dogs puking out all that was in their intestines and cars lifting steam from their fronts it wasn't a day that was too good on the road to Glasgow. After one hour or round about it, she beside me would say I believe they are gaining on the left and if you don't edge in we will not be much back for the Mod never mind the shops. Although I was thinking better myself I would obey and barge to port. No sooner was I on the North Sea side than she would observe they were man after man going before us on the west side. And like that ahead: where ever were we it was slower than the place she had made me leave.

When we saw the sign at Dunblane that said 'Expect delays until December' I said tiny to myself, isn't it good that we have the spuds and herring of Liz in the boot. But it did not take three months as the signs prophesied. If there was a little bit more urgency surrounding Alec Murdo's transmission of prayer it would not have taken the three hours itself that it took. But closing time is not the most that puts care on that fellow.

'Why are you writing in Gàidhlig?' says the daughter. 'Is it to make us more homesick or just for the Mod?'

'Or,' says she, 'are you trying to annoy the three Lady Di look-alikes who marched out on Dick Gaughan?'

'I'm not sure,' *arsa mise* to myself, unless it is to make *one* traffic jam last longer. Gaelic circumnavigation and English are at odds with one another and if there is space to be filled in a hurry you'll save time and gain yardage with the more analytical.

The master once wrote that while the average English speaker gets along with 400 words the Gaelic-speaking peasant uses 4,000. 'The plight of the English speaker,' *ars esan*, 'with his wretched box of 400 vocal beads may be imagined when I say that a really good Irish speaker would blurt out the whole 400 in one cosmic grunt.'

But that was a while ago. Sadly, because I guess death is always sad, the average Gaelic speaker under 44 now has only 40 words, 38 of them being variations on *brosnachadh, farsaingeachd* and *cooltower*, whatever that is. I have 41 myself but I'm not wasting them here when there's money to be made in *Smudge* next week.

Friday, 10 November 1989

Give me a plank of pine, or better still the whole tree, and I'm a happy man.

In this crazy race against time, we must always remember that life is but one short bright day followed by an eternity of darkness. Our insignificant individual consciousness has perhaps more meaning than the 'collective' philosophy of an imagined broederbond, yet it is nonetheless meaningless if there is no God. It is even more meaningless if there is.

My wife often buys me a tree to plant or, sometimes, she brings me a dressed plank from Chippy in Bain 'n Morrison's with which to make something. 'Cllr Macdonald is always hanging shelves and things for Morag – why can't you do anything?' One of these days I might well do a bit of hanging, like many a nagged man before me.

With the sentence of eternal darkness looming ever closer, is there anyone amongst you who would not like to have his grandchildren ask: 'Did my Grandpa really hang that shelf?' When, and if, in the future children play together as we did, will they dredge heroic actions from family lore, like the Barvas Navigator when he claimed that his father, at the age of 56, cleared a six-foot fence in pursuit of a yearling? Perhaps they will, perhaps not. If they do, I don't want to be numbered as the joiner who spoiled more wood than the ranchers of Brazil or DC Thomson.

Gordon, sensing my depression, said: 'Think not of your menopausal flushing as decline; imagine instead that the first bloom of youth is beginning to fade. Take the beautiful Tina to lunch and you'll feel better in the afternoon.'

Greater love hath no man than to sacrifice his secretary for a fiend, but he is a poor psychiatrist. He doesn't understand that contemplation of temporal beauty is but a reminder of how quickly it fades. The morning sun brings joy to some; to the pessimistic realist it is but the harbinger of dusk. This fleeting glimpse of light is gone with the speed of a 5th of November firework, unless you're a hostage in Beirut, in which case the fleeting glimpse is not so fleeting although the fireworks are for real.

Socrates had no hobbies, but if his wife's mail order catalogue had advertised Black and Decker I'm sure he would have been an amateur joiner (*Saor Geal*) like the rest of us. This is, of course, mere speculation like the teasers often thrown up by my learned colleagues, such as: 'Is it better to belong to Martin's Memorial than have no faith at all?' Death would indeed have little sting for most of us but for the worrying thought that the elders of Martin's might beat us to the cushioned seats in the Glorious Stadium (after they had marked up the entrance fee by 55 per cent).

The plank of wood, bought to fit the space measured by the one who bought it, is another matter altogether. It is an unusual text for a sermon,

I know, but the apparent complexity of the sermon – drawing as it does on the very stuff of life itself – is designed to illustrate what a hash the female of the species can make of the easiest task.

When that first operation, the simple removal of a rib, was carried out, we must be thankful there was no ward sister present. 'Five and a bit inches, your Honour, and just a little to the left.' Had a woman been in charge, have no doubt, instead of the shapely beasts they are today they would resemble one of my curtain rails.

Whittling was our only hobby in my youth, in those days long before television had been invented. We would sit in a circle, around the fire in the middle of the floor, whittling and philosophising the long nights away. Wood from wrecks came ashore in abundance, so there was never any shortage of whittling. In 1928 when the fishing was poor I must have whittled my way through half a rain forest. But that is by the way.

In 1989 here I am still whittling because of her. Listen to the way she measures the width of a bathroom. She lies down on the floor. 'When I left Hyndland School I was five-two-and-a-half. Allow half-an-inch shrinkage with age and curvature of the spine, and that's it.' At the other end, in the builder's yard, poor Chippy has to measure her torso, add a little bit for the legs, and cut accordingly.

But I protest too much. There is no challenge I like better than a piece of timber that is too long and I do her an injustice because it is impossible to measure exactly the distance between two walls when there's no holes in the wall. All you can do is buy long then cut plenty off and add wedges. The thin end of two wedges or several rolled *Gazettes*. Above all you must have faith.

If you are without faith, then the thin edge of the fattest wedge will not bridge the gap. You may have to move a wall. When grandchildren and their friends gather to marvel at the primitive carpentry of their ancestors, all that remains in evidence of your existence is one sagging plank. Nothing at all remains of the one who did the measuring, unless she is right about the soul, in which case she gets the last laugh.

*   *   *

Excuse me, I hate to stop in the middle of a sermon but some strange letters have landed on the diary desk (perhaps they were intended for the letters page).

Who is this Press Council, and who are the Councillors? Are they by any chance related to the Yorkshire Ripper's widow? Or do they reside in the House of Lords?

And this Ian Stephen fellow. He must be a crank. Would a non-crank name his house The Last One? But you're quite right, Ian. One rushed into print in a moment of anger. I'm sure dear Jill is a gentle person and it is totally out of character for us to defend ourselves. We were brought up to be silent in the presence of strangers, especially English-speaking strangers. You will notice, though, that I avoided quoting her gross libel of Terry Macguire.

When the entire population of fishermen/weavers are on the dole and the North-West reverts to wilderness I will mount a stuffed seal in my bedroom.

By the way, Mr Harrison, you should look up some late copies of the *Irish Times*. O'Brien became increasingly bitter and twisted towards the end. I have merely aged faster, probably because of cranks.

Friday, 17 November 1989

Almost everyone in the Western hemisphere who can speak English or German has been dragged in front of our television cameras to tell us 'what it all means'. Old and young and those in between, our group whose adulthood is the era of the Berlin Wall, all had their say.

Henry Kissinger, one-time adviser to the Archcrook Richard Milhous Nixon, spoke in English. This must have been reassuring for younger Germans on both sides who probably cannot remember why he won the Nobel Peace Prize. Older Germans would probably prefer to think of him as American: they have enough to live down.

But what does it mean to you and me, the men on the street? Men who grew up to expect too much. Men who never saw a shot fired in anger, except maybe a gamekeeper's, and who grew up in the age of antibiotics. Men, in other words, to whom going over the top meant too much cheap whisky at the Mod. It might just mean that we could live, some of us, to a fair old age without having been at war.

This only applies to relatively few modern nations and to only a single age-group within the few. America took good care to ensure her young men were in constant practice. This in turn meant that those who weren't killed lived through an age of buoyant economy. Captains of the greatest industry lived well and happily paid their taxes. Our government and theirs happily handed back these taxes for more weapons. Sometimes they sold surplus production to Argentinian and other dictatorships.

This seems a good way to keep the world going round and at the same time keep the global population at a manageable number, especially if you are an arms manufacturer in Detroit. It does not seem such a good idea if you are an arms bearer in Vietnam.

The threat of peace spreading uncontrollably throughout the entire world caused a few of our commentators to panic. Many of them were caught short and unrehearsed. There was something very comical, were it not so tragic, about American statesmen being concerned for Russian security. 'Russia cannot pull out of East Germany', said a deeply worried American who couldn't think of anything else to say.

We need the Russians in East Germany so that we can stay in West Germany was more or less what Kissinger said. The most hilarious serious question of the century was asked of some Russian spokesman by one of the Dimblebys: 'Are you not worried, or have you forgotten the 20 million of your fellow countrymen who died fighting against Germany?' We are desperately worried about you, he implied.

A reunited Germany, according to all the experts, is out of the question. 'Absolutely impossible,' said Kissinger. 'We cannot have one neutral Germany.' He wasn't quite sure why, and as a German himself he couldn't say: we are a warlike race (a terribly warlike people, some teacher used to tell us). Kissinger's doubts must give heart to those who would wish reunification. It could happen in our lifetime.

The Germans have certainly been aggressive in the short space of a century; but their history is one of peace and calm compared with, say, the Scots' and the Swedes'. They seem to me to be industrious and honest, although a bit simple and easily led like the English.

They also have a generation (ours) that has never known the ultimate brutality. They are out of practice and a threat to the natural order of things. They do not think of war as inevitable. The longer they live without war, the more unacceptable the horror becomes. The only venue in which I see the Germans becoming irritable and impatient in the near future is the Brussels battlefield. Forced to work constantly with the chaotic Celtic races, they could possibly be driven to re-arm or suicide.

In the meantime, while the East-West truce lasts, we have to find someone to hate or learn to live in a vacuum. Even the Scot Nats have a bit of a problem here since Jimmy Hill was sacked from *Sportscene* (at least we don't see him north of the border, so I presume he is banned in the cause of national unity). We must have someone to hate so we can justify defence spending. Unless we continue to prepare for war there will be millions who cannot continue to pay their mortgages, and that threat has more immediacy.

Right here and now, as far as we crofters are concerned, the outlook is pretty good. According to our economic advisers, our wealth and well-being will from now on become more and more dependent on tourism. At a stroke, as the HIDB would say, an extra 16 million potential tourists have been released into the west. This represents about 800 EXTRA tourists for every croft.

As sheep, salmon and Harris Tweed go out of fashion, all these sheds and outhouses can be filled with well-heeled German tourists. Of course they can only afford to come here as long as we keep buying their motor cars. It seems a crazy way to make the world go round, but less painful than war.

Friday, 24 November 1989

THE PERFECT MURDER

Many a poor deluded fool imagined he had planned the perfect murder, only to be foiled by Hercule Poirot in the dénouement and subsequently hanged by the neck. Poison was a favourite of Agatha's, but the stupid relative always left a trail of clues that a blind Belgian could follow. (Incidentally, I notice that the Lawyer is now almost as deaf as Niall Cheòis. Now that my eyesight is failing perhaps we should partner at bridge.)

But to get back to the perfect murder . . . it is obviously only perfect if you get away with it. The knife is a messy business. Even if you leave no fingerprints 'they' will probably trace the gutting technique back to the fishermen's co-op, and then you're done for. A tricky business, the successful murder.

Yet, it is so easy. I struck upon it 'quite' by accident last Saturday afternoon on the golf course. I have no reason or desire to do away with the Director of Finance: on the contrary, he could be quite useful to us alive if we ever find ourselves in a rebate situation again.

On Saturday he just happened to be in the right place at the wrong time – in this case the exact spot for which I was aiming. Normally this would be the only spot in the Castle Grounds where a man could hold his head up high but, as luck would have it, I very nearly got him on the skull. For one hundred and fifty yards the Grim Reaper had him in his sights but, for some strange reason, decided his number wasn't up.

Stewart, who is going through a rough patch, had a good vantage point and is blessed with a powerful voice, chose not to alert your man with the traditional cry of 'FORE'.

This, I realise now, is where my defence would have been very shaky. Murder on the golf course can be got away with, but only if you remember to shout 'Fore'. Next to not shouting 'Fore', the worst mistake is to hit a wealthy man and only stun him. In this situation you must rush up and finish him off with the club, otherwise he is soon on his feet shouting for his lawyers – and they're not all deaf.

Seven days earlier my young athletic winter league partner, Murdo O'Brien, almost brought down a helicopter pilot. This is a much more serious business than a mere director of shenanigans. A helicopter pilot serves a very useful purpose, and you never know the day. This particular pilot was crouching in the fading light, in what seemed an attitude of futile prayer, as his friends walked away. Murdo, who recently got married, assumes he has lost some strength and length (on the course), but that is an old wives' tale. He is, if anything, more calm, longer and mature. He asks me to apologise in case his outboard ever breaks down.

When men are under fire the Grim Reaper's role should never be underestimated. He can always intervene if He wishes. If Murdo Alec started playing again we would have to give him a handicap of plus 10.

Young Donnie Plumber had a string of threes the other day. Older and wiser, Bronco advised him to stop estimating the value of the sweep money with six holes to go (must be approaching one hundred quid on a Saturday now). 'The Supreme Architect takes a dim view of people counting their chickens,' said the old fellow. I guess he must be in the Lodge.

For a golf club we must be in a unique situation in Stornoway now. We have plutocrats like Dixie and Iain Macritchie, a host of us ordinary folk and at least 30 people on the dole.

Will the fleshy quail-eaters scatter crumbs among the children of the starving poor? I believe they will, because, whether induced by goodness or guilt, a strange sort of socialism will always flourish on the Celtic Fringe. With a large section of the club, the Harris Tweed Clansmen, out of work, they still raised over one thousand pounds for Children in Need on Friday night. Unique is a unique word, Kenny, and should never be qualified.

Excuse me, I have wandered into a room with a television. What do I see but that industry, salmon farming, once again under attack by freaks and cranks. A young woman, Alison – with whom I shared black pudding at breakfast – is talking about the sea bed. She was a student when she first came to become an expert, and to all extents and purposes normal – apart from her concern for the filthy grey seal.

Her latest concern is the sea bed, if you don't mind. Unless I disremember, four-fifths of the planet is covered by sea and on the bottom is mostly mud and slime (out of which we all, especially solicitors, crawled, according to the Church of Scotland). How much longer must we put up with these cranks? With four-fifths of the earth's surface covered by ocean, what effect will a few salmon jobbies have? How do these people gain media space?

Enough is more than enough, as my Grannie used to say. We have to get rough with the cranks. The men of, say, the Scottish Scenic Trust – if so they can be called – we should drag to some remote site and throw them off a 100-ft cliff with 80 ft of string tied to their parts. An eye for an eye, and all that.

In the aftermath of our own MP's brainwashing by Norwegians I have taken the unprecedented step of writing to Heseltine. Tarzan will sort them out.

The unfortunate thing is that none of these cranks takes part in blood sports like golf. Otherwise, I'm telling you . . .

FRIDAY, 15 DECEMBER 1989

A STERN-LIPPED YOUNG MAN LOOKS AT THE SCOTSMAN

It is a dreadful day in Point. Every day is a dreadful day in Point. We had scarcely travelled two hundred yards with the coffin when Charlie Nicolson remarked: 'We have a time-bomb situation here, and the lid is likely to blow off at any minute.' Taking care to avoid the cracks appearing in the island. And stepping carefully over the cliches. We trudged mournfully with the 'box'. A hideous construction cobbled together with timber from disused fishboxes.

Needless to say, the man in the 'box' had died like most Lewismen. In a bizarre accident. Shearing a ram at maniac speed without a verb or a seat belt. We wonder if he has gone straight to hell. Or if he was given a short parley to enjoy his own funeral, as most Lewismen seem to. Ken!

The sun burns low over the Minch *(A rare evening funeral? – Ed)* and reflects, in the cheap brass handles on the box, the sombre shadows of old men rolling cigarettes. There is nothing they like better than a Scotsman funeral. Except maybe an Englishman's. Old and young grow increasingly insular. The bizarrely deceased's nephew shouldered me out of his way when I attempted to take a photograph of the so-called coffin.

They walk in silence. Except for one who had clearly been at the magic mushrooms in the Castle Grounds. 'Are you my cousin twice removed?' he asked. I wasn't. But he insisted on boring me. 'There is nothing a Lewisman likes better than a funeral except perhaps a good fight.' I do not wish to fight. 'That is a pity,' he said, 'It has been a good year for funerals but fights have been scarce.' 'You try to talk like Hemingway but you don't like a fight! Are you sure your father was a Lewisman?'

I refuse to be provoked. I have to save myself for Friday night's disco in the Seaforth.

As the sun sets, the most aggressive elements drift off to wherever aggressive elements drift off to in this last stronghold of the Gospel. But not before we have discovered the coffin is empty. Yes. An all too frequent graveside discovery in Lewis. In the ructions of the wake the corpse has been forgotten. An old man, bent before his time with carrying coffins, says this is a regular occurrence at modern funerals. 'It wouldn't surprise me,' he says, 'if the dead man was sniffing glue. No wonder we are beginning to lose our faith.' Are you my cousin? I am.

But only in the sense that we have both lost what little sense we had. I am marked by my white tie. I am making a mental note to change it for a black one before the disco. There are only two police officers at the funeral. One of them is a man. The other one isn't. The one who isn't confesses to being in secret love with her maiden aunt in Garrabost. I sing two verses of the 23rd Psalm for her because her secret love's no secret anymore. I am wasting my time. She cannot remember Doris Day. Neither can I. I cannot help wondering if some of the youngsters are extracting the water. Do they realise who I am? *(Yes – Ed.)*

At the disco I mingle with the crowd. I imagine the camera is a passable piece of camouflage but a gang of 10-year-old girls – in mini-skirts – yell abuse at me. They should be stoned. Police are helpless, confronted by primary school girls armed with skipping ropes. I am giving thanks I am not a Mormon when a greasy-haired biker from Vatersay disarms the kindergarten mob with a Mo Johnston joke.

He is remarkably civilised, all things considered.

Friday night is horrendous, yet I am still not fully prepared for the atrocities of the Saturday night in Stornoway. If you can imagine 2,000 drunken North Sea oilmen coupling in dark corners, you begin to get the gist of it. Yet that was nothing compared with the horde that poured out of the Cabarfeidh in the early hours of the Sabbath. The Bridge Club's annual dinner.

I am wearing my fixed smile. I am scared. Twenty men of probity with their ladies and bow-ties. Not a pretty sight. It should not surprise us if they were smoking prohibited substances and gambling. I recognised some of them. Their sons could one day be students in the Free Church College. To be ministers. Oh, yes.

The atmosphere in church on Sunday was chilly. Old ladies munching Chop Suey and belching their appreciation is not quite what one expected from Free Presbyterians. Bachelor Buttons it used to be. This is probably a fair reflection on the state of the evangelical movement today.

The text of the sermon escapes me for the moment but unless my nose misleads me the man in the pulpit was a bit the worse for grass. Ranting and raving in the manner of the primitive Gaelic Church. Only two police persons on duty again. 'What can they do,' said Charlie Nicklaus, 'when confronted with 20,000 Free Presbyterians high on Chop Suey and cannabis?'

A Chief Inspector said: 'It's no so bad. They're just letting off steam. They're no worse than rugby players.'

For the first time since I was 10 I tumbled into bed too tired to say my prayers.

FRIDAY, 22 DECEMBER 1989

'S E BEURLA TH' AIG SANTA

Bheil fhios agad air a seo: tha cuimhn' agam air a' chiad Nollaig mar gum b' ann an-dè a bh' ann. Cha robh similear ann. Toll os cionn an teine meadhan an làir. Thuit Santa tron an tughadh 's cnapan sùich an crochadh ris an fheusaig aige, agus mur b' e am paraisiut a bh' air bha e air a mhanachan a losgadh anns an luath.

'Seall sin a-nis,' dh'èigh mo sheanmhair. 'Nach e Santa a bha gu math dhut.'

Who did she think she was kidding. 'S math a dh'aithnich mise spàgan mòr Iain Thormoid. Robh iad a' smaoineachadh gun toireadh iad a chreidse ormsa gun robh size 12 aig Santa. Agus ged a bhitheadh, robh e dol a thighinn à Lapland le toll na bhòtainn. Cha b' e sin a-mhàin, ach bha geansaidh mu chlisich a chunna mi air bioran mo sheanmhar an t-seachdain roimhe sin.

À, Dhia, bha iad a' smaoineachadh gun robh sinn blunt. Co-dhiù, thuit an truaghan tro mhullach an teach (bha e lucky nach robh sinn air an stòbh fhaighinn), thòisich e a' swingeadh air an t-slabhraidh 's a' seinn 'Chingle Bells'. Agus bha e smaoineachadh gun creidinn-sa gur e Santa a bh' ann. Feumaidh e bhith nach robh e buileach aige fhèin; cha do sguir e a sheinn ged a chaidh osan na briogais aige na teine.

Co-dhiù, chaidh do nàbaidh a ghearradh sìos agus a chur na shìneadh air an t-sèis. Ach chuimhnich e orm. 'There's your apple, my boy. Siuthad a-nis, thoir thugam deoch bhùirn.'

Ged nach robh mi ach ceithir, dh'aithnich mi gur e Beurla a bh' aige, agus chuir e iongnadh orm, an uair sin fhèin, na rudan àraid a bhios a' tighinn a-steach air inntinn dhaoine a th' air a thighinn gu aois. Cha b' e a-mhàin gun robh e dhen a' bheachd nach biodh Gàidhlig aig Santa, ach, ma bha cànan idir aige, gum b' e Beurla.

Bha mi rudeigin tàmailteach nach robh a' Bheurla agam fhìn a fhreagaireadh sa chànan, ach co-dhiù thuirt mi, 'Aye, aye, sir.' Rud a bha mi air a chluinntinn aig na bodaich. Cha do leig mi orm gun dh'aithnich mi e, ach shaoil leam gum bu chòir dhomh deoch bhùirn fhaighinn dha co-dhiù.

Bha an Sàtan, an uair ud, a' fuireach anns a' ghleann againn. Co-dhiù, sin a bha mo sheanmhair ag ràdha, agus ged nach robh mi a' creidse ann an Santa, cha robh doubt sam bith agam mu dheidhinn a' bhalaich eile. Agus tha e coltach gur ann an dol fodha na grèine a bha e dùsgadh. Mar sin, bha feagal mo bheatha agam ron dorchadas. Cha bu mhi nam aonar. Dh'fheumainn a bhith coiseachd dhachaigh le na balaich gu lèir, fear mu seach, ged a bha mo ghlùinean a' glagadaich. (Bha an Sàtan anns a h-uile gleann.) Ach cha robh uimhir a dh'eagal air duine 's a bh' ormsa. Nis, feumaidh mi aideachadh gun robh mi rudeigin slaodach up top nach robh mi air mothachadh, aig an àm ud, gur e anagram dhen t-Sàtan a tha ann an Santa – agus, càil as àraide, cha chuala mi aig tidsear a-riamh e. Cha b' e gun rinn mi cus èisteachd ris an traib sin co-dhiù. Agus cha b' fheàirrde mi fhìn sin.

Fhad 's a bha na rudan sin a' dol trom inntinn bha 'Santa' na shìneadh air an t-sèis ag èigheachd, 'Nach toir thu thugam balgam uisg' (a' feuchainn ri toir a chreids' orm gur ann à Lapland a bha e). Nis, anns na làithean a dh'fhalbh, bha na peilichean bùirn air an stòraigeadh anns a' chlòsaid. Cha robh solas na Tilley a' ruigeil doras na clòsaid. (Toll, bha mi cinnteach, às nach robh an Sàtan a' carachadh.) Ach tha rudan ann a dh'fheumas balach a dhèanamh mus bi e na dhuine.

Rug mi air a' mhuga sheipein agus dhaibhig mi dhan dorchadas a' feadalaich 's ag èigheachd, 'Cha bhi mi fada.' Ged a bhiodh an Sàtan gu math smart, cha bhiodh e air breith ormsa an oidhche ud.

Gu mì-fhortanach, an uair a bha mi cho faisg air na peilichean 's a tha mi ortsa an-dràsta, leig cailleach sgreuch ann an ceann eile an taigh a theab mo chur à cochall mo chridhe. Bhuail mi mo ghàirdean dhan a' pheile a b' fhaisge, lìon mi am muga 's thug mi mo chasan leam.

Ch robh tòrr air fhàgail anns a' mhuga sheipein nuair a ruig mi Santa, ach bha an Sàtan air a dhòigh. 'À, Dhia,' ars esan, 'bu tu am balach, a lorg am bainne-tiugh ann an trì mionaidean.'

'Aye, aye, sir,' arsa mise, a' toirt a chreids' a-rithist nach robh fhios a'm cò bh' ann. Ach bha mi cinnteach, ma bha càil mì-nàdarrach mu thimcheall, gun tuigeadh e Beurla.

1990

FRIDAY, 19 JANUARY 1990

Last Saturday morning I awoke to the sort of rumbling in the intestines than can only be caused by haggis matured overnight in stale whisky. For half an hour or so I lay on my back and considered my situation. I figured that if I stayed long enough I might be able to contain the turbulence and salvage the contents of the stomach. The alternative was to risk the hazards, in the half-dark, of the journey to the bathroom.

Long ago I took the precaution of plain walls in the bedroom. Flowers or designs of any kind on a bedroom wall is asking for trouble. At the first hint of daylight flowers begin to swirl and dance, and on severe occasions they can assume hideous and terrifying shapes.

Just when I thought I had gained a measure of control over internal motion, the telephone rang to tell me my brother was waiting in the boat by the pier and to please get a move on. I never cared much for haggis anyway and I certainly wasn't sorry to part with that one. Then, I accidentally caught a glimpse of my face in the mirror. A terrible shock. There staring back at me was my 80-year-old father. I resolved that from then on I would take care of my body. A man *should* take care of his body after a certain age because spare parts are scarce for older models.

After another quick look in the mirror to confirm my suspicions I decided I would see the Lawyer about a will first thing on Monday morning. The last thing you would wish is a horde of relatives squabbling over the bones.

It is now Monday and there doesn't seem to be quite the same urgency. The little bags on the big bags have subsided, a flash of white has returned to the good eye and, in any case, it probably costs a fortune to have a will drawn up.

What I miss most is the smoking. Many of my eminent colleagues do not appreciate the benefits of smoking. Not only is the morning routine completely altered, the morning comes a lot earlier. Without a soothing draught of malt and nicotine, sleep becomes elusive and the few winks snatched tend to be restless. The once-attractive dawn brings little joy. You no longer even have the pleasure of half an hour's serious coughing to kick-start the lungs.

The benefits of vigorous coughing are hardly ever acknowledged by the profession, although the evidence is there for all to see. The taut abdominal muscles, the 32-inch waist – where else do you find these except in the heavy smoker and dedicated morning cougher. If I could give you a living example (rather than the customary cadavers prefered by medicinemen), look at George Prince. Once as lean and hungry as Kesting or Donald Dewar, and a fine golfer in his day, he now casts a shadow on the golf course like a well-developed cumulonimbus – the obvious result of a lifetime of little coughing. He can now only hook round his extension. *(That's enough living examples – Ed.)*

Perhaps you're right, but the alternative is too painful. There are, as always, exceptions to the rule. My old friend Johnny Walker who sat beside me in School(s) for 11 years (until the authorities decided we were wasting their time) has called in to see me tonight and he still has a figure like a conger eel, although he stopped smoking 10 years ago. How has he done it?

That's an easy one. He has started a second family with a younger second wife, and he seems to be thriving on it. For most of us this is far too costly an exercise, as Maggie pointed out to me. 'Carry on coughing,' she added, mysteriously.

While moping about the house, far sunk in self-pity, did my eye not fall on an advertising feature in the local paper: *'Nomie's Body Shop, Competitive Prices, Free Estimates'*.

That, *arsa mise*, is the place for us. I think I've read about these Body Shops. Nancy Reagan and people like that go regularly. I took Maggie in for an estimate. Nothing too elaborate, I suggested, a tuck here and a fold there, perhaps a little burned off, gently? He promised he would see what he could do to keep the price down – as long, said he, as you don't want any major reconstruction like a bum-lift. I'm sorry, he added, impertinently and unnecessarily, I cannot do anything about your eyes. See young Doig, whose folk used to believe in the NHS.

No, thanks, I don't think I can afford to talk to someone who gets his braces hand-stitched in Switzerland.

Talking, in passing, of the NHS: many of us are puzzled about miraculous manifestations in South Lochs. How do so many nonagenarians still hunt deer? What is Dr Rambo's secret? Is he into some sort of unnatural transplantation?

Not that we on the North Side of the Loch disapprove; we would just like to be in on whatever it is. Although, to be serious for a moment, I believe one can take this sort of youth phobia and redecoration too far. I would hate to call on one of my old relatives in South Lochs only to discover that, like Nancy Reagan, they have to uncross their legs to smile.

Having emerged temporarily from gloom, I called on the old man to wish him a happy 80th birthday and found him rolling the Golden Virginia, looser and thicker than ever, to absorb more poison. I brought up the subject of the will, purely in the interests of tidy administration, but all he said was: 'OK, you can take the rest of the ounce.'

FRIDAY, 26 JANUARY 1990

Here I am pounding the hard streets of Glasgow, in the Millionaire Cobbler's 80-dollar shoes. I am not suited to hard pavements, or the shoes and the shoes weren't made for walking. I suppose it is too late to take them back now, three years later, when they're nearly done.

The Cobbler did promise me they would see me out, which means I have not got long to go or else he intends to patch them up from time to time. I'm determined to outlive these shoes even if I have to wear them to the fishing. The main thing is that the crofter is not suited to the city.

As I walk along Byres Road I notice the indig tend to mince; only the balls of their feet seem to touch the ground, and then only very briefly.

This obviously enables them to take quick evasive action, so that untold thousands of them can pass each other on narrow streets at great speed without collision – like a colony of soldier ants.

The crofter's style needs a lot more space. His stride gives the impression of circular motion, like a long-legged gerbil in a barrel. Once set on a particular course he cannot change direction easily. This, I explain to my daughter, is why I often walk into people and have to spend so much time apologising. The occasional black eye is the price we have to pay for our easy going way of life and our wall-to-wall heather carpet.

Each time I swear I'll never step on a city street again, but we cannot have our own way all the time. The reason for my visit this time was to check up on the brats, Liz and Fiona, and see that they're learning their lessons.

But first I must tell you about some weathermen I ran into. They were on their way to Glasgow to be told why it would be in their interests to accept a pay cut, and this was on the day after someone at the Butt of Lewis had misread an instrument. Swift retribution, indeed.

We lost Leslie once or twice between the Airport and the city centre, but he is not too difficult to spot in a crowd.

People tend to give him a wide berth because he is so obviously not watching where he is going. Look for the empty space in a crowd and there you will find Leslie. As he gets his kicks from trains, we found a place where we could leave him in Central Station for a couple of hours. He seemed safe and happy sitting there, and some people threw him a few coppers.

For what seemed like a very long day I trudged these hard pavements with the daughter, looking for Lolita. I mean the Book, of course. I never knew a Lolita personally; the name is a bit too fancy even in Glasgow where they were given some very flowery names in the Sixties. Lolita the Book is what the brats were ordered to study this term and what I was ordered to buy, although, as a Presbyterian and concerned father, I do not approve. Whether or not it had anything to do with recent television publicity for the author I don't know, but there wasn't a copy to be found among the mountain of Penguin Classics in Glasgow.

We had to give up on *Lolita* in the end but I found a few books I'd been meaning to read for 20 years. Unfortunately, I could only afford to buy one of them because the brat is such a drain on resources. I chose a book by Tobias Smollett because he had dabbled in medicine like myself. Also, I like to think of myself as an eighteenth-century man. Smollett, it says in the introduction, practised – unsuccessfully – as a surgeon. I like that 'unsuccessfully', and I wonder how his lack of success manifested itself and who suffered. An unsuccessful medicineman of any kind is bad news, but an unsuccessful surgeon sounds like a dangerous man.

But I must get back to the brats, who claim to be permanently broke and hungry, because I promised to report to other anxious parents. Young Malky Macrae bought me a whisky and left. If he went home you have a very sensible boy there, Robbie; if, on the other hand, as I suspect, he went to some den they call the Overflow you must have a word with him. By the way, Debbie passed a statistics exam. There you are, Debbie, we now have your achievement on record in case you never pass another exam. And believe me, if you carry on mixing with that gang, the chances are you won't. They will drag you down to their own level, which, as you know, is at a very low elevation indeed. Liz, Fiona, Big Alex, David and Steve look to me the sort to avoid if you want to study seriously. Catherine Docherty looks a stable sort, though, and I wish I was a little bit younger.

Fiona's friends were at great pains to explain to me what a steadying influence she is. How sensible and studious, etc. As a reward I fed her three or four times in two days. One of these times was in an Indian restaurant where she was severely poisoned. On the second night we ate a few pheasants in the Ubiquitous Chip at the reasonable price of £4 each. After this I was dragged to a debate on the abolition of the House of Lords. I was cheered after this because, although I couldn't hear very well, even some young Tories seemed to be for it.

I like to surround myself with young people, especially when they take me to discos and feed me Scrumpy – a sort of lethal cider, which, in retrospect,

I find difficult to recommend. On Saturday morning I did not feel at all well disposed towards young people. I couldn't help wondering why, if the brat is so sensible, she is known by name to so many barmen and cab drivers?

Back at the ranch, sitting by the fire writing with a biro by candlelight, I wonder how we are going to make it through the winter. To the accompaniment of nightly hurricanes and power-cuts I must contemplate the cost of the brats' education, of which the cost of taxis and the Union make up a great part, and I can only conclude it is not worth it. I fear I must chase her out to work or persuade some unfortunate man to take her for a wife. I hold very little hope for the future: I am now right through the soles of the 8o-dollar shoes.

FRIDAY, 24 FEBRUARY 1990

One hesitates to criticise fellow members of one's club, especially in this our centenary year, but there comes a time when one must speak out.

There was a time when one went to one's club of a Saturday afternoon to relax in the company of gentlemen. One could perhaps read one's *Weekend Guardian*, do the *Times* crossword or indulge in learned disputation with one's eminent colleagues. Sadly, as things stand at the moment, one might as well belong to the Sea Angling Club.

No, I am not exaggerating. It is that bad. A few years ago some of us let our guard down and allowed a ruffian element to gain entry. Hooligans from Uig, Falkirk, inner cities and various other deprived quarters slipped in during the reign of a committee that was desperate to take anyone's money. One alarming result of our lack of vigilance is that it is now not uncommon to hear bad language on the premises.

My gentleman neighbour Dixie has drawn up a list of immigrants to be prohibited and, much as it grieves me to report this, the Captain is on the list. A tireless worker (could anyone get tired at Main & Borison's?) but nevertheless a thug.

Having been let down once again by our League partners, Dixie and I had to play with the Captain and the Match Secretary. Presumably no one else would play with them. Now, I'm not surprised. Even after several years in the company, albeit dwindling in number, of honourable gentlemen, the rough edges haven't begun to wear off that pair.

Walking on ahead of a man about to make a lunge at the ball was the cause of my old friend Bill Maclean's first breakdown. If only he were still alive, I'm sure he could instill a modicum of etiquette in these louts. As for taking a line on the opposition's ball, it is perhaps as well they don't bother, for they would only trample on if it they found it. But that is not the worst.

We don't expect this type of person to be sociable but they could at least try to join in polite conversation about the feeding of ewes or the falling Yen. But not them. While rummaging in the rough for balls, they have radio receivers clamped to their ears in case Rangers score a goal. Is it any wonder the North Lochs crowd have applied to join the Harris Club. Dixie is at this very moment calculating the extra petrol cost and, of course: 'Will I still get 42,000 miles out of my tyres?'

Worth every penny of it, says Robbie, to get away from *them*. Murdo Morrison has taken the extreme action of moving to Tipperary, and who can blame him. (He worries a little about his Donegal lady, Jenny: will they be able to understand her Gaelic down in the deep south? Don't worry, Murdo, I once knew a family who moved to Skye.)

Sorry, I seem to have been diverted again. Back in the Clubhouse, after three hours of torrential rain and a Force Eight that always seems to blow in your face, there is no respite. The roar of the wind abates but my sad story of trouble at the 10th is drowned by the roar of the 'new members' gathered round the *satellite television*. God help us all. I'm not sure who to blame.

People like Whiteford, from whom you would expect something, are as bad as any of them. Glued to this devilish instrument of Murdoch and shouting encouragement like a mindless rugby fan, he forgets himself – as they all do. Most of us like to see Rangers lose, but do we care all that much? I sometimes wonder if the Sea Angling could be any worse.

Mark my words, it is only a matter of very short time until you see members reading the *Sun* and the *News of the World*. Who knows what next – perhaps drunkeness itself.

Talking of the Scribe Whiteford, we had a brief conversation before the football hooligans started shouting. And what did we talk about? What else do writers talk about but money. Are we getting paid enough, Allan wondered. I think I managed to reassure him, dear Ed.

Cunninghame North himself is coming up soon and will take us all out to the Cabarfeidh for a feed. This will worry him when he reads it, but Joni will fix things; she loves to spend his money. In case he takes fright I must set his mind at ease. I recently had wealthy relatives for a weekend who decided to take us out for Sunday dinner to save us cooking. I said, I'm sorry Horace Capaldi is closed on Sunday, I'll throw on a few salt herring. They wouldn't hear of it, so they dragged us, reluctantly, to the Caberfeidh. I was a trifle or two apprehensive because I've been left with the tab too often. Now I wish I'd grabbed it because at six pounds something a skull it's no bad. There is no washing up and the waitresses are all broody and love to look after babies, Brian.

Again we seem to have drifted away from urgent issues, but people like that even if editors don't.

The Club and Cultar was to have been the theme. Some time has now passed since we first spoke of taking culture to Barra. I think it was the Lawyer who set the wheels in motion, while temporarily mesmerised by visitor Jane's accent. Some said: it's no use, you cannot do anything with the Barrach. But others persevered. Look at the way we have brought the people of Ness out of a state of darkness.

When Iain Gordon and company first started coming down from Ness to the Club for Bridge, boy, were they rough. Bidding in Gaelic and the cards sticking to their peaty fingers. But look at them now. There is no reason why we couldn't do the same for Barra.

Loganair, or as the cailleach in Tong calls it, Localair, must do their bit. They will surely ferry the Honourable Company of Stornoway Bridge Players to Barra for the advertising advantages of being associated with such a worthy group. The company's image is already enhanced simply because we have mentioned them in committee. If we manage to do some good missionary work while down there, that is a bonus. They need have no fear that we'll bring any of the people mentioned in the golf notes. They seldom move far from home.

The timing of the visitation is difficult. There is no doubt that we will win, but I think we should tackle them at Easter while they are still weak from Lent.

FRIDAY, 27 APRIL 1990

I often wonder what the Granny would have thought of the flushing lavatory. 'She would probably have taken it in her stride,' says the wife, in a waggish mood. Okay, if that's her form tonight, I will not consult her again. I'll fill this space on my own. Smart Alexinas I can do without.

(Wee aside) My intention this week was to dwell on not so ancient islands history and maybe become a bit sentimental. I've often felt that this is the sort of stuff the Wee Paper has lacked. Unlike the Greysheet, *we* have no history.

We weren't even born until 1972, when James Shaw Grant already had his telegram from the Queen. Telegram, did I say? Isn't that quaint. 'What is a telegram?' asks the overgrown lout of a son who still hangs about the house. I explain, as best I can, that it was an urgent message brought on a bicycle by the most important man in the world, The Postman. No fax then, I sigh (wistfully), but what's the use.

In the face of hostility and mockery I retire to my attic to think on the peaceful past. When the ace electrician of that bygone age, Starchy, switched on the first 40-watt bulb the Granny, who'd said, 'I won't live to see it', saw it and eyed it warily. She clearly suspected a trick. Being an expert practitioner in the black arts herself, she probably realised she couldn't keep abreast of modern jiggery-pokery. I won't know for some time, because she died very soon afterwards.

(It is interesting to note here that my friend Archie, in South Uist, didn't see the magic lantern until nearly half a century later. This was a mixed blessing because, although it kept the television at bay, his eyes were ruined trying to read in the light of the Tilley.)

Any minute now I'll remember what we were talking about, and I thank you for being so patient. Ah, yes, I had just stumbled out of the Greysheet office, where I'd been trying to sell some Gaelic poetry, and I spotted one of those magnificent science-fiction bogs, which is why the late Granny sprang to mind – and, my God, spring she would.

Now look here, there is nothing I like better than a good laugh, but this is going too far. Whoever is the latter-day Girondist responsible for this joke, he must be exposed.

As luck would have it, several technicians were doing some final tuning to the timewarp mechanism and the 'door' was open. Naturally I was offered a bribe, in the form of strong drink, to keep my gob shut, but I declined. The public must know about this one, because who are the public conveniences for if not the public.

In the electronics compartment of the machine I saw some equipment that would make your eyes water, never mind the other thing. Among levers, springs and old-fashioned valves there is a devilish contraption that can only be a guillotine. This implement could serve the innocent purpose of chopping the 'roll', but who is going to take a chance on it. A fraction this way or that and you're only fit for steeplechasing.

But that's nothing. The ejector seat is automatic. *You have no control over motion duration.*

I have no wish to re-engage, in learned disputation, some of my eminent colleagues who seem to think that a high-fibre diet guarantees speedy delivery. Some of them know nothing. But let me tell them now that daily feeding on rough oatmeal can bake a blockage you would have no chance of passing in the 'programmed time'. It would not surprise me in the least to learn the Council had engaged a very young doctor as 'superloo consultant'. But, had they asked me, I could have advised with sincerity and for a very small fee that the only safe way of getting out of them things before you are ejected is Guinness.

But all that is by the way; wait till I tell you this one. I seen a phone in there: a direct line to the Director of Environment. And tapes that play music. Mood Music, they call it. (The Granny must be laughing.)

Imagine for a moment – if youse will – the springs are creaking, your 50 pee is running out and Calum is singing 'She Moved Through the Fair'. Your bag doesn't respond to the air, so you start dialling frantically for a Bobby Macleod reel. What do you get? A BT voice telling you she cannot get you the Director of Environment unless you can prove you're related to Fred. That's a fine how-do-you-do, with seconds remaining until the populace see you ejected in your dirty underwear.

I think, at this stage, it should be recorded that Skye and Lochalsh told them where to stick their £6,600 privies. Only Stornoway councillors thought they should be in the advance guard of turditecture.

All this is fine, but remember some poor boy must perform at the opening ceremony. Sandy's not daft. He knew when to get out. So, he has left the new Convener with the gruesome task. And what a test of character.

I asked Big Carloway how he might tackle it. 'I have nothing to be ashamed of', quoth he. 'I'll strip first. Remember, I lived in your Granny's time.'

FRIDAY, 7 JUNE 1990

THE WORST DAY IN MY LIFE
There are some people who will not trust their wives with the simplest tasks. I'm pleased to say I am not one of them. Painting, decorating, electrical wiring and that sort of thing I am not too proud to leave in her hands. My one big mistake, 10 years ago when we were building the house with a little help from Kenny Dhòmhnaill Fhionnlaigh, was allowing her to finish the plumbing.

The other day in the middle of the Brazil-Argentina game her handiwork came undone. The hand of God! Perhaps. Who knows?

The Brazilians were moving the ball about with some confidence and should have been three up. The Argies were up to their usual filthy tricks – much the same as in the Falklands (now I believe the *Sun*). The whole first half was a bit like watching the highlights of an English international match.

When the noise of the samba drums died down with the half-time whistle the wife said, *ars ise:* 'What a terrible downpour.' Having more than a passing interest in meteorological phenomena, I made a quick observation of the celestial dome. 'Much as I hate to disagree with you, *a ghràidh*, it cannot be raining from that speck of altostratus over Keose,' *arsa mise rithese.*

Like the rest of her tribe, she is very far in the head. 'It is lashing down,' she maintained. 'It cannot be,' I would return with all the confidence that comes from 25 years' study of cloud physics.

At this point the daughter, who was in the spare public room playing with the dog, screamed. When someone screams, normally, people become alarmed and rush to the scene. *We* learned to ignore Fiona's screams when she was four months old.

This didn't cure her. *She* learned to stop crying through being continually neglected, but she carried on screaming. Now she screams the way other people laugh or sigh. I guess she is so highly strung and emotional that conventional '*obh, obhs*' just will not do.

So, when she let out a bloodcurdling screech, at half-time, the wife and I continued with our learned discourse on the Bergeron Process of droplet formation as if everything was in its own place.

Very soon, though, I felt a far from cold drop on my bald patch. Meg may be slow in many ways but, in a crisis, she can put two and two together with the best of them. The daughter by then had stopped screaming and had started crying. As the wife and I tried to leave the room together we got jammed, going out, by the daughter coming in.

Perhaps if I hadn't stopped on the stairs to recite an old Rhodesian ditty about a Zambian bricklayer who let go the rope (since plagiarised by an Irishman) the ceiling could have been saved.

By the time we reached the upper floor, wrestling with each other on the landing, the insulation had given way on the boiling cylinder and we had the sort of catastrophe on our hands you sometimes hear of on the news.

At such a time a clear head is essential. The daughter and wife rushed back and fore thoughtlessly with buckets, the way women do, occasionally snarling at me to call a plumber or something. Of course, all the time I was thinking.

Above the 25 gallons of boiling water I remembered there were 50 gallons of cold water waiting to come down. They hadn't thought of that. 'Get me some string,' I yelled at the daughter. At the same time the wife, who had so many strange experiences in Gartnavel Hospital, ordered us to haul in some blankets.

However, I'm pleased to say, my voice carries more authority than hers. Armed with string and torch, I was assisted into that narrow passage underneath the ridge tiles that leads to the cold water tank. That dark tunnel was Kenny the Plumber's final dirty trick. Having spent his life crawling through drainpipes, he probably thought: 'Some day he'll have to come up here: he should have paid me.' I guess plumbers, like good golfers, are all deformed.

By the time I gained the apex of the western gable-end rafters had torn the skin from my skinny hips and the protruding cartilage on the left knee had made a sort of horizontal step-ladder of the joists, I don't mind telling you I was as near prayer as I've been since that night in the Mozambique mountains. I could see no way back unless Karachi could be called out to knock down the gable-end.

For a time my pain and suffering made me forget my lifelong terror of enclosed spaces. I had one hand on the vital ballcock, the torch in the other hand and the piece of string in my mouth. It is possible, I suppose, to tie a knot with your mouth if it's big enough; but you must have a nail to tie it on. There is no shortage of dangerous 'speaks' protruding where they shouldn't, but damn the one near that tank.

Never mind, I had just managed a sort of temporary noose round a spare copper pipe that seemed to be going nowhere in particular when I heard a voice from below. 'It's OK,' she shouted, 'don't bother. There's a valve under the kitchen sink.'

I have no doubt in my own mind that she and Kenny planned my end some 10 years ago. If I ever get out of here alive I will exact a terrible vengeance.

A friend, one of the few left, has tapped a message through on the pipes, that Brazil lost.

FRIDAY, 3 AUGUST 1990

GOD BLESS THE ROYAL DOLE

I cannot remember how the conversation started, unless it was sparked by the news that the Royal Families no longer have to plead for dole in-increases. One thing led to another, and the Honourable Company of Stornoway Golfers was soon embroiled in a heated discussion on poverty in general.

In a matter of seconds Bronco had taken over with his childhood history of cruel want in the slums of Scotland Street. 'Poverty is it, now,' *ars esan*. 'Is it me you're talking to about poverty.'

'What about Point Street with 10 of us in a closet,' claimed George O'Brien. And so it went on, each trying to outdo the other with horrific tales of hunger and overcrowding.

According to Mr MacArthur, something of an authority on Stornowegian history, one block on Scotland Street housed about 12 families – and he named them, adding that he might have forgotten some. And families in those dark wartime days were far from small – rubber being as scarce as everything else.

If we assume that the average family numbered seven and only half of them got up in the morning we still have 40-odd persons fighting for the single toilet. 'There was no question of letting an old bodach dally for a smoke,' says your man. 'In desperate times you would haul him through the keyhole.'

This one block, incidentally, has since been turned into a mansion by the Millionaire Cobbler. He lives there all alone and I wouldn't be surprised to learn he has several bathrooms. He will never qualify now for membership of the Red Circle.

I noticed Warrior kept very quiet while the poor children of the Town reminisced. Can he possibly be hiding aristocratic ancestry?

Naturally, I too said very little. These guys think they had hard times!!

I did dare to interrupt once. I told them I was 10 years old before I tasted a spoon of porridge the hen hadn't had its beak in first, but I was dismissed more or less as a lunatic given to wild exaggeration. They have no conception of what we in the country suffered.

They had running water and gas and the butcher Seonaidh Bhragaidh nearby where they no doubt bagged the occasional tasty morsel of offal. And never forget the fry from the boats.

What did we have? We had nothing or next to nothing. Cuckoo wrasse soup on Saturday night was a rare autumn treat. The wrasse bones, stuck in the gum, was not a Sunday breakfast we relished, but it had to do.

Now and again in midwinter a calf would die of starvation, Aha, I hear the Stornoway boys shout, a Sunday roast! But what were we going to roast it on? We weren't pampered by the Council with fancy gas ovens. We boiled the beast on the fire in the middle of the floor and, true enough, there was a meagre Sunday meal in it. On Monday I got the bones to gnaw, being the eldest brat. On Tuesday I would pass them on to the next in line to the throne. Come Saturday when the youngest got his turn, there was very little nourishment left even in the thigh bone (the poor child has always blamed the rest of us for his stunted growth).

Please don't run away with the idea that *we* were the worst off. We were all more or less in the same leaky boat. It was not unusual to call next door on a Tuesday and get a shot of an only child's 'bone'. I was always envious of Coinneach. He was so well off he would often miss a scrap of marrow or even a sliver of meat in a crevice.

Aye, cove, it was tough. Rare moments of good luck stick in the memory like that one long hot summer. I cannot remember who caught the 40lb ling, but it had a gullet the size of a woman's nylon stocking and a basinful of liver. This mammoth sausage lasted several days and every child in the glen had a sook at it – even the younger ones. It probably pulled them through.

I'll tell these boys in the Golf Club something, the ones who complain nowadays about the cost of going private for a new hip – 45 years ago we would have been bidding for Whiteford's *old* hip, perchance to make a watery soup with it (as it is, Nina says, he now has nothing to 'trade in').

Lean and hungry these country boys may have been, but when King George called they didn't hesitate. One hundred and twenty men slung together in hammocks on a small corvette didn't seem like overcrowding to them.

Who could blame the menfolk for staying in Singapore pretending the war hadn't ended. Eventually, though, they had to come home and go to work for the Hydro. These were times of relative plenty, with Presents at Christmas in the form of red or yellow fuse wire. Who needed food when we had these magic vivid-coloured toys with which to make moorings for little boats made out of National Dried Milk tins.

Perhaps even more than the fuse wire and the giant ling, the high-water mark of an exciting childhood was the Coronation of Queen Elizabeth No. 2. How we got to hear of that imminent event and had time to prepare for it is a bit of a mystery. We had no radio or newspapers, and anyway we couldn't understand her language. Still, we were ready for it. Skinny little urchins in rags pushed heavy tyres and old timber to high hilltops (also, unfortunately, a roll of felt meant for someone's hen shed – I'm sure if he were alive he would forgive us). We laboured and lit our bonfires to celebrate that joyful occasion just like the children of Sussex.

It astonishes me still how we somehow grasped without fully understanding that this unknown Englishwoman was essential to our happiness and wellbeing. Nothing has changed very much. As she temporarily lit up our blighted childhood, so she continues to comfort us in middle age.

I'm quite certain if she knew of the waiting list for plastic hips in Stornoway Golf Club she would open her purse without hesitation. I feel I speak for us all when I say how delighted I am that she will no longer have to suffer the indignity of bargaining for Social Security increases. It is all quite wonderful.

FRIDAY, 31 AUGUST 1990

COGADH BEAG FAD' ÀS

'And I saw another sign in heaven great and marvellous, seven angels having the seven last plagues, for in them is filled up the wrath of God.'

(Revelation, Ch. 15, v. 1)

'And the fourth angel poured out his vial upon the sun; and power was given unto him to scorch men with fire.'

(Rev., Ch. 16, v. 8)

'And he gathered them together unto a place called in the Hebrew tongue Armageddon.'

(Rev., Ch. 16, v. 16)

I quote these three verses from the Last Book merely to jolt your memories. I'm sure the rest of St John the Divine's Revelation will come flooding back with a terrible foreboding once you tie it in with current affairs and recent Rupert Murdoch headlines.

Rupert's hacks will not, of course, be familiar with the Bible, otherwise they would have dredged up many more colourful headlines. The Butcher of Baghdad appeals to them, but it hardly conveys the same fundamental terror as the Beast of Mesopotamia.

I realise as I start my sermon that we, who have climbed the steps, are discouraged nowadays from dabbling in politics, but Armageddon is not a town you see on television every night. At the risk of incurring Presidential fiery wrath, we must alert the congregation. We must, though we be struck down this instant, expose the first angel for the slippery snake he is.

Until several weeks ago President George Herbert Bush, like his ancestors before him, was happy to think: 'He is the Bastard of Baghdad, but at least he is *our* Bastard of Baghdad.' And he believed it. In the name of Jesus, he sent him as many weapons of destruction as he thought would keep him amused.

Suddenly he realised, and cried in exceeding anguish: 'Gawd, we've sent the son of a bitch too much.' But Gawd answered him not. Yet still his children believed they were the children of Gawd: they gathered at the foothills of Armageddon and prepared to slaughter the circumcised.

All this time his friends the Israelites kept their peace and said very little, but just in case they should decide to do a little smiting he ordered a Pentagon deacon to say unto them: 'You guys keep the hell out of this lest we should get any bad gospel. And by the way,' he said, 'where the hell is this place Armageddon?'

All the wise men of Tel Aviv pored over the Murdoch Atlas of the Financial World, but no way could they find this place called Armageddon. 'Gawdamn place,' said the holy men, 'ain't even got a Stock Exchange.'

However, at this time there lived in the far west a man called Reagan, an old cowboy. He knew about them Gawdamn places – John Wayne had told him. He called Herbert on the phone and he whispered 'Kuwait.' Kuwait, that's where Armageddon was at.

At the mention of this name President George Herbert grew exceeding wroth and called for the head of the CIA. Why, he demanded, had they not told him this Beast of Mesopotamia was mentioned in the Bible? Why had they not arranged to have him assassinated like a Latin American stooge? But the leader of the CIA-ites was an angst-ridden mid-Western Calvinist manufacturer of guided missiles. Angst, my ass, said the President.

By the way, I hope none of you will be offended by my language tonight, but I am merely trying to tell it like it was in the letter from our missionaries in the Bronx. I am pleased to welcome back tonight one of those selfless servants of the state, Dixie MacLean. He went to have a look for himself at Donald Trump's evil empire in Atlantic City, and he says the Harlot of Babylon was never in it compared with what he witnessed with his own two eyes and Matie's good one.

Next door to the glittering satanic streets of one-armed bandits he saw tin-shacked poverty he could only compare with Mombasa's shanty towns. Thank goodness, he said, we did not accept that creep's money for Bethesda. I would rather, *ars esan*, go into the County.

Meanwhile, Dixie like all good patriots is doing some light training in case the call comes. This is the difference between his generation and young, fit Main and Borrison layabouts who claim they are in a reserved occupation because of Trish's Grant and Loan.

Dear me, I seem to have moved a long way from Armageddon. But this is not a quick, convenient Catholic sermon. You can go to the pub tomorrow.

Revelation, you may have noticed, is closer in style to the earlier tales of the Hebrews like Judges and Kings. This is not mere coincidence. The 'Ghost' writer lives forever.

This, however, does not make it any easier for us, in the Pentagon or wherever, to place Armageddon geographically. And it's no use looking at your wristwatches. My Friends in Barra place Megiddo with typical Jesuit arrogance on the plain of Esdraelon so many miles SSE of the city of Palestine in 608 BC. This is a typical Jesuit trick to impress the infidel with scholarship. They try to detract when they can from ancient Phoenician Freemason authority.

However, we all know how the desert sands shift. Who can doubt that the place where the last great battle shall be fought was recently called Kuwait.

OK, so we have now established our whereabouts; so what are we going to do? If I were a God-fearing President of the US of A, I would go and have a game of golf. Then, by Gawd, I would zzap them.

In the meantime, while the Commander-in-Chief is playing golf, someone has to take on the role of angel number one and direct the distribution of the seven plagues. Who can possibly keep control of all these fighting men who speak in different tongues? The Syrians with their hooked noses and black evil eyes could easily be mistaken for Iraquis, and the Italians with their hooked noses and narrow eyes might end up firing at the French, who also have hooked noses and evil eyes like the Arabs.

The Good Book promises that Armageddon will be a fight to the finish between good and evil, in which case it would be simpler if the Americans and the British with their regular features and open honest eyes take on the rest of the world.

Like the old fellow in South Lochs who wanted a '*cogadh beag fad*' *às a chuireas an-àird pris nan caorach*', so it was with the Americans and the British and especially the French in their fattening of the Beast of Mesopotamia. It will take a long time to starve him, so it has to be Armageddon. And we are led by a gomerel called Herbert. Lord help us.

Friday, 21 September 1990

SATURDAY FERRY

Until recently I have taken little interest in the Great Ferry Debate because, quite frankly, my travelling days are over. However, as a Christian, I feel I must express my wholehearted support for a Sunday sailing between Stornoway and Ullapool. I would actually prefer a sailing between Stornoway and Liverpool but I realise this is too much to ask of the reactionary yahoos who control our way of life.

Our much written-about 'unique way of life' is neither unique nor for the most part much of a way of life. More of the African under the tree later, but first we must examine the Christian aspect of the Minch Crisis.

If you are a serious evangelist, as most of our ministers would claim to be, you have a duty to reach the maximum number of sinners with the Word. I realise this is no easy task because those most in need just will not sit still and listen. Consequently you, the minister, have to make do with the same audience every Sunday – an audience already converted. It must be a bit like being married for 40 years to a woman who agrees with every word you say.

So where can you hope to reach the ungodly? Obviously the public houses are out of the question. Not only is the congregation likely to walk out to another pub, you could easily get a dart in your eye. Forgive me if the Sunday Ferry seems too obvious an answer, but where else could you be so certain of a gathering of sinners – as defined in the Deacons' Court.

During a four-hour crossing from Ullapool to Stornoway, at 10 knots, you could lay into them with a terrible vengeance and there would be no walking out. You could rain fire and brimstone from the crow's nest for the duration of a rough crossing and even hardened sinners like Cromarty would think twice before taking to the lifeboats.

There are many other good reasons why the Christian should welcome a Sunday Ferry. I can think of no better example of keeping the Sunday peace than a Minch voyage at 10 knots. But these are reasons *for*. Reasons *for* have hardly been aired at all. Those who would deny have done all the talking, and I have never heard so much nonsense talked by so many.

Possibly the people of Tarbert have an excuse for their anti-social protest, for theirs is a peaceful little village on Sundays. The solid citizens of Stornoway have no excuse. Saddam Hussein could land a division on Number One pier in Stornoway on a Sunday afternoon and nobody would notice. The noise from the motor racing track on North Beach Street would drown the rumbling of tanks, never mind the quiet arrival of a few Christians in their Ford Escorts.

And do you know what I'm going to tell you, the boys making the noise are the ones who arrived on the Saturday night ferry with loads o' money and XR several numerals on their motor cars. Ban the Saturday ferries and you have gone some way towards the preservation of our not-so-unique-way-of-life. Keep these young warriors on the mainland for an extra 24 hours and let them contemplate spiritual matters as they cross the Minch on Sunday at 10 knots.

As for the notorious poll, so much publicised by one of the local papers, I will treat it with the contempt it deserves. I know a little about these market research groups because I worked for them once. I'll let you into a secret. They often employ local people to do their so-called research, and rumour in North Lochs has it this latest telephone poll was conducted by Calum Russell – a man of the Church who works part-time for the *Stornoway Gazette*. Mind you, I'm not saying for one moment that there was any deviation from the standard parameters.

So, 66 per cent of those who can afford to pay the recent increase in BT extortion do not want to enjoy their Sunday on the ocean wave. Why should we care. We live in a democracy: we have no wish to herd them on to ferries.

In a hurried poll, conducted by myself personally among my Orthodox Jewish friends, 75 per cent were in favour of the immediate withdrawal of the Saturday ferry. The other two were out of town on business and could not be contacted.

But if they had been available and the poll was 100 per cent *for*, would it have been right to deny the rest freedom to travel? Why did we fight the Battle of Britain? *(You vant to fly also? Ed.)*

Make mock if you must, but I wish to be serious this week. Let us suppose for the moment that the *Suilven* makes the crossing from Ullapool to Stornoway on a Sunday at 10 knots, slowing down to the customary two knots at Bayble Island, what devastating upheaval would result? If the boat sticks to the present timetable (at the same speed), the 30 per cent or so who attend church would be blissfully unaware of its arrival. Their way of life would certainly not be affected.

What about the other crowd who see a Sunday ferry as a vague threat they cannot quite identify, far less articulate? The card-playing dinner-partying heathens who would hate to see their 'Lewis Sunday' change – *their unique way of life*. How is the quiet arrival of a ferry, at two knots, going to disrupt their pagan practices? What is their fear?

I'll tell you what it is. They have been alarmed by the propaganda expertly spread by the young Iranians in our midst that a Sunday ferry would somehow mean *work*. This threat strikes the same terror into those who spend all day Sunday in bed recovering from the previous evening's grand debauch.

This 65 per cent grouping of guilt-ridden 'againsts' do not really enjoy a pleasant way of life at all, far less a unique one. They have become far removed from our old friend, The African Under The Tree. There is nothing peaceful about their existence, and even if there was, a Sunday ferry would seem the least of their worries.

It need never interfere with *Eastenders* and, in any case, a walk on the golf course with a stick and a ball might be better for the soul.

Friday, 28 September 1990

TERRORS OF THE DAWN

Half-past-six on a Monday morning is psychological low water mark for most people. The damage done to the psyche by the night's dreaming can take hours or sometimes days to repair.

Start slowly and work back from death. Gradually lay your concrete bricks against the terrors of the dawn, build a solid wall between you and reality, and perhaps in an hour or so you can get out of bed. That is if you woke up *in* bed. If nocturnal activities were as frenzied as they sometimes can be, perhaps you came round under the bed or in a cupboard.

The trouble with our household is that you have to share the entire family's nightmares. I usually warn people who come to stay with us that a night's rest is not guaranteed. Disturbances of a noisy and violent nature can erupt at intervals throughout the night.

When the daughter is at home she can cause great alarm to strangers, although *we* learned to ignore her 10 years ago. She often takes a stroll through the house in her nightgown, but it is no ordinary sleepwalking because she asks and answers questions and even conducts lengthy conversations. Our friends find her behaviour rather odd but are usually too polite to comment.

She shouts and screams a lot. Someone called Elizabeth gets a lot of abuse for locking her out of her room, and she occasionally rearranges the furniture. Yet she never seems to come to any harm, even when she tries to climb the curtains.

'You don't look very well,' people tell me in the mornings. Do you wonder? I sleep next door to her, and I also have my own and Iain's nightmares to cope with.

These have taken a turn for the worse recently. The other night I had a terrifying encounter with some polar bears, possibly brought on by my increasing preoccupation with the disappearing ozone layer. I had consumed only two oatcakes with cheese washed down with a moderate measure of brandy.

It was about two o'clock real time but 6am dream time and a fine, calm morning. I'd just set a net at Ceann Thabhaidh and had gone ashore to tie the head-rope. I climbed up high to keep a look out for the *Moidart*, but I must have fallen asleep.

I woke up with a shock to a vision of startling clarity. I could see the Faroes and Jan Mayen to the left, Bear Island and Spitsbergen on the right and then the Polar icecap in fine detail. Tiumpan Head had disappeared or was too close to focus on (probably a result of the removal of the Earth's curvature).

The scene at the Pole was one of unimaginable tranquillity. Polar bears and their young frolicked like lambs in spring. The occasional Eskimo, in sharp relief against the blinding snow, dragged a seal's carcass on a sledge.

In a moment the scene was transformed from total peace to utter chaos. Gigantic waves rose up from the other side (presumably the Pacific in this two-dimensional picture). Foaming crests towered high above the white plain and smashed the ice with awesome cracking noises. A hundred ice floes, strangely uniform in size, broke loose from the main field. Each one carried a marooned bear. In no time at all these rafts were carried past the Butt of Lewis as if someone had stood the picture upright. This surging torrent ended abruptly at Loch Erisort in a slow-moving whirlpool. The ice melted rapidly and all around me swam one hundred bears.

Determined to save the net, I took to the boat but quickly found the bears could swim faster than I could row. I hurriedly returned to shore but discovered the gently-sloping nose of Tabhaidh had become a vertical sky-high cliff. Desperately I hauled myself up with hungry bears snapping at my heels, but I knew all was lost. The bears' blood-soaked jaws opened wider than a man's shoulders and their snarling froze blood and muscle.

It was about then I realised a certain snarl sounded familiar. Apparently as I tried to climb the wall I stood on her hair spread out on the pillow. Accustomed as she is to my ways, she quickly went back to sleep. Sleep for the 'normal' person was out of the question.

The dog Smut, sensing all was not well up above, had set up a sad drawn-out howling. Fiona chose the same moment to float through our room claiming someone was trying to knock down the east gable-end. To humour her I went along with her to investigate and found, for once, she was awake and something unusual, if not abnormal, had taken place in Iain's room.

He, who clearly takes after *her*, was sound asleep; but the scene in his room was one of devastation. The bedside table was overturned, a lamp had smashed, and the bed – normally lying north–south – was now positioned east–west. The boy was entwined in bedclothes twisted into a knotted rope. A fierce struggle had obviously taken place, but whatever 'it' was had fled.

We shook him gently and he told us his dream, still real and vivid enough to make him tremble. *They* had tied him to his bed somewhere near Carlisle and set the bed off at a great speed down the motorway. Unable to steer or dodge traffic in the normal way, he could only manoeuvre his 'vehicle' by throwing his weight violently from side to side. Again the two-dimensional picture must have been upended at the north end, so that, as he 'drove' south, his speed increased. Through superhuman effort he negotiated the bed to the south of England, bringing it to rest dangerously close to the Channel – or, as it happened, Fiona's wall.

The very next day, in real life, he passed his driving test. His dreams are easy to analyse.

In my own case, I've started staying up all night and already people have begun saying: 'You look better'. The daughter has left home and the dog sleeps all night. Some night soon I may risk closing my eyes again.

FRIDAY, 2 NOVEMBER 1990

I shouldn't be here this week, of course; I should be in Austria. But the wife broke down on me. I have no doubt it was a judgement from on high for having squandered her life's savings on an excursion to Vienna with the potatoes still in the ground and the sheep undipped.

As luck would have it, I found myself in another city of culture during the National Mod, but I couldn't find thon Ballygovan. I asked several people in Partick the way to the Mod but they'd never heard of it. It is a sure sign the town is too big if you meet people there who haven't heard of our great folk festival.

Yet the Bodachan is probably right. Ballygovan deserved their turn. There are probably still more Gaelic speakers in Glasgow than in the Western Isles, and they exiles like to speak the language in their own funny way.

I wouldn't have minded so much not getting to Vienna if I could have found someone in Glasgow with whom I could have conversed in German. You see! It's not the money she wasted that bothers me, it's the time spent studying a foreign language. Two weeks, night and day, I listened to 16 long tapes in the German tongue, and I thought I was doing fine. I had mastered simple sentences of polite conversation like 'Would you like something to drink at my place?' and now it is all wasted unless they start another war.

I'm not sure if the German language course is a reflection on the German-speaking nations or on the sort of tourists who go there, but for some strange reason my tutor assumed I intended to spend my holiday meeting strange women and force-feeding them. How on earth did the Germans manage to become such a mighty industrial power when they are obsessed with food? 'Would you like something to eat now or later?' 'Yes, please, thank you. I will eat now *and* later. In fact I like to eat all the time.' No wonder they lost so many wars, with their noses permanently in the trough.

Never mind, some day I'll find my way to Vienna and I'll tell you what these people are really like. And she need not think I didn't know what her game was. Keep him away from Ballygovan at any cost in case he meets Tormod a' Bhocsair and people like that. You know what *they* are like. Serves her right.

Yet despite her I did meet some teuchters in Paisley. The guid sister who lives in Paisley Golf Club arranged a game for myself and three so-called friends who let me down badly. Cunninghame North and the Macleod brothers, Iain and John Neil, got us thrown out of the club for being improperly dressed.

You would have expected by now that these Macleod guys – who've been around a bit, who are probably related to members of the Lodge and who have done well for themselves – would know how to dress properly. But no, the crofting genes shine through the bottoms of the most expensive trousers.

As for the sartorially dyslexic Cunninghame North, there is nothing much can be done with him. Although he has taken to wearing suits and ties, there always seems to be a piece missing. There's something about these boys from the southern tip of Argyll. You could spend money – let Hardy Amies loose on them – but they'd still manage to look like a half-sheared sheep.

From the moment we entered the premises people stared at us as if we had carried something in on our shoes. Cunninghame North flourished a rare tenner at the bar, but before he could say 'Do you realise who I am?' we got the bum's rush.

Still, we made someone's day. Someone who had probably joined the club 30 years ago so that one day he could throw some scruff out. Very likely he had been blackballed by the most important club of all. Golf clubs often have to take rejects from the Lodge. As a last resort I suppose one could always join a sea-angling or a shinty club, but who could you throw out?

There was nothing for it then but to watch the Mod on television.

It has to be said that Catherine MacDonald made a fine job of presenting in the short time allocated, and the Hearach fellow is not so bad either (although for some strange reason I kept expecting to hear him sing that old ditty 'I used to be a Hearach but I'm all right now'). I see Michael has become as temperamental as an Italian tenor now. He threw some terrible tantrums, but it worked. He frightened them into giving him the Gold.

It never ceases to amaze me what some children achieve despite their parents. We have often discussed, over a Saturday afternoon pint, the children of our 'friends' and how they turn out (this, by the way, comes under scientific research and not gossip). I first spotted this anomaly long ago when one of Dixie's daughters won a beauty contest. Even more mysteriously, they went on to get good degrees. Similarly, Robbie and Norrie Macgregor's children all did well at university. It makes you wonder if they are the real fathers at all when these people couldn't scrape an ounce of brain between the lot of them. And how could a growler like Rodney Mackenzie produce girls with such sweet voices? Mysterious indeed are His ways.

It was all rather depressing being stuck in the house with so much going on all around, but there you are. I suppose I could have gone out on my own but, of course, I couldn't enjoy myself thinking of her at home and unwell.

At the end of the day I was consoled to discover in Ullapool that the *Suilven* was in dry dock. After a quarter of a century of being transported in a cattle boat it is difficult to adjust to the luxury of the *Isle of Mull*. Do you suppose that one day we will be able to afford to cross the Minch regularly in comfort, or are we being punished for something?

Sadly, despite the cheerful surroundings, it seems all MacBrayne's cooks went to the same catering school – somewhere in Siberia. I risked a curry, but I'm afraid it defies description. I cannot imagine what they did to it unless perhaps it had already passed through some lorry driver's digestive tract. We will never attract many German tourists unless we teach Mr MacBrayne to cook.

FRIDAY, 9 NOVEMBER 1990

For two years or so Stornoway has been infamous for its Saturday nights. According to the gentlemen of the National Press it takes a brave man, and a braver woman, to venture out on the streets of Stornoway after dark. I cannot remember who wrote the first tall tale, unless it was John MacLeod. Whoever it was, and I'm not saying it was him, he sure did start something.

Intrepid reporters armed with notebooks and cameras sneak in on the Saturday ferry and lie in ambush at dusk waiting for the Carloway boys to ride into town firing their pistols in the air. Alas for the reporters, this doesn't happen. The wild men of Harris leave their irons at Marybank, and even those who come from South Lochs are mighty peaceable nowadays. They haven't run a sheriff outa town for years. This is a great disappointment for those who have come a long way at great expense. But, having done so, they must go back with a story.

The story generally goes that policemen are frightened to mingle with the young desperadoes who roam the main streets threatening to riot and lay the town waste. This blatant lie has gained much credence and is believed not only by distant readers of tabloids but by natives who cannot be bothered to have a look at the real thing for themselves.

Pity the poor 'journalist' serving an apprenticeship for greater things who still hasn't seen any blood spilled at 1 am, far less a drunken riot!

Here we must give credit to a recent visiting scribe – from the *Glasgow Herald*, I seem to remember – who turned down the offer of 'a bit of fun'. He happened to mention to a couple of young Siarachs, who had taken a couple of drams against the autumn cold, that things were very quiet. 'That's no problem,' said one Jack the lad. 'Do you want us to start a fight?' The boyo was unlucky. Had he stumbled on one of Murdoch's vermin he might have earned a few bucks for a bloody nose, but fortunately the *Herald* man wasn't into blood sports. Nevertheless, a column had to be filled, so the budding war correspondent became a temporary preacher and went on to draw attention to several revellers who seemed a bit young to be out so late.

He had a good story, but he let it slip through his inexperienced paws. Are there many places in these dark days where 14-year-olds can gather in small town centres in relative safety? But, no; our reporter hadn't the imagination. Having been sent to look for a riot, he had, at the very least, to find something of which his readers would disapprove.

Hot on the *Herald* boy's heels came our own Grampian Television with preconceived notions of evil. The theme of their promising new programme was '*cron*'. Perhaps it doesn't translate accurately as 'evil', but it is near enough to damn the programme. Grampian let their very competent camera crew loose in the late hours and the resulting pictures were, or will be, a collector's item (well done, Sam). The yellow late-night glow probably didn't need any filtering, because that is the way peat smoke diffuses – vaguely reminiscent of Jack the Ripper's London.

While scenes of Saturday night Stornoway were being filmed on the streets, dear Angela MacHector had to chair a discussion on the depravity 'they' expected to see revealed when the movie was developed, or whatever they do with moving pictures.

Unbeknown to the poor victims in the studio, the camera had captured truth.

In this case the truth, or picture, did not come anywhere near fulfilment of tabloid promise. On the contrary, the film showed a harmless *(gun chron)* gathering of young people that is common in the squares of many continental *(ECU)* towns.

In the meantime poor Angela has to referee a learned disputation among a team of four good men and true – the Revolutionary Murdo Alec, a Free Church minister; a youth worker, Dòcas; a superintendent of police from Glasgow; and Norma, Director of Social Work.

Naturally the question to be answered was: 'What are we going to do about it?' Please remember, at this stage, the poor people being asked hadn't seen what was essentially a joyful gathering of young men and women with no '*cron*' intent. There was no 'it' to do anything about.

To be honest, I did catch a glimpse on film of a very young man showing off with a can of lager, but this hardly warranted a call-out for ministers and social workers. But there you are.

The responses from the minister and the polis were fairly predictable – beat them with the Bible, and if that doesn't work beat their parents with the Bible. The social workers were a terrible disappointment to me. Inbred fear of the minister and his polis deacon forced them into a defence of the innocent.

So we are all, broadcasters and audience, forced into debate on a '*cron*' that doesn't exist. For the purposes of entertainment it is merely essential to have two differing opinions about imagined, or conveniently created, evil intent.

So far as I can judge, from my mingulaying with youth, this much publicised Saturday night seems a joyful gathering together of teenagers with no more malevolent purpose than the obvious joy of being together.

The film shown by Grampian TV during the debate proves my point. Unfortunately this leaves us short of conflict. There is nothing much wrong with a great gathering of youngsters in the so-called Narrows (a small prize is offered for the first young hooligan to date correctly the earliest recorded mention in literary lore of the Narrows, now an accepted definition of which street?).

If in the absence of recognisable disorder we have to pretend for televisual purposes to have a problem, and have to employ Carloway boys to start a fight, well, let's spend a few quid. Otherwise the studio discussion lacks punch.

If, despite evidence, we must persist with the notion of 'cron', I'm afraid we have to go back to the old country dances to find it.

When Shawbost, Leurbost and Back village halls were at their peak, dancing took a poor third place to the main events. Fighting came first, or perhaps second-equal with the guzzling of strong drink. Dancing as such only entered into proceedings when there was no other way to steer a young woman towards the back door of the hall and inevitable procreation.

To continue the comparison with 'cron' past and present, take a look at a letter from our files of 70 years ago. A huge gathering at the Mullach Mòr resulted in a young man being hauled in front of the judge for playing the melodeon. This Pied Piper of Crossbost enticed so many young people to gather from all points between Balallan and Ranish that an entire field of corn was flattened. Now it is well known that folk didn't dance in the corn: they danced in the road. Yet they disappeared into the corn at every pause of his fingers. He got severely fined by the magistrates for resting his fingers between dances.

It is a great pity we no longer grow corn on Cromwell Street. That is what the country boys are really looking for.

1991

FRIDAY, 11 JANUARY 1991

TYPES

During the period we call Hogmanay, I spent much of the time in the company of young folk. By young folk I mean boys and girls even younger than myself – the 17–23 age-group that still maintains the tradition of wandering through the villages calling wherever the signs seem welcoming.

Seventeen to 23 has always been a great drinking age. One half-bottle has a lot of mileage in it, and the idea of drinking is more important than the drink. The shame of dependence is such a long way off that it is not uncommon to see a young buck pretending to be drunk. This acting is good practice for a certain type who will very likely, 16 years later, often have to pretend to be sober (absolutely essential if he is to become a surgeon: could never act, myself, which is part of the reason I remained a plain Dr).

I am privileged to have been allowed to travel on this youth train wearing my sociologist's bonnet, so naturally I cannot name names. Still, it is interesting to identify, at such an early age, those who are going to survive and those who are going to fall down a lot.

Although this culture of ours is still very much based on strong drink, the group I studied seemed to have a much more civilised attitude than their counterparts in '61. For instance, it is rare nowadays to meet a young person on all fours – still wanting to fight. It is almost as if the change from Gaelic to English has taken the competitive edge off them. Or it could be that Stornoway's joyful Saturday night gatherings have had a pacifying effect.

It would be foolish to pretend they have all been transformed into little angels. A certain amount of fighting will be inevitable among the bucks while two or more are attracted to the same female. The male display will always retain some violence and will come to the fore when excessive sobriety loosens its unnatural rein. Primitive possessiveness is given vent with loud threats of 'Get your hands off my woman – take that, you swine . . . and that.'

One type that has always fascinated me is the 'careful type'. Like the others, he is easier to study these days because of the much less frantic rush to oblivion.

But first you must understand that the days of neat whisky by the neck are gone forever. As a matter of fact, whisky, neat or otherwise, has become a rarity. Instead of a bottle on the hip your young first-footer now has his portable cocktail cabinet. You are likely to be offered strange-coloured drinks with exotic names topped up and softened with fizzy additives. Unlike an old friend in Ranish, I don't believe this means they are all homosexual. There is nothing written in Leviticus or anywhere else that says a man can prove his innocence under the old laws through drinking raw whisky.

Anyway, to get back to the careful type. He has been with us throughout the ages. He is classed as dull by his contemporaries, and they are probably right. However, he will never get the jail and he will never get religion – except maybe very late in life, as insurance. He derives a certain amount of satisfaction from the knowledge that his friends are doomed. He is superior and smug and tends to smirk like a Salmond.

The sad case of the young man with the shattered heart is perhaps the saddest of all. His love is lost. He is inconsolable and very vulnerable. His pain can only be dulled by alcohol. In the two or three years it takes to forget he will probably acquire the costly habit. His type will always be with us. He has no equivalent in the ranks of the opposite sex because their broken hearts are easily mended and their affections easily transferred.

I have no idea how this type survives in non-alcoholic cultures such as the Jewish. Perhaps scars are healed through energetic and creative activity. Time sometimes heals. Sometimes not.

I like the extrovert, the life and soul of the party. He is uneasy if the company is unhappy. Because he cares deeply about how you feel, he is always under a great deal of stress and has to drink a lot. He often injures himself while trying to entertain, but these physical wounds are nothing compared to the remorse this type suffers in the aftermath.

You will often find a sullen unsociable sort drinking steadily on the fringe, as if his task was some sort of unpleasant duty he was forced to perform against his will. This is a man who will almost certainly, in the fullness of time, take to religion and preaching against the miseries of strong drink. He will be speaking from experience and telling the truth as he saw it.

Fortunately, a certain type of hooligan, common in '61, seems to have become extinct. Perhaps this shouldn't surprise us because his behaviour pattern was not geared towards survival. He wasn't the worst type; he sometimes couldn't avoid hurting others, but he inflicted a lot of pain on himself. He was sure he was the strongest, toughest fighting man in the world, and he became paranoid when others seemed unconvinced. He had to lash out at the world and the world often lashed back, which is probably why the type is now scarce.

Often during this period of great rejoicing you will come across someone who has isolated himself in the bathroom to the great annoyance of those who have been drinking beer. This fellow just wants a little cry. He wants to weep the old year out. Unfortunately, very often he will carry on long after the bathroom door has been broken down. If trapped by this fiend, you may be forced to spend the night looking at old photographs and be expected to mutter sympathetic noises (I assume you yourself are completely teetotal).

Finally, there is one type who should be expelled from civilised company for all time, and that is the wife. They are far too common who insist on bringing in tea and buns when all present are in the grip of alcohol. Many strong men in the past have left home over this type.

Although you will probably still be able to find all these types in 1991, they are less extreme in every way than the class of '61. I'm sure you will take my word for this and do not expect any proof, yet I must mention that a sizeable gathering of Leurbost youth was playing charades in my house at 2 o'clock in the morning of the second. Strangest of all, they seemed to welcome tea and sandwiches. Give them a break.

FRIDAY, 25 JANUARY 1991

SUNDAY After my customary Sunday afternoon run in the Castle Grounds with my own little Rubens lady and the dog Smut, I chanced to tune in to a Gaelic sermon from the BBC. Sweeter, tastier Gaelic I have seldom heard, although the minister was a Tolsta man. I would guess from the tone of the sermon this was a man of the reformed faith. He asked us, the listeners, if we had been chosen – were we children of Christ? This was a far from easy question to answer.

Earlier in the day I heard another preacher, this time from America, praying and claiming to be of the chosen few. Somehow he didn't seem very persuasive because he spoke in what I imagine to be a low-caste New York accent – a bit like Walter Matthau acting a tough guy. But who knows?

To confuse matters further, television showed Saddam Hussein praying to his God, presumably recorded in happier times, and he seemed to have received an instant reply assuring him that God was on his side and would smite the infidel forthwith.

Meanwhile, in Israel they have no doubt, but they still go to bed wearing their gas masks.

MONDAY Having been totally confused on Sunday, it was a great relief to leave theology and return to weekday politics. The first preacher I heard on Monday was a Lowland Tory called Gerry Malone. His enthusiasm for the war seemed all-consuming. I couldn't understand how he managed to restrain himself from charging immediately to the front, unless he has ingrowing toenails or something. Another old warrior who sounded as if he desperately wished he was a little bit younger was my old friend in the tartan trews, Auld Nick Fairbairn.

No one has ever explained to me satisfactorily why young boys and girls should be sacrificed rather than the middle-aged and older. Nineteen-year-olds can perhaps run a little faster than we can but they have so much more to live for. We who have lived a little could perhaps stand a little more heat, and in any case we are past our best, have lost our ideals and would be no great loss. If we want to perpetuate the myth that we are concerned with the future of the human race we should try to preserve our teenagers, humanity's only hope. Of course we could never trust them to make decisions.

TUESDAY The outcome of the war is not in doubt. It may take a long time but eventually might will win. The problem then is how to manage an uneasy peace.

The obvious solution would be to recolonise the Third World, but this would probably be unacceptable to the colonised because we made a mess of it the last time. But perhaps next time our approach would be different. Perhaps we could save Africa from the Africans and Asia from the Asians if we attempted some sort of partnership. Naturally, the suffering poor in the colonies would be junior partners until such time as they mastered the intricacies of the stock market.

We would not have to fight the French and Germans over colonial resources this time because we stripped those the first time round.

WEDNESDAY On the domestic scene I see the little politicians have made some significant moves while we were all preoccupied with the Monster of Mesopotamia. I phoned our Member, Calum Macdonald, with the news that a Cockney Seceeder, Mr Andrew Price, was to be his Tory opponent at the next election. He said: 'I ain't worried.' I'm afraid I take a dim view of his complacency. Bearing in mind that the outcome of all modern battles hinges on which side God is on, I would advise Calum to keep his powder dry. We are after all a conservative people and we are getting older.

It is no secret that I have never managed totally to suppress my nationalist tendency, and now that Ms MacFarlane seems to be the

Crown Princess I must re-examine my position. It is quite possible that she may not want my support but I feel, as my children were once grateful for her hand-me-downs, I should at least offer it. And, of course, I went to school with her old man. My great fear is that she may have been a victim of Jesuit indoctrination down there in Barra.

THURSDAY Ironically, my own literary research assistant – a colleague who used to dig with the other foot – is now going through a phase of intense interest in Judaism. Much of our time is spent in the Old Testament, particularly on Levitical law and ritual. This alternates with readings of Knox and Calvin, but I fear that my colleague's discovery that we still eat cormorants and eels has proved a great spiritual stumbling-block towards 'coming over'.

But to get back to the new SNP candidate . . . I want her to assure me that she never met my friend Jackson. I would hate to think that her politics are based on disappointing encounters with Englishmen. The subject of Englishmen was being emotionally discussed by some of my eminent colleagues the other day. Sadly, the conclusions reached were not at all in favour and in fact were barely printable. Horrid, beastly, ghastly cads were some of the terms I overheard. Yet they were unanimous in declaring that English women were quite wonderful and thought this was nature's way of compensating for English men. Captain and Mrs O'Shea were cited as typical examples, although they might have been Anglo-Irish.

FRIDAY Before I go the whole hog on this nationalism business. I have to know where stands the new independent Scotland on war. If we fall out badly with England and have to take up arms, what proportion of Tornados can Scotland claim? Will the bankers and accountants who run the City of London be allowed back to Scotland? Will they want to come back? What if they are held hostage in strategic border posts like Newcastle? Can we rely on members of the British Legion to sing 'Flower of Scotland'? Is North Sea oil important enough for America to come in on our side? Remember how they hesitated over Hitler. Minor points, you may think, but they must be answered.

SATURDAY Am I alone in thinking that Mr Bush is motivated merely by fair play?

FRIDAY, 22 FEBRUARY 1991

THURSDAY On this the third day of the trial separation all goes well. She seems quite happy to be back in the tenement, and I have the house to myself.

I cannot make up my mind what gives me greater pleasure – the rolled-up damp towel on the kitchen floor, or contemplating the empty hook where it should hang. There are many important questions still to be answered, like who gets custody of the dog Smut. Perhaps we should let him decide. He certainly seems much happier when I'm in charge and, contrary to what she has always maintained, chicken bones do not seem to do him any harm provided they're alive when he catches them.

FRIDAY The towel on the floor has become the symbol of my freedom, so I'll leave it there until it moves of its own volition. Already I've managed to save a lot of peat and coal. It is clearly unnecessary to light a fire in the early morning if one wears enough clothes. As a matter of fact, I seem to have made savings in all departments. On a visit to the supermarket I replenish the larder at a fraction of the usual cost. I can only think she must consume an awful lot of junk food *and wine*.

After 21 years of constant nagging can you imagine what bliss it is to stretch out on the sofa in the early afternoon, fully booted and spurred, with a good novel? By the way, try to avoid these cans of so-called draught Guinness. They are 90 per cent gas and make a terrible mess, especially when you try to open them in the reclining position.

SATURDAY Sadly, there are men who need managing and who are unable, without guidance, to plan a day in their own lives. They approach the simple tasks required to run a household without a system, so they waste their mornings running around in circles.

Now pay attention, you bachelors. As soon as you open your bleary eyes in the morning, stop to think. There is no sense in crippling yourselves with anxiety. After a few moments' debate with the inner man, it becomes clear there is really very little to do. There are hardly any of those jobs, which women with their little minds think essential, that cannot be postponed indefinitely. If you haven't washed anything, there is no washing to hang out. Stay in your warm bed with the novel.

That towel on the floor is beginning to annoy me. Somehow, it no longer lends any satisfaction, so I hang it up in its proper place.

In case I succumb to further urges to do some work, I decide to visit the Barvas Navigator.

Where he is or what he is doing I cannot of course reveal in these sensitive times. However, he is in a very belligerent mood, so I wouldn't like to be in Saddam Hussein's shoes at this moment. I expect him back very soon with his mission accomplished, and it shouldn't surprise us if he emerges as the modern Lawrence.

SUNDAY After a hazy night of soul talk with Lawrence I seriously think of going to church. For sad reasons, during the last few months, I have been exposed to more than my usual ration of prayer.

But instead of going to church, despite my burden of guilt and remorse, I lie in bed and meditate. After two hours in the prone position I have to reject prayer as a solution to the human predicament.

In desperation I telephone several friends renowned for their preoccupation with matters spiritual. All I ask for is one small shred of evidence that prayer is ever answered. Just a single instance of His intervention on behalf of the demanding individual was all I wanted. No one could help.

MONDAY Still in the blackest of moods, I resume my quest. At last I find a friend with proof – an Anglican who once considered taking Holy Orders but who has since lapsed badly. In fact, as lapses go, his is unsurpassed: he married into the Catholic Church.

Yet he showed me proof. Apparently an aged in-law of his prayed for Russia. Every night for 30 years she prayed for these poor people to be delivered, and look at Russia now. So there, he said.

Although far from convinced, I had to admit he had hit on something. Hardly proof, but then again who can say this good woman did not bring about the liberation of Eastern Europe with her persistence.

As my friend is obviously familiar with Romish practices, I asked him if he had noticed a trend, on that side, that I had begun to suspect on our own.

Was there a conspiracy among clergy of all denominations to devalue the importance of Hell? He thought so.

Promises of eternal happiness are no longer counterbalanced by threats of damnation.

This worries me because, unless you terrorise the flock with fear of the flames, I don't see how they can be kept under control. We need to train more brimstone preachers without delay if the social fabric is not to be rent asunder.

TUESDAY Although it is very much against the terms of our trial separation, I phone the wife to ask: how's Glasgow? The poor woman is obviously finding it hard to cope without me. In search of peace and assurance she had gone to Partick Highland Free Church on the Sunday.

The congregation is now diminished to six pews of women, many of them even older than herself. I wonder if they have driven a generation away with traditional threatening sermons, or do they need a star attraction on detachment? Or have they moved to the Church of Scotland, where it is easier to be good? In a moment of weakness I ask her to come back on probation and she agrees.

WEDNESDAY In an attempt to draw closer to nature I drive to the hills of Uig and am immediately rewarded with further proof of miraculous gifts. A smooth network of immaculate motorway stretches in all directions. Their councillor is, as everyone knows, a Priest. Although only of the Church of Scotland, his prayers have been answered with a million tons of tarmacadam. I resolve to contact DHM on my return to the dirt tracks of North Lochs and ask him to try prayer.

FRIDAY, 8 MARCH 1991

CRISIS IN NORTH LOCHS

The North Lochs councillor's resignation on grounds of ill-health has left us once again unrepresented in the Chamber of Horrors. DHM is the third councillor in recent times who couldn't take the strain, which should show us that we cannot be too careful when it comes to the selection of a person sound in body.

There is not a moment to be lost if we are to find the right man for the job (a woman is naturally out of the question – it's too rough in there). In the run-up to previous elections we tended to concentrate on candidates with vision. Men with ideas and the ability to articulate them. Men, we hoped, who could think on their feet, raise the level of debate around the purse and then come back to the parish with the loot.

We pinned our hopes on DHM's great command of language when we should have been examining his physical parts. Now that we know mental agility is not required in the Grande Chambre, we will carefully scan potential candidates for bunions and palpitations. When I say brains and powers of speech are not necessary, I mean they are a positive disadvantage.

If you can bear to look for a moment at the most successful councillors in the present collection, you will notice they are all fine physical specimens – ugly, certainly, but big and strong. South Lochs, Shawbost, Carloway, Gress and Uig have all relied on men of might, with spectacular results. Roads and new schools can be had if you have diplomats who can hold their own in street thuggery. I wouldn't like to tackle that Mary Bremner either.

We must immediately start weeding out wimps in our search for the 'right man'. Although I say the mind doesn't matter, I still think a smattering of education might help. Perhaps the least we should demand in this sphere is that our man should be able to read the *Sun* without moving his lips or following the lines with his fingers. But that is not the main qualification. The first simple test of strength would be to wrestle Carloway to the ground, and then perhaps two rounds with Shawbost.

Perhaps I have set my sights too high, but how else are we to get roads and schools?

As luck would have it, when the news of DHM's 'ill-health' broke last Friday afternoon I was fighting a losing battle with Dixie on the Golf Course, where he inadvertently revealed some of the qualities we want in our representative.

Mac Sheomag sounds a lot younger than he is, although he looks a lot older. He got the name Dixie during his brief spell as football star for Lochs in the Thirties. I know, it *is* hard to believe when you see him sprinting up the Dardanelles with a heavy bag on his back – in 1991. But there you are.

His physical fitness is not in doubt, but he possesses even more important characteristics that would not go amiss at Comhairle nan Eilean.

He is, how shall I put it, rather careful with his money. Let me give you an example.

Kenny Murray, brother of millionaire tweed baron Derek, marked his ball on the rough edge of a green with a penny (typical). Of course the penny couldn't be found, which led to an unseemly squabble about where the ball should be replaced. Fortunately Dixie was in the vicinity, and, as you would expect, he found the penny in no time at all. This is the sort of man we need. Someone who takes great care of his own money is not likely to squander *your* poll tax.

Apart from other considerations, Dixie, late in life, has had to join the dole queue. There is no shame in this, for who knows when it might come to us all. The problem with this fellow is that he has become a pest. A naturally active man who abhors idleness, he now has time to annoy his neighbours. Having redecorated his entire house with these old white fivers, he is at a loose end. Much as he would like to, he cannot call meetings of the Grazings Comedy every day, so he calls honest civil servants away from their work for the Queen.

I understand when he ran Keose Co-op as a dictator the men had to apply in writing to go for a pee. Yes, I think he could be our man.

Another strong contender in every sense of the word is Wee Angus. Not tall, certainly, but few ever got the better of him in a tight corner. My one misgiving is his habit of buying out of turn. He was never one to hoard. He believed money was made to go round, and consequently he has not piled much under the bed. Originally he came from Ranish, where we despised the acquisitiveness of Leurbostians.

However, who knows? He is another who doesn't encourage layabouts, and he is curious to know why certain departments exist in the big house.

Still, I suspect the winner has to be a native of Leurbost. It was said of the wealthy merchants of Leurbost, when they were at the height of their power in the Thirties, that if diamonds rained from the sky and knocked their eyes out they wouldn't mind if they got their hands on them.

I hear Norman Mackenzie's name mentioned, but I doubt this story. He already owns the Cabarfeidh, the Seaforth, the Royal and the Lewis Hotels (perhaps more since last weekend), so I shouldn't think he is interested in Council – unless, perhaps, gossips misunderstood and he intends to buy the Comhairle and run it profitably. Yet he is another who came up the hard road, and a man who handled a few toughs in Glasgow in his day. He is still fairly robust.

My attention has been drawn to changes in Robbie Macrae's behaviour patterns. Although an East Coaster, he has lived in Leurbost now for 20 years and could soon be eligible to drop the title *srainnsear*.

Robbie is reputed to have caught a slight dose of the *cùram*, and that is no bad affliction in someone who aspires to Council.

Down in Ranish I hear my friend Coinneach's name mentioned. Physical qualifications are fine – he bends steel girders on his sturdy knees. But as an ex-trade unionist he thrives on debate. The Grande Chambre is no place for that sort of thing, and there is always the danger Council meetings would clash with sheep fanks.

Some have talked of Calum Russell, but the parish is full of comedians.

Last but not least, I have, as they say, allowed my own name to go forward. Although I may be considered a poor physical example of the species, I could always carry a gun.

All in all, an interesting seven-cornered battle is in prospect.

FRIDAY, 15 MARCH 1991

'IN THERE'

Now that a date for the North Lochs election has been fixed with indecent haste, it seems only right that I should take over the column for the duration of hostilities. Believe me, for I should know, he is not above using this public platform to further his political ambition.

I date say regular readers are well aware of his 'view', but with only seven weeks to go it would be unethical to let him fill this space with a list of his personal accomplishments. Although he is not entirely wanting in the meanest of, they would scarcely run to a full column. Well, otherwise I wouldn't have to go out to work, would I?

Please don't imagine I wouldn't like him to win, because I would – if for no other reason than there is a lot of mazuma to be gathered in there. Quite apart from blatant bribery and shiny trinkets for favours rendered, all of which appeal to me, there is the £52 per night subsistence. Subsistence, by Dr George: that would cover many a grand hotel, let alone a doss-house in Benbecula (including a stake for the poker game or whatever it is they play).

Yet, having said I want him to win, what I mean is I don't want him to lose. One can take only so many years of being tied to a loser. When I think now how I foolishly turned down D Campbell, turf accountant, in his prime – and his promise of every winter in Mombasa – I could spit. Even Dr Taylor, despite his mother, held some promise of position in small-circumference society. But that is by the way. Sylvia now has the Hyndland Dux and I have a drake in decline.

Still, decline or incline, as I promised in church all these years ago, I will support him when he wilts. With more candidates staking a claim every day, we could end up with 10 hopefuls and not a decent body amongst them. I nearly said throwing their hats in the ring, but he hates them things – it's OK if cliches date from the Alaskan Gold Rush.

The unfortunate outcome of close scrutiny is that all candidates cannot bear it. If you're talking about skeletons in cupboards, I have a small alcove that is sealed up. If the bones therein were to rattle, they would sing a sorrowful song. But is there one amongst the candidates who has not spotted his garment?

Alasdair Neileag, one of my old boy-friends (and I mean old), has a mind to stand. This comes as a great surprise to me. He was never one of the friskiest, even in his younger days; and, as a nurse, I must strongly advise him against futile attempts to regain his youth at this stage. For all that, he is a charming man, moderate with alcohol and possessed of infinite patience. I may still vote for him if he can convince me he is up to it. I am told he is not a Freemason, but that is not important because there are only three of them 'in there' now.

Please excuse the old-fashioned fountain pen, dear Ed, but I'm afraid I disapprove of modern technology. Sitting bolt upright at a keyboard is fine if you're musical, but I'm afraid it is not conducive to creativity. I do not claim to be a mechanical genius. But if forced to write a business letter I can manage a typewriter and, unlike Allan Whiteford, I can wind my own watch – and tie *his* bootlaces. Still, when it comes to literature, the pen is your only man.

I think I'm beginning to enjoy this, and I wonder if I shouldn't finish his novel myself. Naturally, I would have to redevelop some of the characters to show women in a better light. It probably wouldn't be a bad idea to have some of them fully clothed for a change.

Sorry. I seem to have drifted away from Council business, as we women do. Oh, by the way, while I'm on this diversion, I have a fleshy bone to pick with Ted Brocklebank. I don't know if you saw that programme on Chan 4 the other night where a gang of chauvinist males tried to make out all island women were fat with big bouncy mammaries. I'll have them know that God intended women to be well-padded. We still outlive our skinny husbands by an average of 20 years. So there.

Now, what can one say about candidate number eight? Coch has tried everything, so why not the Council? As a baby I dangled him on my knee and changed his nappies. I knew then that here was an unusual character. I watched him take his first steps and heard his first words. He still cannot say cloch, but what does that matter. His grandfather Dòmhnall Barney supervised his boisterous youth and often said he was born to be hanged. Hanging is no longer permitted, but I suppose the next best sentence is four years in the Grande Chambre. Coch can get you anything *now*, as a lay person; imagine what he could achieve in a position of authority.

By the age of 22 Coch had owned 40 cars. He was – still is – a painter, a mechanic, a weaver, a warper, a fisherman, a taxi owner, a chef and many other things besides. A truly self-made man who is at peace with his maker.

There is a rumour in church circles that Torquil Òg has expressed an interest in doing good work for the parish, and I would certainly approve. Unfortunately, I don't see how this can be true, because he is still a Council official. As owner of a granny farm, we sincerely hope there are no skeletons in his cupboards.

Torcuil Aost in Grimshader would be my ideal candidate. He is one of the few people in North Lochs who writes and speaks sense. A most eligible bachelor with loads of money. Yes, I think we could rely on Torcuil to do the right thing.

In the final analysis, having examined the lot of them through the eye of a nurse, I will probably have to choose between the man who occasionally shares my bed and Aonghas Beag, who is generally much more useful to me nowadays. And usefulness, when assessing potential councillors, is what we have to consider. When you need a man, do you vote for someone who can write you a love poem or for the person who can fix things and keep your old car going? A difficult decision. I will not be rushed into it.

I do not, of course, agree with what he said last week about 'in there' being no place for a women. Thuggery is not at all the only means of getting one's own way. I still think a glimpse of stocking, or even support tights, would go a long way towards a new road.

Next week, if I can get my hands on his files, I intend to publish some of the letters he wrote to the Council over the years. And perhaps, unless there is some law against, I will also show you the ridiculous replies. Must go and do my hair now.

FRIDAY, 5 APRIL 1991

MONDAY This morning, April 1st, I had a very close shave with the Grim Reaper. Had it been any other day I would have been addressing youse from the other side. I can only think he is saving me for something worse.

A Hydro van parked on the Harris-Stornoway road, between Murdie Siarach's and Dòmhnall Chuilidh's, obscured my view to the right of Elders' Corner (so called because 30 years ago we very nearly lost five North Lochs Free Kirk elders – *nach maireann* – who were, also, attempting to climb out of Leurbost).

Anyway, I did as Moley's School of Motoring taught me. I looked right and left and right again. To the left I could see all the way to Harris, but no matter how often I looked to the right I could only see the Hydro van. Much as I like looking at the noble superiors' Soval Lodge set against the Clisham backdrop, I can only obey the Highway Code for so long. I held her back against the brakes, closed the right eye and launched myself onto the main road. Had the Grim Reaper been in an older vehicle without ABS steering, or whatever they cry it, well . . .

TUESDAY Now I don't blame the man who was driving south at 96mph: he probably had a ferry to catch, and was too young to know the corner's history. And of course there are no signs bewaring of stray natives crossing.

In the absence of a councillor someone *has to speak out.* Fifteen years ago, Dr Cement spent 60,000 dollars on Elders' Corner so that we, his wife's relatives, could join the main traffic with peace of mind. The hump was removed and the road was widened. The engineering department did what they could, but their great mistake was to widen the road.

The lure of this artificial 'hard shoulder' is too much for the average driver. Whether he is a taxi driver, a milkman or one of those chocolate-munching articulated train drivers, they cannot resist that first breathtaking glimpse of Lochs. They pull in and abandon their cabs. Where they go, no one knows. We only know the result. Death soon. Not in itself a great tragedy, if quick and clean, were it not for the desperate grief of those left to grieve.

WEDNESDAY There is not much to laugh at in North Lochs nowadays, except the Saga of Sandy's Cows. When the poor man decided to raise some beef he thought Leurbost was still a crofting village. Someone should have told him ours has been a bedroom village for the past 20 years. We work in Stornoway, sleep in Leurbost, and on Saturdays we tend our sheep and mow our lawns. We take a dim view of Crossbost eccentrics who still keep cattle.

Unless Dixie decides otherwise, I'm afraid the village is open to all manner of animals until the 10th of May or until the corn is three inches high. The 10th of May was when we traditionalists left for the herring fishing, and we are great boys for tradition. If the cows eat your Veronica before the 10th, the only course open to you is to plant some more. I'm pleased to say, though, that any sheep worrying your roses can be shot on sight.

Some years ago when I had some trouble with Atch's cattle I had to resort to extreme measures. Atch had of course trained his animals to break down fences, but I fixed him in the end. Every Sunday morning when I found his beasts in my back garden I took a sharp knife and sliced a steak of the best rump. Atch himself was renowned for his gargantuan appetite in those days, and pretty soon he had to get rid of his cattle to stop nasty gossip.

THURSDAY Easter, somehow, is not the great religious festival it once was. It doesn't rate a mention in the Free Church. Our refusal to acknowledge the Resurrection is a constant sign of concern for foreigners who have considered 'coming over'. I must confess this lack of spirituality in the Free Church was one of the chief reasons I myself decided to join the Catholic Church.

Like the Anglicans and the Church of Scotland, we hold the Resurrection to be of supreme importance to our faith. As a matter of fact, without Easter Sunday I cannot understand how the Free-men can consider themselves to be Christians at all.

Maunday Thursday is one of my favourite days, and I very nearly decided on the Anglican Church because of it. This is the day the Queen of England pretends to be Pope and goes around washing Cockney feet and drying them with her hair. I understand she also hands out money to the poor. I'm very surpised my fundamentalist brothers haven't latched onto this bonanza.

To my great astonishment I have discovered that the Catholics seem to enjoy the Easter festival. This worries me a little, because any hint of enjoyment seems to me to be at odds with belief. On the other hand, a good *ho-rò* when it's all over is something with which I am in complete agreement.

FRIDAY One of the most pleasing aspects of my new faith is that the clergy have nothing against a wee flutter on the horses. I can now feel free to go into print on that other great festival – Aintree. Listen carefully and I'll tell you how you can take D Campbell, turf accountant, to the cleaners on Saturday.

Go to the Bank and say you want to buy a car or something. Don't bother to haggle about interest rates because you'll be paying back on Monday. In fact, you may be able to go into the lending business yourself after this one. I had a dream the other night where I saw that old donkey Durham Edition coming home by 10 lengths at a very fancy price.

The problem now is that after this revelation the odds are likely to shorten somewhat, so get in early and demand your 40–1. I have already booked a table for 20 in the Cabarfeidh on the strength of my dream, and dreams seldom let me down. Reality sometimes does, though.

SATURDAY I had another dream last night about a ferocious row in D Campbell's after the Grand National. There wasn't enough money in the till for the hordes collecting, and some Siarachs had taken the law into their own horny hands.

FRIDAY, 12 APRIL 1991

MONDAY On this particularly gloomy Monday I desperately searched the airwaves for a glimmer of hope. Just one tiny item of happy news would have done me, but I searched in vain.

Radio was bad, but television was ten times worse. The BBC insisted on showing me the bloody bodies of slain Arabs while I practised my golf swing. As if that was not enough, they remind me – with more gory pictures – of the alarming number of children who die on our highways. A snippet in my newspaper says more people were murdered in the State of Washington in the last few months than died in our recent moral war against Hussein.

And so it goes on. By early evening I was so distracted I gouged large chunks out of the living room carpet with my nine iron.

As luck would have it, I happened to tune in to ITV for the early evening news. I feel so much better now, and I will retail their message so that you too will cheer up.

'Prince Harry today paid his first visit to the ski slopes. His ski instructor was delighted with his progress and described him as a natural. Unfortunately he developed a coughing bout and was forced to abandon the slopes. However, after a hot drink, he felt better and was soon smiling again.'

TUESDAY After a ferocious half-hour's coughing bout I had three cups of coffee and three fags and now I feel good. I'm smiling again. If only we had more happy news instead of aerial film of freezing Kurds, how much better would our golf be.

I am constantly hounded by the media for comment on the massacre of the Kurds. Sometimes I am interrupted on my backswing by impudent reporters asking silly questions about the carnage in Iraq and what am I going to do about it. Let me see now . . . how can I put this so you'll all understand. Perhaps if I say to you that Kurds are not Kuwaitis . . . I hope I have made my point clear. Thank you.

WEDNESDAY At last I hear something that cheers me enormously. My little friend John MacLeod has been awarded Young Journalist of the Year by the Bank of Scotland. Particular mention was made of his in-depth peep at Stornoway on a Saturday night. The young man should not be too despondent about this award – I won it myself in 1948. The fact that this appreciation comes from bankers, who normally only read figures, in no way detracts from the honour.

At the time MacLeod wrote his piece on Saturday night fever the gatherings in the Narrows were happy affairs. Since his reportage started to attract TV cameras the young bucks feel they have to live up to their reputation and things have taken a turn for the worse. I think if MacLeod turned his attention now to Sunday ferries, we would soon have a flotilla of fast vessels running a shuttle service across the Minch.

When we contacted our own TC, who won a similar award last year, he said from the south of France: 'I must seriously consider sending it back.'

THURSDAY An urgent message from one of my diary assistants tells me David Icke has approached the Tory Party with a view to standing.

I would like to examine this man's credentials at length, but we must postpone his profile until another time.

The post has just arrived, and with it another tale of woe from our South Uist observer, claiming he's come across the odd crofter with a Kalashnikov slung over his shoulder the way the casual kids of Kuwait carry it off. This apparently has nothing to do with poll-tax collectors, too much Sky-watching or a surplus of dumped kit.

FRIDAY It seems the island has become infested with a plague of deer thought to have swum in from North Uist or Skye or bred from one-time children's pets like the frogs and hedgehogs which, though locally extinct since the Vikings burnt them all as witches, now add a bit of variety to the customary assortment of squashed meats on the roadway.

This is tree-planting time for the born-again crofter, and it is difficult enough to resign oneself to waiting 20-odd years to see a tree grow tall even if these rapacious beasts didn't haul them out, strip them down and off with their heads quicker than you can say 'wonky social worker'. Thus the magnificent 50ft maples of your forest dreams are sadly and ineluctably reduced to ashes, and schoolkids in a thousand years will be taught it was the Vikings what did it all. That's larnin' fur yuh.

It seems these deer belong to no one in particular, as historically there is no deer forest in South Uist. All the hill ground is in crofting tenure, let out to the cow and sheep keepers at an average souming of 29.17 sheep and 2.98 cows per share. Whatever flies or swims in or is under the ground thereof belongs to the lord, except the midges and acid rain, which belong to us all. Whether a deer becomes a fish when it swims or a bird when it soars over fences could tax mediaeval ecclesiastics or Land Court lawyers. But were deer to speak they surely would agree that a tree forest should precede a deer forest.

Meanwhile, Kalashnikov-flashing notwithstanding, there is little hope of them being hunted down. Few would resort to the local poisoning speciality, and the bulk of the peasantry has long since grown soft on Audrey's Black Forest gateau (secret weapon?) and are now in distinct danger of rescinding grazing birthrights in favour of the vocal pottage industries of language reanimation, military installation minding and sundry jobbies around the big hoose.

Closer inquiry reveals a combination of short-sightedness and sentimentality consolidating this *de facto* encroachment (*deja vu, an tuirt thu*). The position may change next year when the pesticide Arborguard will be in surplus, but how much better were wolves subsidy brought back – must mention it to Calum for his forest thing.

FRIDAY, 19 APRIL 1991

FOOD AND SMOKE

Some very old readers will probably remember when I used to write a column on food and drink. That was a happy time before the children arrived and I could afford fish and chips. The ironic bit (you must have that) was that during my period of relative affluence there was no shortage of willing hosts to dine me out. Now that I am a gentleman in reduced circumstances, there are no 'friends' to pick up the tab. Sad, but is that not always the way.

While I was wallowing in this Slough of Despond, anchored firmly on self-pity and weighed down by Celtic introspection, a real friend came along and said: 'Let me treat you in the Crown Inn to a feast to raise your spirits'.

I always go fortified in expectation of disappointment, but now I regret that extra slice of duff I had before the off. The flounder on my plate was as fresh as anything I ever had from the Granny. If Derek Cooper comes to visit soon I will not be ashamed to let him take me to the Crown. At a mere £6 a skull I wouldn't be surprised if he takes the whole of Leurbost.

As often happens, within a very short time of my happy experience in the Crown I was sadly disappointed in the same town. Tough, overcooked beef is fine, if you're at a wedding and totally anaesthetised; but when you're paying yourself it is impossible to digest.

I first suspected the meat was not as it should be when Sylvia, that gentle lady from Milngavie, started spitting her gold fillings into her doily. 'Donald,' she whispered, 'if you don't do something I'm going in there to damage the cook.' 'You mean the chef, dear, to damage the chef,' said Donald, correct as ever.

The cook, as often happens, blamed the butcher, as if North West Meats had ossified the beast for three days in a microwave. If this is how they treat the Bridge Club, what sort of fare do they serve the yeomen? Perhaps if the Lawyer had a palate like Stewart's we could seek redress through channels.

Often it is safer to invite your poor friends to eat in your home. Do not despair if your larder is at a low level, for there is always that old favourite, sliced sausage and corned beef soup (with egg) – a solid standby at communions and other festivals.

Open a tin of corned beef, take the plastic off the sausages, throw in some stale vegetables and water and simmer for an afternoon. Towards the end spread a beaten egg on the surface to camouflage your stock. You don't have to worry about the egg sinking. You can serve this wonderful meal as a soup or allow it to cool for a while and dish it up as a knife and fork job. If there is anything left over it makes a fine foundation for fenceposts or clothesline poles. Friends who sampled this wonderful creation last Christmas still talk about it.

Anyway, what does food matter when you're talking. While talking very seriously to my eminent colleague Dr Taylor, about the early stages of eternity (the worrying warming-up period, because after that we will presumably have become acclimatised), I remembered the time Dr T and my learned friend Sam Maynard were shipwrecked on an isolated island in the South Minch.

It was one of the smaller isles with no cover or shelter in the way of trees, and totally bereft of a 'hideout' where you could have a secret smoke.

In the desperate wake of the storm they had managed to salvage, from the emergency box, a certain amount of food and enough Multivite to keep body and soul together. This they shared quite willingly and drew up a 'daily ration' quota. Loneliness and hunger were not a problem: their Crusoe existence was fairly comfortable until the craving for nicotine began to manifest itself in bad temper.

Of course they had both managed to keep a packet dry because they keep them close to the vest. And each thought the other had none, yet they couldn't be sure. After two days of self-inflicted torment – two days of constant spying on one another – each was finally convinced his was the only packet on the island. On the third day Sam began to weaken. He said he thought they should light a heather fire to attract attention. He asked Donald if he had a match. The alchemist's suspicions were immediately aroused. He had a lighter, but he denied it. 'I must have dropped my lighter where we beached,' he said. 'I'll go and have a look.' He had quickly sussed he could have a sneaky drag in the heather smoke.

Unluckily, a dry north-easterly had completely dehydrated the soil and in no time at all the island was a raging inferno. DT had scarcely managed to fill his lungs with cigarette smoke before he and his mate had to swim to the nearest rocky outcrop. There they sat shamefacedly drying their fags in the sun for 10 days until Sylvia raised the alarm.

When the lifeboat found them they were, according to the bosun, haggard and hungry after two weeks on raw mussels, but still arguing fiercely about the 'missing fag'.

Suddenly I am dreadfully upset and ashamed to be classed Scottish. The boy has just brought me a new publication called the *Sunday Scot* owned, I understand, by Rangers Football Club.

If you thought the *Sun* was as low as these rags could sink you are wrong, because in the *Sunday Scot* journalism has dug even deeper into the mire.

In this one issue they manage to insult my old Gordonstoun pal, Charles, and the entire population of the Highlands. These two institutions form the basis of Rangers support, and consequently the only two symbols of hope for the Central Belt hordes.

An interesting point is that this 'paper' is mostly written by women who are very likely married to Rangers supporters. I fear, this time, they have underestimated the intelligence of their husbands. There can be little doubt that the *Sunday Scot* is the cause of Graeme Souness's preference for the bleak deserts of Lancashire.

FRIDAY, 17 MAY 1991

MONDAY Rewards are so meagre in the National Health Service these days that I have been reduced to working part-time for another paper – as a blood sports reporter. The money is good, but it has to be. Not that I care much about money, but careless sub-editing and loose printing can lead to a great deal of aggravation.

One little word missed from a sentence could easily lead to a black eye or even a costly libel writ. And then there is the good name of the paper.

The dangerous little word 'not' worries me most of all. A missing 'not' could get a man hanged. If I write that a certain Mr Kelso is not a fool and the 'not' gets lost in the complex industrial cogs of a modern newspaper, a friend is lost. But for the fact that few of those involved in our particular blood sport can read, well . . .

The only parallel I can draw is the word 'not' escaping the sub-editors when the Ten Commandments were being carved, or perhaps if the 'ands' had been plucked from WB Yeats. You see. Chaos!

TUESDAY My eminent colleague Dr Vishu continues to set a bad example, constantly puffing away at that evil pipe of his, but the smoking of nicotine is now generally very much in decline. If only more would try to emulate my friends Sam Maynard and Dr Taylor.

One day DT slipped out of his laboratory for a few minutes to inhale some tranquillising smoke. While he surreptitiously dragged and socialised on Stornoway's main street he spotted Sam approaching from a downwind direction.

That day Sam had acquired a box of matches and had been prowling the Narrows hoping to offer some acquaintance a light.

Sam has a keen nose, but DT has a sharper eye. When he sensed Sam beaming in on him, his cigarette was only half smoked – much too long to throw away, but still too short to share. He cupped the dout in his right hand and plunged his fist into the pocket of a new pair of trousers.

The other fellow, who has all the time in the world, twigged and proceeded to engage DT in a lengthy debate on atmospheric pollution. The discussion was prolonged and painful. DT burnt a large hole in the new trousers and lost several inches of skin off his right leg. But he didn't mind.

'I got the better of that battle of Wills,' he chortled from his hospital bed.

WEDNESDAY The following is a synopsis of a lengthy work soon to be published in *Sociology Today*.

I have had in mind for a long time to do something for my friends in Stornoway. Now, when I have so much time on my hands, would seem to be the moment.

My concern is mainly for men who live in Newton, on Matheson Road and among the copper beeches of Goathill. Men without roots in soil or language. Men left behind when time marched on. I say men, and only men; because their wives are, in the main, enlightened women who still have cousins outside the cattle grids.

I hate to name names, and I pick on Brother Fred's merely to illustrate their plight.

That plight attracts little sympathy from those of us who live 'at home'. We can understand their loneliness, but how many of us appreciate how deeply alienated *they* feel in what they imagined to be their town. From the moment they arise in the morning they are instantly made aware of their exclusion from the mainstream of life.

The morning news on their local radio station could be broadcast, for all they know, in Serbo-Croat, if such a thing exists (their own 'English' is a strange mixture of Dickensian Cockney and American Cowboy slang picked up in the old Picture House). They arrive at their place of work to hear colleagues chatting away in Gaelic.

Until very recently this didn't worry them, for they had inherited the Crown. They were the sons of the city fathers of the commercial capital of Northern Scotland. Now they are outnumbered by the indigenous even in their own clubs.

Suddenly you hear them talk of long-lost relatives in Marvig and other equally outlandish corners. One MacLennan of Newton was heard recently trying to claim cousins with no less than that famous son of Marvig, the Millionaire Cobbler (or, as they call him now in Stornoway, our Ratner).

His pal, the Captain of Industry MacIver, has failed to find any country cousins. No amount of research can trace his family tree past the Ma and Da. He is possibly a changeling. Even the famous gynaecologist *(mistake?)* Bill Lawson cannot find as much as a distant Hearach. All *we* can do, to make them feel better, is to try not to speak Gaelic in the Town of the Lost Tribe.

THURSDAY Although we haven't heard much about him recently, some very old readers will probably remember my ancient colleague Dr Fingalstein. Incidentally, this fellow cannot be numbered among the Lost Tribe because he knows who he is and his Gaelic is fine despite many years in the Stornoway Gaelic Choir.

On a recent holiday in Botswana looking, as it happened, for his wife's relatives, he contracted some dreadful tropical disease. Fortunately, I still had some special medicine in my Kalahari chest that did the business – in conjunction with long rest and extensive bleeding. But it was a close call.

This was the latest of Fingalstein's long history of misfortune abroad. 'Even worse,' he said, 'than the time I fell down the steps of the Kremlin.' He swears that is the last time he'll cross the Minch.

FRIDAY I don't mind in the least helping Alec Dan or Councillor Macdonald with their sheep, because they are neither of them much good with animals. Coming on duty after Councillor Macdonald is another matter, though.

The smell of sheep in the surgery doesn't bother *me* much, but some of my patients, who perhaps had weak stomachs on admission, start to display symptoms of dysentery. This makes diagnosis difficult.

This very day I found two pages of my register stuck together with what looked suspiciously like animal waste. Yesterday I had the devil of a job cleaning tufts of wool from my instruments and the rest room is no place for a ram. I am a tolerant man, but sometimes he goes too far.

Friday, 14 June 1991

MONDAY A few minutes ago I heard my large friend Councillor Macdonald being quoted by Radio nan Gàidheal. 'I'll have to send an official to investigate,' he said. Unfortunately, I missed the lead into this story, but I figured if the big fellow was sending someone to investigate we should know all about it. He is not the sort of councillor who would set the costly wheels of investigation in motion without good reason.

My researchers tell me it is the troublesome people of Barra again. They are apparently unhappy that the Ludag Ferry can only carry 12 passengers per voyage. Did you ever hear the likes of it? Do you mean to tell me that more than 12 people on MacNeil's Sgeir would be travelling on the same day, unless perhaps they were all trying to escape together?

Since 1975 I have persistently warned the Council about making life too easy for those who were yoked to Inverness-shire for a hundred years. Give them a taste of liberty and democracy and in a very short time they begin to take these notions seriously. It is just as well they have no teeth left in Barra, otherwise I wouldn't be surprised to hear them demanding their own dentist soon.

TUESDAY When my councillor friend said he would send someone to investigate, I had a quiet chuckle to myself. What he meant, presumably, was that he would call on someone to touch down. At any one time 95 per cent of Council officials are airborne, like taxi-drivers. His message would read: 'If numbers one to nine-nine-nine are flying anywhere near 'Bene' at the moment, could they please ask the pilot to divert to South Uist. Walk about with the briefcase for a couple of days, at £56 per night subsistence, and write a report.'

Perhaps that is a wee bit unfair. After all, fair play to your man is all we want. Scattered islands are difficult to rule. Repeated attempts to learn from the French, by sending deputations to Indian Ocean outcrops, have yet to yield results. But these things take time. It is quite possible that lessons learned on holidays in Reunion will one day be of great benefit to our grandchildren. If not, perhaps the recent 'executive' hooley in France itself will lead to some sort of revolution. We have much to learn from history if we live long enough. When Chairman Mao Tse-Tung was asked what he thought of the French Revolution, he said: 'It's too early to say.'

WEDNESDAY Today, Loganair announced a yearly profit of half a million pounds, and good luck to them. From my unique vantage point, here in my surgery, I am able to account for this company's cheerful cash flow chart. Daily, or even twice daily, I count them all out and I count the Council officials in again. I am certain our airsick officials would rather stay at home, because if they've seen Glasgow and Benbecula once why would they want a second look. Having familiarised themselves with the geography of these far-flung places, in the early days of their employment, could they perhaps retain the picture in their little minds and use the telephone for urgent business? No, they say, there is nothing like personal contact – and besides, there is no £56 per night for telephone calls.

Call it the politics of envy it you like, but I feel I must ask the Western Isles Council to publish the cost of unnecessary travel before I ask my parishioners to pay another penny in Poll Tax. They say nothing broadens the mind like travel and *they* are probably right. The very least we might expect from our well-travelled councillors and officials should be a regular public explanation of how their view of local government has been enhanced from the air and how the long-suffering electorate might be enriched through their experience. Now bear in mind that, unlike many critics, I never once claimed that anyone in the Big House ever undertook an unnecessary voyage.

THURSDAY Much as I hate being strapped in an aeroplane *ohm-ché* for any length of time, I hope to spend most of July in Indonesia – if my dear colleague Leslie will cover surgery for me (I'll pay him back in the winter as usual).

Java is dangerously close to Australia, a country that has always terrified me, but I cannot let the opportunity pass. I mention my mission here only because of the astronomical cost. The Council will, I am sure, feel they must reimburse me for any intelligence I can add to their 'maritime-archipelago archive', and there is always the chance I may get lost. And CNAG must have a small budget for essential travel, what? Failing that, I must persuade some discerning editor that my educational, entertaining account of the adventure is worth paying through the nose for.

If I'm still short of a few bob I have one one last card to play – a trick I learned from Coinneach Mòr in the early days. Somewhere out East there has to be some descendant of a Siarach who once worked for the Dutch East Indies Company. That should be good for a whole season of *Thall Thairis*. If that doesn't work there is always the straightforward begging letter.

FRIDAY I don't care very much for television (although that could change soon) and in any case I am much too busy. However, I am as nosy as the next person, which is why I pay Leslie well to watch for me – just in case. He insisted I should see Alan Bleasdale's latest effort, *GBH*.

Mr Bleasdale is a hard-working craftsman, although lacking in subtlety. I was disappointed in his latest effort, but what made me laugh was the nationwide misconception that his inspiration was Liverpool and Derek Hatton. *We* know very well he has kept abreast of Hebridean shenanigans and that his story is based on *our* Education department.

FRIDAY, 9 AUGUST 1991

'The Lochs football team sets new world record' . . . I would like that to be our front-page headline, but I suppose it is too much to expect. Will 'Four In A Row' do instead? The Eilean an Fhraoich Cup must surely be ours to keep now.

I thought on Friday night some of our players looked well past their sell-by date, but at the end o' the day experience and brute force proved too much for the skilful little Point players.

In the quarter century that has slipped by since I did all the running for Barts and Roddy G the game has become much faster. The pace is furious and the players are fitter, but I wonder about the skills. Where have all the ball players gone? Would the likes of Billy Urquhart still find time to beat three, draw a fourth and set someone up? Why are there no wingers? Please excuse those of us who are caught in a time-warp.

Let's look at Angus Beattie. Robbie Macrae says: 'Man, he's rough but he's a gentleman. He mows them down, but at least he always offers to carry them to the Ospadal.' With only a one-goal advantage going into the second half, and a setting sun in their eyes, we were worried about Lochs. Blinded by the sun and old age, Angus seemed certain to be sent off. The maroon of Lochs and the red of Point were easily confused in the gloaming. As Angus swept up all oncoming traffic he probably gathered as many of our own players on the scythe as he did Rubhachs. But the policy of not letting anyone through is a sound one. You don't even risk an own goal.

There was a moment of panic towards the end when our goalie had to limp off and Calum, who must be nearing 50, took over. But we need not have feared. Beattie just glowered at anyone who threatened to shoot.

Would you believe she's still there 25 years on? From amidst a gang of roaring Lochs supporters (or it might have been Iain Skelly on his own) I heard her: 'Come on de reds. Tha 'n Cupan air a dhol meirgeach anns an Rubha 's cha toir duine eas e.'

'Chan e as duile dhut,' ars esan.

Up front several of our players have grown much too heavy for their knees. A certain centre-forward who shall be nameless spent the evening bandaging alternate legs, while fit young substitutes warmed up in vain. Still, his considerable physical presence might have helped to intimidate the opposition.

Iain Murdo Matheson appears to have not only inherited the old man's stopping power, he can also go forward and create. If he wants to, he is probably ready to step up a class. I feel I must write to the Celtic management and draw their attention to ra boy. Hector Martin looks like another who could probably earn a living at the game rather than waste his energy on fish farming.

The Point numbers two, eight and ten also caught the eye. They would benefit greatly from a transfer to a more successful club, like Lochs. While we are at the business of identifying individuals worthy of praise, we must not overlook Angie Hogg's major role in the drama. As the only linesman ever to be shown the red card by a referee, he must be due some award. His excuse for being tired – that he had sheared 370 sheep in the afternoon – sounds rather weak.

I've waited a long time for revenge, but it was worth it. I cannot remember exactly how long it is since Bayble under-14s drubbed Leurbost 21–0, but neither can I forget it. The Babylonian centre-forward, Croesus, later shared a flat in Glasgow with the Leurbost centre-half, the West End Tory. I never understood how they could live with each other, unless it was their shared knack of amassing vast wealth. I tell them it will do no good in the Real Final, but they will not listen.

Back at the ranch I have time at last to catch up with the great gamble that went wrong. Maggie recorded some of our leaders' television performances, but I find it impossible to sit through them in cold sobriety. Anyway, the responses from different men on the croft are much more interesting.

I thought Norman 'Brot' Macarthur had the whole sordid mess in perspective, but he spoiled his letter towards the end by letting his narrow political view shine through. The Chief Executive's comments were misunderstood by the nation because they couldn't know he has been trying to emulate Margaret Thatcher's habit of refering to *herself* in the third person.

My old friend Sandy Matheson had a narrow escape because there was no one around to point out that he *was* the Council when the gambling started. When the Leader, the Reverend Convener, spoke I couldn't help but recall Sandy's part in a recent play: 'Dear Lord, please help, the mind is numb, humour me this once and strike him dumb.'

Alas, the Lord has left us to stew. Over the years we have had occasion to identify and slag the leaders of various committees. I see references in my files to Transportation, Education, Housing, Development and Social Work, but never a word about the Finance Committee. Who is Chairman, and why isn't he dangling from a tree in the Castle Grounds? If anyone can fill this void in our intelligence, the usual reward awaits.

Next to Brot's I would place wee Maggie's comments. Her urgent fax to Java read: 'Think of the football team we might have had with 23 million. We could have bought the entire Rangers Club and still have enough left over for Maradona.'

Sadly, it looks as if Major is not going to come across; so the time has come to shed weight, to lighten the load, to sacrifice luxuries. There is no need to mention the two departments that can be scrapped immediately. They know who they are. Like the rest of us, they have children and mortgages, but they should be able to find jobs with the Councils who could afford to lend us the stake at the start of the game.

FRIDAY, 13 SEPTEMBER 1991

FOR THE INNER MAN

Recently, as the *Sunday Post* might say, Ali opened an Indian take-away in Stornoway. Ali invited D Campbell, turf accountant, and various wealthy men about town to the opening night. Good for D Campbell. He has been around a bit and served his Queen on foreign hostile soil. But did he ever employ Ceylonese cooks as I did in better times and warmer climes? Of course he didn't. He couldn't afford to then as a lowly marine.

Still, I think highly of his assessment of fiery food. Having just been released from an Edinburgh hospital, where he was having his burnt-out pipes relined, the Bookie's opinion on curry has to be respected. He said Ali's bhuna wasn't bad. Asked about the cost he said: 'Do people really still notice these things!'

Did I mention that I wasn't invited? Never mind.

Still smarting from the snub, I passed Ali's twice a day savouring the aroma, yet determined not to set foot in the place until I had a report from a forksman who knows the value of money. As luck would have it, Cunninghame North dropped in for one of his short-stay visits to the island. He ferried a busload of Uigeachs over to Ali's for to treat the country cousins.

He fed all of Mangersta and half of Breinish for 50 quid and he thought it 'reasonable value'.

Like his colleague Sam Galbraith, who fancies himself at the Indian table, North's knowledge and experience of spice from the East was gained in Gibson Street, Glasgow. The only proper Uigeach I could pin down for comment was Murdanie, who thought the portions were adequate, but he had consumed several bowls of his Ma's potato soup in the afternoon 'just in case'.

Imagine our dilemma in the Crofter's Club, hungry and curious after 18 holes in a cloud of midges. Whether to stick to Charlie Barley's Cow Pies or try Ali's Tandoori Oven?

Who should walk in but the undisputed Prince of Trenchermen, the

Lawyer himself. He ordered a cow pie and a couple of packets of crisps and casually let dab that he'd been to the new Indian.

Here, *arsa mise rium fhìn*, we have the proof of the pakora. 'The pakora was fine,' he burped. 'The nan bread and paratha were fair, the main course was comforting, the pudding slipped down and you can't complain at 16 quid.'

'Sounds reasonable for two,' said a visitor. '*For two*,' says the Lawyer. 'Don't be ridiculous. Nora doesn't eat between meals.'

We were back where we were, more or less, and wistfully remembering the days when you could get a fresh fish supper in Stornoway.

After a restless night dreaming of curried Maldivian tuna I was wakened by the mellifluous tones of my old friend Ciorstag Ruadh on Rodeo nan Eilean. She was not at all impressed with the new Indian. Now I knew Ciorstag well when she was young. But, with respect, can we seriously expect a person from Carloway to pass judgement on Indian food? It's like asking a Tibetan monk for his opinion on boiled guga.

There was nothing for it but to try it ourselves. My Javanese host and Dear Moria had flown 6,000 miles for a weekend on Lewis lamb. Perhaps it was unfair to ask people who had dined recently on fruit from the Garden of Eden to sample Ali's take-away, but what could I do. With Lewis lamb selling at six pounds the beast, it is difficult to appear hospitable with sheep nowadays unless they can eat one apiece. Not that Macpherson would leave much if left alone in a kitchen.

So, we ordered in Ali's. For the price of four fat Lewis lambs we had a good night out. Maggie thought the various dishes tended towards the mild, but that is probably down to her asbestos Partick palate.

Personally, I deplore and despair of my sybaritic anaesthetic friends. I get my nourishment from the sound of the sea and the sight of the diving gannet.

Talking of gannets . . . Thanks, Calum, for the bird. I shouldn't have phoned so soon, while the wife was hosing you down with Dettol after two weeks on the Rock, but the Historian in Inverness is uncontrollable once he gets a whiff of the westerly wind. How you managed to get the bird on British Airways *that same day* before the salt had reached the bone is a mystery that must remain Niseach.

I called the Garrabost Historian in the early evening to make sure the bird hadn't been apprehended at Customs, and damn the bit of thanks I got. He had sent the wife and children to Aberdeen for the day so he could concentrate on the 'bird'. 'Spend as much as you like,' his neighbours heard him shout, before a lengthy grace.

I said I was truly sorry I had interrupted, but he didn't hear. 'My eyes and my ears are closed to the sounds and sights of your tasteless world. Call back in an hour.'

I called back in half an hour in case he had done himself an injury, and sure enough he had devoured all but the wings. I tried to tell him the boys in Ness had done a deal with Ali to have all the gannets on Sùlaisgeir curried next year. I cannot be certain if he was being sick or merely his usual argumentative Bobbie Neilly self . . . 'Salt, salt, salt is the only cure, my boy . . .' Or something like that. *Dè math dhaibh a bhith tighinn an seo le stamagan pàipeir.*

FRIDAY, 4 OCTOBER 1991

MONDAY Before we launch into the uncertainties of a new week I have a few words left over from last.

While we, the gullible innocents, were preoccupied with familiar splits in the Kirk and settling old scores, a powerful new clique has taken control of our lives. When I say new, I mean fresh out of the closet.

The Siarach Mafia has always been in existence in a quiet, sneaky way, but now they are the top cats. Having duped the rest of the country boys into belief in some kind of Maw Brotherhood, with Sandy Matheson as number one enemy, the Lieutenants can flaunt their power in public.

Just as soon as the new ruling class has recovered the £23 million (they have their ways), we will see even more new motorways and schools on the West Side. Probably the seat of government, and perhaps the airport, will be moved to Carlobost. All of this of course will be at the expense of the impoverished east coast of Lewis. Whether or not a few crumbs of reward will drop down south for services rendered we'll have to wait and see.

TUESDAY When Sandy Matheson ran the Outer Hebrides as a benevolent dictatorship, I think it is safe to say he was as wise and fair a ruler as any dictator can be. He encouraged education in scattered rural communities (thus ensuring the welly-booted stayed as far away from Stornoway as possible) and he was not ill-disposed towards the native language. He even once spoke a few words to me in the Gaelic. He did all this and much more, yet damn the bit of thanks he got.

Tonight, in what I am assured will be a packed Town Hall, Sandy addresses an audience on matters of great interest to students of history. Yet less than a mile away, in the Golf Club, Bridge Night has not been postponed. Why is this? When Rangers FC are performing on television on a Tuesday evening, bridge is banned by a certain element with no consultation of the majority. Are we to assume a lecture by Mr Matheson is considered less important than a football match?

I've long suspected there is some destructive trait in the Hebridean temperament that means we are far from ready for democracy. Say the word, Sandy, and I'll mobilise the boys for a swift return to sensible authority.

WEDNESDAY Talking of dictators, I'm pleased to hear Ol' Blue Eyes is making another comeback. All these years he spoke of looking forward to retirement he was obviously whistling in the dark. A whole summer of daily golf was turning him into a dull boy.

I guess once a man gets seaweed in the blood it's a terminal disease. He will be easier to live with now, and he can stop worrying about getting 40,000 miles out of his car tyres. Perhaps he will cease hounding me for that dubious fiver in '89 and give me the benefit of the doubt. But Dixie was always careful. He was the only man in Leurbost, apart from the tweed barons, who had a bank account before the war. The Council could do worse than approach him for financial assistance in the present crisis.

It is good to hear that the Keose seaweed factory might open again very soon, but a word of warning for the new workers. If you've been accustomed to the easy-going ways of JA Mackenzie, do not expect them to continue in Keose. The gulag will be run by Blue Eyes in the same old fashion, only this time he hopes to introduce Japanese early morning practices. The workers will be expected to assemble on the pier at 0600 for physical exercises while singing the Company Anthem. Anyone found carrying seaweed away in his pocket will be severely lashed and then sacked. But we wish them well. The Calvinist abhors an empty factory.

THURSDAY After 30 years as a member of a party that threatened to implement some sort of social justice, it gives me no pleasure to announce my resignation. So where to now? I know there is no natural justice, but I cannot go all the way over to the party that practises the law of the jungle. We cannot go around eating the less fortunate – at least, not yet. That leaves me with only Charlie Kennedy and his crowd.

I realise my resignation will cause dismay – nay, devastation – in the bosom of old friends like John Smith. After all, they would have looked to me for advice when the horrible reality of power fell in their laps. Not since Bevan stopped being a Bevanite have they been struck such a blow. I'm sorry, but my mind is made up.

Perhaps the least I should do is offer some explanation. The sad day dawned as I drove home from a hard nightshift wondering how many more years of unremitting toil my feeble body could take. A posh public school Labourite was speeching from Brighton, reassuring those who have to scratch a living on a mere £40,000 a year they need have nothing to fear from a Labour taxman. Bad enough, you might think, but then he went on to encourage the vultures at the top of the manure heap. These connoisseurs in avarice will be allowed to keep 40 per cent of their so-called earnings – idle layabout chairpersons who contribute nothing yet pocket the wages of 15 working men. And all this while schoolchildren round about me share one textbook among 20. Ninety per cent tax on incomes over £60,000 does not seem excessive to me.

Ol' Blue Eyes says it wouldn't go far if shared out. That's not true; it would go a fair distance. But that is beside the point: to reduce these parasites' waistbands would give a great deal of satisfaction. What do you think, Charles?

FRIDAY The last of our children has left the nest and Maggie is uneasy. Perhaps she feels she has reached the end of her useful life, so I try to console her. She still has Smut the spaniel.

He uttered his first word the other day; he already understands two languages, he can spell and he watches *Dòtaman*. He can do wonderful things with his 'hands', and he knows 'Daddy'. I wonder what life has in store for the poor boy?

FRIDAY, 18 OCTOBER 1991

BUT IS IT ART?

I drove down to Slèite the other day to have a dram with Sorley on his 8oth birthday, but I only got wine.

This was not Sorley's fault – he didn't know I was coming. It was the fault of the new Gaels, men in suits and ties who are trying to forge a new sober image of Gaeldom while the old crowd are out in Dingwall revving up in the traditional fashion. We are in serious danger of losing our quintessential quaintness if this goes any further. But never mind that, let us have a look at Sorley at 80.

Is he any good as a poet? Obviously Angus Peter and the rest of the groupies think he is. Well, *they* naturally would. But what does Sorley himself think? He doubts it, because he is still alive, and I have to agree with him. If he was really very, very good, this torrent of adulation would not have half-drowned him until he was dead. It has never been known in the Celtic world for a man to be praised while he was still alive, or even until he's been dead for 200 years.

There is another serious question we must ask, while we are at it. Remember Sorley is 80 and he's not an alcoholic. How can a sensitive

Celtic bard tolerate cold sobriety for 80 years? The truly great should all die of the drink at the age of 38 (sorry, Sam, but that's the way it is). And he has another flaw . . . but is he flawed enough?

Sorley is complex, but not as difficult to understand (if you have the English translation) as Dylan Thomas. We can understand him. He is tough enough for the under-70s with all these old words, but yet we can just about grasp it. I shudder to think what he could have done had he been a drinking man. Of course he wouldn't have lived till 80, but think of how much sooner he would have been famous. Not that he would want to be famous, because he likes people and sees only the good in them. That is not a flaw; it is a desperate want in his philosophy.

We must pause here for the learned reader and ask: what is poetry? A difficult enough question in English, but if you ask it in *our* language it is doubly difficult. Seamus Heaney is not ashamed to rhyme in his English poem for Sorley, yet it is still poetry. We don't have that same problem in Gaelic because with our wealth of words we have no rhyme in the English sense. We have nothing to be ashamed of.

We have the heather and the weather ever-changing that drives us all insane, but when does it become poetry? God and Sorley only know. My own guess is that the poet is a frustrated prose-writer who never got the hang of conjunction.

'The distilled essence', some call it, but I think they are merely scared to come out with it. The poets are greedy with words. 'Make of it what you will,' they say, 'because I'm not sure myself.' Take Sorley, for instance. What has he written? Perhaps one hundred thousand words, while I have used up over one million to say the same. He must be lazy. Still, he says I sometimes make him laugh and he always makes me cry.

The arts will always remain a mystery to us philistines, and Lindsay isn't helping. Her sculpted tribute to Sorley is in the finest tradition of Gaelic art. What was once a fine piece of wood was lovingly whittled into a wonderfully mysterious mantle piece. I asked several of my learned Gaelic friends what they made of it, and their interpretations diverged towards every point on the compass.

Quite clearly, to me, it was a heavenly harp enclosing a swivelling flintstone poetry book. But after one glass of wine Rusty thought it was a ship's rudder. Maggie, who' had a few on the ferry, thought it was something with which the outlandish people of Laxay used to decorate rams' heads. Come to think, I realise now, it was all of these things and much more.

Compared with the sculpture, the painting was simplicity itself. Some saw fiery serpents' tongues licking the celestial dome (the Cuillins), and the boys from Ness thought it was an IDP fence gone wrong. Fortunately, Angus Peter – who was *an làthair* at the conception – explained to me that what appeared to be the sky started off as the Minch. If you turned it upside down the 'Cuillins' were clearly the birth of creation – anemones on the seabed. *Seo a-nis.*

My old pal Angus Peter asked me how the novel was coming along. I cannot bear these impatient people with no sense of eternity. I sometimes wonder if he's a Gael at all. As it happens, I have temporarily shelved the major work and started on a minor novel in praise of older women. They know so much. Unlike Humbert Humbert, my passion is neither perverted nor illegal. But, just in case, I took the precaution of marrying one.

After the party I thought I would call at the *Free Press* to open the annual round of pay negotiations, and who should I meet there but Mary Beith on the same quest. My eminent colleague, Aristotle, is Mary's number one fan. You won't believe this, Alex, because she looks so innocent. Have I got stories to tell you. The great consolation is, if the paper doesn't come across she will put a spell on them. She is also much younger than we thought.

The hospitality of my colleagues at the *Free Press* knows no bounds – especially Torcuil's. So I spent the night in Oban with Sgiobair nan Eathraichean Loibhte and Morag MacIntosh. Calum Iain is a typical ageing member of the teaching profession – three years now since anyone got a Higher Maths in Oban, and he has taken to carrying a gun.

A quick visit to the Barras to stock up with winter clothing and I'm ready for Dingwall and the old Gaels. Must have a word with the

Bodhan (A' Bhòchain, *shurely? – Ed*) to see how his Gaelic's coming on. Malky now speaks the language like a native. Must also look up my old Gordonstoun buddy Charlie to measure his Gaelic now that Rhoda has taken him in hand.

I hear as we go to press that he didn't feel up to using the Gaelic while addressing the masses at the Mod. That raises the question of what he and Rhoda were *really* doing.

FRIDAY, 29 NOVEMBER 1991

Ever since Shergar (the second) was delivered one night last week I've been crippled with anxiety. With the IRA getting more and more desperate, a kidnapping attempt was very much on the cards. We took all the usual precautions you would associate with the transportation of an animal worth more, according to the owner, 'than any ram in this country or probably any other'.

Councillor Macdonald hired an unknown face from the Dun (what they call a Duna) for the job, a man who 'wouldn't talk'. But you can never be sure. I appointed several friends to watch the beast around the clock and I warned them to be mindful of an approach from the sea.

On Saturday the sister-in-law phoned to tell me some strange cars had driven past the croft slowly, and two of them had driven into the ditch when they caught their first glimpse of Shergar II. On Sunday Coinneach called and asked me if I'd seen Shergar II in the daylight, and then he laughed. Sabbath or no, I thought I'd better go and have a look.

Quite clearly I've been the victim of the sort of cruel practical joke the people of Dun take great delight in. Somewhere between Carloway and Ranish the costly beast of superior breed was switched. The changeling with false horns left in its place almost defies description.

The shape, from the side, is not unlike old rams we have seen in Ranish ('*eil cuimhne agad, Dougie?*) when they used to keep them till the age of 21 – short back and one side. The one side, the port belly, is grossly distended – obviously some kind of hernia, very likely dating back to the time it escaped on the Airport and the owner fell upon it in anger. Or perhaps it has merely reached the age when the large intestine knows it is only fit for white pudding.

Without further ado I called the owner and reopened negotiation on the lease. First he tried to tell me it had been badly sheared by an Englishman called Badley, then he suggested it could be wind. He thinks I'll believe anything. A friend at the Butt who knows about these things said: "*'S dòcha g' eil uan ann.*" I'll tell you wan thing. If they'd seen this animal in Point there would be a song in it. I'm fed up with the lot of them. Perhaps I'll eat it.

Almost every morning now on Radio Highland I hear terrifying stories of crime in Inverness. And the criminals, it seems, hold the police force in utter contempt. When they break into houses they often cook a meal, wash their clothes and have a bath, while their friends play requests for them on Moray Firth Radio. My old friend Detective Macuaireigin says he's at his wits' end but thinks it would help if people turned the water and electricity off at the mains.

Luckily, this is one type of crime that is unlikely to trouble us here in the islands. Since we went onto the national grid the power is off most of the time, and no self-respecting burglar would immerse his body in our water.

Every other morning I hear my colleague Pàdraig talking to some High Tory from Highland Region. Pàdraig, like many people who have reached the age of accumulation, has veered somewhat to the right. But, give him his due, he often asks these liars: 'Why should we believe you when you tell us the people of Inverness have never had it so good?' Normally very few listeners would believe them, but these are very far from normal times.

When burglars are so concerned with personal hygiene, what are the working classes like? Wealthy and clean enough to believe Tories?

*　　*　　*

For a little while after French and Russian Revolutions our noble superiors quieten down a bit. But it doesn't take them very long to forget. In a few generations they come to the fore again in sufficient numbers to make outrageous demands of the suffering poor.

Who is this guy somewhere in the Highlands who wants three million pounds of the taxpayers' money to maintain his estate? Is Cunninghame North pulling my leg? Thank goodness we are all too civilised nowadays to rise up and start chopping off heads, but perhaps a hand here and there would do no harm.

One way or another they'll get us. They cannot afford to poison us to a sudden death, but they will ensure the food they produce will leave us much too weakened to revolt. Look at the bacon, for instance.

For 20 years I made it a rule not to stir from bed until the smell of bacon had wafted up the stairs. Sadly, this is no longer possible, for the simple reason that it's not possible to fry bacon: it can only be boiled. Whether it be Danish or Ayrshire, it is mostly water. I have written to our MP on this matter but I don't expect much help there. He looks like one of those vegetarians.

Just recently I took the notion to start the day with a steak pie. It means she has to get up at six instead of seven, and I thought she didn't mind. But then I discovered to my astonishment that she minded very much. This morning she tried to slip me something that was evidently out of a tin. I had my suspicions but said nothing, because the pastry looked real – until I stabbed it and the whole thing collapsed and half a pint of thin fluid ran onto the plate. I was left with a disgusting-looking pancake smelling of offal.

Later on when things calmed down, I found the container of the so-called pie in the bin. The Co-op's own steak pie, it claimed – *a new improved recipe*. We must deduce from this ludicrous claim that they had at some time made a worse pie. Unless Derek Cooper or Terry Waite can help us, we'll be poisoned in our own kitchens.

* * *

The news from the croft is a mixture of good and bad.

The glad tidings are that the animal is doing the business, but this does not bring everyone comfort and joy. At a hastily-convened meeting of the Grazings Comedy many of those present were reported to be exceeding wroth. I have a message from them saying that if Shergar II gets out among the village sheep he will be shot down like a mad dog.

In case the matter should reach the courts, I have commissioned Sam Maynard for a portrait – at enormous expense.

FRIDAY, 13 DECEMBER 1991

For several days now I've been trying to write a ghost story for Hogmanay, and the going is far from easy. A long time ago I remember Roald Dahl had the same problem. He had an idea for a television series of ghost stories and sold the idea to Hollywood.

All he had to do was collect 24 of the best stories from the best writers and then write the screenplays. He filled his house with 'practically every ghost story ever written' and began to read. He read stories by the famous writers of all ages and rejected them all. He couldn't find the spookiness he was looking for. He even tried writing some himself but gave up in despair. Eventually, after several hundred stories, he found he had a few good ones and, astonishingly, the few good ones were all written by women. We should have known.

With this in mind I asked Maggie to have a go, but hers is a practical nature. She can frighten people in many ways, but she is not at one with the spirit world. I was on the verge of telling the BBC it couldn't be done when the obvious dawned. Why not tell the truth? Why not a true story from the hills and glens of my birth where the unnatural and the bloodless constantly roamed the night.

My problem now is the opposite of Roald Dahl's. I have too many to choose from. The first couple I tried to write down, imagining them for some reason in Mairead Ros's voice, were too spooky altogether. We don't want people too scared to go out first-footing. I have finally settled on a creepy little tale, but I can only work on it during the few minutes of wintry daylight. Even then my typewriter mysteriously keeps sliding off the desk.

The people of Barvas are not normally the sort who get excited. But these are not normal times. The Barvas Navigator, with a little help from Christine, has at last begotten an heir to the estate.

When I called on Sunday morning to see if he could handle a six-pounder I found him surprisingly relaxed. By the way, there is no doubt the child is his: it's as bald as a coot and he's left-handed (Clendy is now in the clear).

As I was saying, the Navigator was lying back with a large cigar. 'How is wee John Alexander?' I inquired, as people do. 'Couldn't be better,' he said. 'When I went to feed him at six this morning he asked not to be disturbed until nine. He spoke in Gaelic, of course.'

While Christine gathers strength the Navigator has been doing little chores with which he is clearly not familiar. Maggie bumped into him in Presto's, where she had to point out that it is not necessary to go to the cash desk with each individual item. But he's getting on fine, he says. 'Christine has drawn him a wee map of the kitchen showing where cups and things are kept.'

Every year I say I refuse to join in the so-called fun, but in the end it is easier to fall in with the herd. I refer, of course, to the Christmas parties. Civil Aviation (far from civil), Coastguard, Golf Club, Masonic, Bridge Club, Doctors, Witchdoctors and even the Labour Party – they all must have their *ho-rós* at this time of year. Why? Why not, say the wives who have new frocks to show off.

I don't mind so much when some of the booze necessary to get through the ordeal can be worked off with vigorous dancing (what, Nora?), but when the main event is steak what is the point? With all respect to the cooks, is it possible to cater for a mob? Only Roddy on the *Suilven* is honest enough to admit he doesn't try.

To give the girls in the Cabarfeidh their due, they go through the routine and ask how you would like it done, Cur, as they have been told to do. But we all know it means nothing when the beast has been simmering since Friday morning. At times like this you miss old Bill Low, whose idea of a good 'medium' steak was to cut the horns off and wipe its arse.

Yet, I suppose these functions do serve a purpose. When the wine comes on stream you often see husbands and wives talking to each other like young courting couples. In the morning, oh dear, the morning, what a relief only to have to grunt.

Having said all that, I must now get into my best gear and head for Flodigarry and the *Free Press* festive bash. Can you begin to imagine it? A horde of journalists and politicians! People who cannot stop talking when they're sober! Will I get a chance to say all I have to say? My own idea of a good time is a few pints in the Criterion and someone nips out for a fish supper, then off to the country dancing. But that's not good enough for them.

I am tired of it all and desperately need a rest.

Young Torc and the rest of the boys will be there, of course, pretending to enter into the spirit of the season. But I know their game. They are there to keep a close watch on Cunninghame North in case he's shaping to do a Maxwell with the pension fund.

Rumour on the streets has it some renegades from the old Smudge Committee have produced a Wet Highland Free Press. I might have been quite interested in this sheet, because Gaeldom needs new talent like never before. However, I'm told this publication is unlikely to become a collector's treasure. Others who are not so kind say it is so boring it could have been written by the present *Punch* editor.

1992

FRIDAY, 17 JANUARY 1992

While having a moderate measure of alcohol with Aly Bain the other night, I think we may have solved a serious problem for Shetland and the Hebrides at one cosmic stroke. As so often happens, the hour was late when the mists cleared and solutions came easy. But more of that later: first, the formal early part of the night.

Perhaps for those of us in whom primitive instincts have never been blunted it is all too formal. Tables, chairs, pints and polite clapping are all very well for serious students of the fiddle and the box; but what about the dancing? Dance music, never forget, is what Aly Bain and Phil Cunningham play. Do away with the BBC props, clear the floor, tighten the trusses and fling yourselves about. Start at midnight and go on until the last woman drops. By all means pay them more money. They deserve it.

And can I please say a long overdue thank you to wee Roddy An Lanntair, who continues to bring us entertainment we *don't* deserve. Anyone who can wrench a Shetlander away from home between New Year and Uphellya should be properly rewarded. If Mairi Macmillan, a self-confessed housewife (albeit a dentist's housewife) is worth an MBE, what price Roddy? *An crùn le bhith na sholais!*

The later grows the night, the better Aly's playing. But that assessment could be based on a want in my own musical appreciation developed between the bothan and Shawbost village hall – a short track strewn with wrecks of every description.

Phil Cunningham has taken to telling wee stories while Aly gets his breath back. We all need a break, but this is a ploy that normally doesn't work. You wish most of them, having been gifted with one glorious means of expression, would stick to it. However, in Master Cunningham's case, we can forgive; his short, gentle anecdotes are well edited and are aimed at the wry smile rather than the rugby club guffaw. Of course, Morningside breeding will out.

As for Bain Fastbow – half Cajun, half Spanish and the other half Viking – not since Murd 'An Lui resisted Free Church fiddle-burning has anyone gained more command of this Devil's instrument. In any other than an island culture he would probably nowadays employ agents to talk to ordinary folk, yet, still, he will go and play for sick friends in Ranish at three in the morning and would willingly carry on to Dunvegan if there was anyone left who could row a boat.

And, lo, it came to pass, when sensible people were going to bed, Aly mentioned an old and extremely eminent colleague by the name of Cavy. I once shared a house with this Cavy, a boy from the outer islands of Shetland. My share of the accommodation was, of necessity, small, because although Cavy only weighed 19 stone then he was still growing at 65 and needed much space. He was very handy at staggering-home time. I used to nip round corners and abuse dangerous gangs, secure in the knowledge that the giant was lumbering along behind.

According to Aly Bain, Cavy has a bevy of beautiful sisters. Coming from anyone else, I would have rejected this statement because, may the Lord forgive me, Cavy is the ugliest man you could meet in a long day's walk. And in any case, why were the sisters not mentioned in the early Sixties? Surely Brot would have known.

However, we have to take Aly's word. They must exist. And if they do, how many others? How many sleeping beauties are at this moment languishing in distant skerries (*tha beagan Gaelic aca*) while their young men fish the deeper oceans?

At the same desperate time our own young and not so young lonely men have no tweeds to weave and no women to console them. Do you see where we're heading now? A casual remark in the small hours, if properly understood and acted upon by the emigration department of Comhairle nan Eilean, could lead to a brand-new race of sea-going weavers who can subsist on seals and gannets.

I didn't think it was very long since I counted the bachelors in North Lochs, but having had a quick look at my files, I see I numbered Karachi. He now has an heir going to school. Can I have been asleep for five years? Down in Ranish where Duncan worried and often told the bachelors '*Fàsaichidh sibh an ceann baile*', they blossomed and brought forth frantically for 10 years. For a while Fidigarry was as full as a Catholic school, but now it seems the women at the Mouth of the Loch are past breeding age. Or could it be that satanic invention the Pill? 'Is that the one,' *arsa Coinneach*, 'she puts in my shoe and it makes me limp?' What would I know? We didn't have these things in our day; we only wore wellies.

So, we haven't many active bachelors left to send up north. But never mind, there is still Vatersay. Now they have a causeway, these notorious brigands are free to roam and pillage in Barra with alarming consequences. The obvious solution is to dispatch a boatload to Shetland where – according to Aly, remember – one thousand fair-skinned Viking ladies pine on vacant crofts. My only worry is that these mammies' boys on Vatersay couldn't handle strong women.

Nevertheless I'm sure you'll agree my plan is worth a glance by the newly-formed Council Committee of What To Do Next.

Friday, 7 February 1992

Another time Dr T and Wee Sammy were engaged in a fierce battle of Wills along in the shelter of the Woolworth's entrance. Neither had had a drag for some time and they were prepared to abase themselves rather than nip across the road to Capaldi's where cigarettes can be bought. After several minutes Wee Sammy, who never carries, realised DT, who has less willpower, must also be without.

They stood there yarning for some time, more or less back-to-back and scanning the horizon for a victim. But the weather was against them. It happened to be a day of excellent visibility, so their acquaintances could spot them from a distance and take evasive action. Clearly a better plan had to be hatched if they were going to hunt as a pair. Sam took command and suggested that DT move back into the shadows while he, Sam, would move down near the Clachan. An unsuspecting 'friend' would spot DT and turn swiftly round the corner into the fire.

Sure enough, with only minutes left of the dinner hour, who should come strolling along but young John Mackinnon, at that time a poorly paid photographer with the Stornoway Greysheet. Donald stepped out and drove John straight into Sam's arms, where he has remained to this day.

John was then unmarried and carried as many cigarettes as he liked. He accidentally revealed two packs, and this was two too many for Sam – he immediately proposed a business partnership. John learned very quickly. They sit all day in their office called Eòlas waiting for a call to go and film anyone who smokes.

DT didn't do so badly either. He teamed up with a guy called Kenny Fags and they lived quite happily for quite a long time – until Kenny stopped smoking.

Quite frankly, I wish they would all stop smoking and look after their bodies. Whether you call it the Temple of the Soul or the Tabernacle of the Holy Spirit, depending on which foot you favour, you should take great care of it. Look after the body, because it is the only one you'll ever have. You might not be very happy with its outward appearance, but remember the beauty within. That bony shell with its covering of corrugated flesh, its folds and stretchmarks, must be nourished and protected for the micro-second of its existence. But remember, you must never take too much pride in it.

I mention these things because some of my contemporaries have reached an age when they begin to feel the occasional twinge of pain. Having abused their bodies for nigh on half a century, they seem surprised when it starts to complain.

My oldest friend, the Garrabost Historian, called the other night from what he imagined was his death bed. Every square inch of his corp was screeching in protest, but he would not consult any of our eminent colleagues. He knew best. He figured he'd been poisoned at a Burns Supper and intended to sue a certain distillery in Campbeltown. His pride would not allow him to admit that age was getting the upper hand. A man who used to breakfast with Bobby Neilly on broth seasoned with salt herring – what virus would dare to invade *his* intestines?

I must admit I wasn't too worried about the Historian. The only other time he complained of ill-health we were on holiday in France. We were strolling on one of the bridges of Paris on a warm summer's day, walking several paces ahead of the women, when he suddenly grabbed my arm and whispered: 'Don't say anything. I don't want to alarm the women, but I think I'm having a heart attack.' We made it to the other side and to the nearest cafe, where we ordered some medicine. We ordered so much it lasted into the small hours, and next morning he was in much better health than I was. The trouble now is that if he ever catches anything of a serious nature no one will pay any attention.

Nearer home my learned colleague Councillor Macdonald refuses to admit his body is beginning to let him down. We found him writhing in agony clutching the incinerator he calls 'the stomach', but he refuses to see a doctor. He claims he must have been poisoned at a recent wedding. A quick check with his suffering wife revealed that he had indeed had the customary 12 chops and had taken 'a small snack' with him. Also, he had averaged four hours' sleep per night for the last six months.

When I challenged him on his destructive lifestyle and advised him to cut down to six chops and only two fried eggs, he said: 'That is all very well, but what if you're hungry?' On his sleeping routine he pointed out that George Bernard Shaw lived till 94 on four hours' sleep a night. But, *arsa mise*, Bernard Shaw had no sheep and he wasn't a councillor with WIIC.

For years I have lectured these 'boys' on the Temple of the Soul, but sadly they seem to have as little concern for the latter element as they have for the body itself. This is why I have now changed tack to the Tabernacle of the Holy Spirit. Perhaps if they pause to think on this awesome dimension they might go to bed at night.

*　　*　　*

Down in Ranish, Coinneach, who has been far from protective of the Temple, struck a rich seam last week of the best medicine yet discovered – a rare and plentiful shoal of herring.

Alas, it is so rare nowadays that the young women of the Isles don't know how to handle it. I actually caught my own imported wife *discarding the roe*. May the Saints look down on us with compassion.

Fortunately, the supply far exceeds demand and the female of the species far exceeds the male in number. We are in the happy position of being able to sacrifice the bony parts of the fish and fill our barrels with roe (whatever about the soul, that should take care of the Temple for the spring). The roe is fine salted, but even better smoked. My only fear is that the Chemist and Eòlas might misunderstand.

Friday, 21 February 1992

Under normal circumstances I wouldn't dream of exposing a case history to the public gaze. However, I'm sure you will agree that the results of my recent surgical probing of an old friend are far from normal. My 'discovery' deserves a wider audience than the *British Medical Journal*.

When Councillor Macdonald first admitted to his wife that all was not well with his intestines she called me immediately. He doesn't trust 'other doctors' and refused to place himself in their hands.

He has a horror of surgeries but agreed reluctantly to let himself be examined in his garage – with Dennis of Dennis Autos standing by. We eased him onto the workbench with the forklift and commenced exploration. With long sensitive fingers I probed hither and thither amongst the folds of wasted muscle. And, sure enough, I soon found it. An ulcer, we thought, gnawing hungrily at the neck of the duodenum. We had to tell him there was nothing for it but to go under the knife.

The operation had to be performed this very day in the short time between a transportation committee meeting and a sheep fank in Callanish. The theatre was cleared and less urgent cases sent home. The operation itself was straightforward and surprisingly simple, but I was momentarily shaken by his lack of faith when he turned to his wife at the last minute and said: 'Remember he owes me some money.'

(Thug e na mo chuimhne fear à Grabhair a bh' anns a' Home Guard. Bhiodh e g' èigheachd, 's am baile ga chluinntinn: 'Nis, a Mhàiri, mura till mise a-nochd, tha fios agad fhèin far 'eil an t-airgead.') (Parenthesis, dear Ed, in case we give offence to Leslie.)

I must confess the gory lump we removed had the team puzzled. But for the presence of a trainee vet, who was let in for the experience, I might not have recognised 'Woolball'.

'Woolball' is, of course, normally a problem in young lambs. There can only be one explanation: rough butchering in the byre forced upon us by the imminent closure of the slaughterhouse. I hope the appropriate authorities take note.

The patient 'himself' has a passionate interest in science, and I'm certain he will not object to publication if he comes round.

Many people have written to the paper pleading for my thoughts on fox hunting, so I cannot avoid the issue for a minute longer.

As every schoolboy knows, we have no foxes on our island: we drove them off Lewis and onto Skye the way St Patrick drove the snakes out of Ireland. But still we have plenty women, which is a species that has much in common with the fox; and God gave us dominion over both. If you know (in the Biblical sense) and have hunted one, you know the other.

What I am trying to say is that I cannot object to the hunting. However, I draw the line at tearing to pieces. When in the full bloom of youth I hunted for all I was worth, but with never anything worse in mind than the intent to molest. Molestation of this nature was for many a huntsman an obsession that has lingered on long after the ageing process has diminished the ability to molest.

Sometimes we hunted in packs because many of the hunters, then as now, were scared of women and would fall back when the prey was run to ground, or into the cloakroom of Laxdale village hall.

As for the hunted, though they sometimes squealed, they seldom organised protest marches far less go in for sabotage. Some, crazier than any fox, would lead the pack into Stornoway's Castle Grounds only to frustrate and lose the braves on horseback in the rhododendrons. Occasionally a flighty vixen would allow herself to be caught, and in no time at all a hairy brute with a shotgun would appear to terminate the hunter's career.

What we are talking about here, in our old-fashioned way, is what John MacLeod of the *Herald* calls rumpy-pumpy. I'm pleased to see that unlike many of his colleagues on the paper, but like many of his friends in the Church, he has some enthusiasm for The Hunt.

Personally, I like this new and vivid Lowland expression, rumpy-pumpy, but, alas, it has caused some distress in the Highlands. Middle-aged women come home from communion demanding their share of this 'rumpy-pumpy', thinking they are missing out on some modern mainland caper. Their husbands, although they know very well, pretend it is some kind of culinary invention in the pudding line, simply because they are well past the rumpy, never mind the pumpy.

I'm afraid the Churnalist of the Year has a lot to answer for, and I've written to his old fellow (through the Deacons' Court). Mind you, what he does in the shower is his business.

When I intimated a few minutes ago that I was never scared of women, I forgot a certain type of woman that frightens me so much I wilt at the very thought of her. That is the type with total recall. Compared with this lady, Margaret Thatcher is a cuddly sucklepuss.

I picked her up some time ago in her own car on the east side of Loch Lomond. We had perhaps an hour's drive to Paisley if one could drive well and knew the road.

Now, don't get me wrong: I'm very fond of the girl, and she is easy to look at, but her stories drive me insane. Once launched into a narrative, she cannot be diverted by fair play or foul.

She kicked off on a promising yarn in Drymen about a fisherman who had spoken to her for one whole hour on the previous night. Somewhere in Balloch I took a wrong turning. She stopped to direct me for perhaps two minutes (no, I tell a lie, it was three minutes . . . stop, I'm wrong, it was one-and-a-half . . .). Do you see what I mean?

Two or three, what does it matter, she resumed her yarn as if my drive round the block had been a semi-colon. At the Erskine Bridge I thought I had her beat. There was a delay – a long delay – and a search for change, but no matter. I tried to create a diversion by asking about this rumpy-pumpy business but I might as well have addressed Dumbarton Rock. Somewhere over the Clyde – she must keep a finger on the mental page – she said, 'So I said to him and he says to me . . .'

I arrived at Gleniffers Brae a broke man. If all Lowland women are like that, they can keep their rumpy-pumpy.

Friday, 22 May 1992

I thought this week I might pass on a few notes of guidance for islanders who, for one reason or another, have to travel to places like England. But first I would like to thank everyone who came to Shergar's funeral and those who attended the wake.

This prize beast was imported from Falkirk, remember, at enormous cost, and was hired for the courting season by Councillor Macdonald at even greater cost. The business of importing soft rams from the Falkirk sales is not a practice I would recommend. The only other import from Falkirk for procreative purposes I can recollect is Chris Kelso, and he too winters badly.

Well, folks, to cut a long story fairly short, Shergar died of a broken heart. He did the business, as I told you last week, and the lambs were perfectly formed – or, at least, better formed than the daddy. And like most modern daddies he attended the births. He was kept with sheep until lambing finished, but then the sheep were taken to Ranish and Shergar was left on his own in Leurbost. He only lasted three days after the separation. I can understand this, although people scoff, because when I was wrenched from Ranish at the age of 11 and taken to Leurbost

I didn't think I would last three days. Apart from Daniel, the people seemed cold and unfriendly, although better fed.

So there we are, then. Shergar was a romantic soul. Faced with the prospect of not going back to Ranish with his girlfriends, or, even worse, being sent to Carloway (worse than Coventry), he chose to pass on. I didn't have the heart to close his eyes, so he was still staring at me accusingly as I laid him under the sod.

So, fare thee well, Shergar; you did the job . . . I feel a dose of the divine afflatus coming on, but the mood is too sad (come back to this one).

When I said islanders, back there a bit, I meant the ordinary man on the croft and not the people who work for WIIC and spend most of their lives at ten thousand feet or more. I understand there are folk *in there* who have difficulty adjusting to surface oxygen levels. But never mind *them*; let's talk about us.

Supposing you haven't been off the island for a year or so, perhaps not even out of the wellies, how do you adjust? Now, then, the first step is to take the wellies off. You see very few wellies when travelling south (coming north is another story; and by the way, the green buckled type is no longer fashionable – black with a red rim is the new style if you want to be with-it).

Wellington removal is not as simple as it sounds. On the contrary, it is an extremely complex operation. You've probably heard of people who have had a limb removed but the pain is still there. That is how it is.

If your first stop is Glasgow Airport, it is but a small step on the cosmic scale but a great step for crofterkind. You are probably still looking for familiar faces to say 'Aye, aye' to, but *they* always look away. This unsociable behaviour makes you instantly suspicious, so you glance down to see if perhaps you've left one welly on or maybe there is a clinker of sheep dirt in the turn-ups of your demob suit. You must learn to examine yourself in an inconspicuous manner, by which I mean *not* like the guy who isn't sure if he is zipped up.

The simple truth, although difficult to accept, is that nobody is looking at you nor is anyone in the slightest bit interested. By the time you reach London Airport you'll have developed the knack yourself. You can almost walk through people. I'll give you a for instance.

Coming back through security at Heathrow, who is in front of me but George Best himself. He is being given a hard time. They have his underpants and socks spread out like nobody's business, but he can take it because he is used to this sort of treatment. He looks slim, fit and sober. The boys in Glasgow wanted to know if I had actually touched him or even spoken. But, no, I hadn't. Your man is such a seasoned traveller he was able to pretend he didn't know who I was.

A two-day visit to the South-East of England is enough for most of us, yet people somehow adapt. They very quickly adjust to prison life. I met some Celts who have spent years in a depressing town called Bracknell, but still they seemed quite normal.

Personally, I doubt very much if I could retain my sanity, although there is one blessing – Bracknell's sole redeeming feature – in that you cannot see the ocean. As a matter of fact, you cannot see very much of anything. Because of the way the town is built, the maximum visibility in any one direction is only a few hundred yards. This is not good for those of us who have always been accustomed to getting up in the morning and scanning a horizon that is 70 miles away.

I was quite pleased to escape to Glasgow, which is only slightly less depressing. There is one big consolation, though, in Mrs Wong's Chinese restaurant. You'll find this one in Maryhill, and it is well worthwhile taking a chance. I had asked my dear daughter to book us in for Friday night. She must have misunderstood or misheard – I didn't ask her to invite every student in Hillhead. To make matters worse, I reached home to discover the Indonesian crowd had emptied my freezer. It's going to be a long thin summer.

Fortunately, Terry in the Park Bar appreciated my predicament and poured free drink into me. I see the place is as popular as ever, but they have the strangest way of attracting customers.

Where other nightclubs might employ dancing girls, the Park has Sgadan. He has been taken on to attract young girls, and this seems to be working. It's probably the way Sgadan smiles.

I came across a new 'language' down there, and I hope to try it out on youse next week when I understand it a bit better. Must go now and see if I can borrow a loaf from Dolly next door.

FRIDAY, 29 MAY 1992

Lingerabay quarry in Harris has been the subject of several years' angst. DHM's development in Uig has fuelled several column miles in this paper alone. But without as much as an 'Excuse *me*, by the way' to the natives of North Lochs, our 'own' Western Isles Council has started to quarry Ceann Eustapar 'just because it's handy'.

Ceann Eustapar is not just another hill. It is sacred. It is sacred in more ways than one, but the one should be enough. Ceann Eustapar at sunset, before it was vandalised, was a spectacularly beautiful little hill on the flat, lonely stretch between Crossbost and Leurbost. After the sun set it was a terrifying landmark. Grown-ups wouldn't walk alone past Eustapar at night; little boys might, to prove their courage, expecting at any moment to feel the cold, clammy hand of a long-dead ancestor on the nape of the neck (I felt them myself and saw them, but I never told anyone).

Eustapar is, of course, as every schoolboy knows, one of our oldest burial grounds. Generations of men and women from Ranish including Montgomerys have rested peacefully on top of this secure plateau, with scarcely a murmur, until the contractors moved in last week with earth-moving equipment.

Planning and development didn't know, but let me tell them this: God knows.

It is doubtful if we in North Lochs will ever again experience a peaceful night. Even as I write the steel claws of JCBs are mangling the bones of my forefathers.

That is all bad enough, but wait till I tell you the worst. I might not have noticed the upheaval but my first wife (the slim one) called me in the middle of last night to draw my attention to the atrocity being perpetrated in the name of progress. 'Get up quickly and do something,' she screamed. 'There is an ugly bulldozer parked on our special ledge, halfway up Eustapar.' *(This needs some explanation – Ed.)*

Fair enough, you shall have it.

When we, the young bucks of the parish, were 12 or thereabouts we used to entice the girls away from Sunday School with promises of much more exciting spiritual encounters on Eustapar. I will not mention any girls' names here because that wouldn't be fair, but I'm sure *they* will all remember; anyway, Alice is on holiday in Cyprus. The Crossbost boys, Sandy, Johnny Walker and Tabaidh, were much more advanced than those of us from Leurbost and Ranish. We had a much more sheltered upbringing, but we were easily led.

Who knows what people thought, because we were within sight of the Free Church manse. Perhaps they suspected we were picking nits from the girls' hair, but it wasn't that simple. Far from it. We were engaged in the only work that is both necessary and merciful. The occasional maiden's scream did not signal fear: it was merely her unrestrained delight at the discovery of the mysterious nature of her being.

A couple of years later we had progressed to more advanced biology. We had learned to be ashamed and had moved away from Eustapar, but it is doubtful if any of us will ever again come as close to an understanding of the universe as we did all these years ago on the hill now being desecrated.

My second wife (the plump one) would like Eustapar designated an area of Special Scientific Interest, although it is probably too late.

There is a very funny English guy *(Aren't they all? – Ed.)* . . . I know, but this fellow Harry Enfield is a comic genius. Some critics have complained that he has overdone one of his creations – the man who says: 'You don't wanna do that, you must do it this way'. Please let me assure you, he most certainly has not overcooked this pest. I know one in real life who has him beat.

A gentleman fish farmer from South Uist and I had more or less completed the organisation of a simple towing job from Loch Leurbost to Loch Carnan in South Uist when, lo, there appeared from the east one Macpherson. 'You don't want to do it that way,' said the wise man. 'Let's do it my way.'

What could we say? If the First Secretary in Dacca – the man who is going to revolutionise the fishing industry in the Bay of Bengal – says do it my way, I guess we have to do it his way.

Every schoolboy, again, knows the simple mathematical formula for the maximum speed attainable by the mass being towed. Every schoolboy, that is, except those who have found jobs in fisheries development. I will not confuse you with complex algebra, but let me put it this way . . . The First Secretary set off on a 70-mile voyage towing a kite – a single tow in the diagonal.

For goodness's sake, every girl in Cromore knows this is the way to create maximum resistance. The same girls could also have told him you must organise the bulk being towed to its maximum length and minimum width. And of course there are able lassies in Primary 7 in South Lochs who know you must make an isosceles triangle of the bridle with the equal sides being 1.4 times the length of the base, thus making the best steering angle of 47 degrees. But not your man. He knows best. You want to do it my way. I seem to remember a similar problem in Java last year.

To cut the painter short, after two days on the high seas the womenfolk were getting worried and the Coastguard had to be alerted. Personally I would have waited four days before alerting Bristow's, but I'm not a wife with uncertain insurance cover.

Captain Bob of Loganair was very helpful as he flew back and fore from Barra for several days. He reported sightings of many cages, but there was no way he could tell which were being towed and which were firmly anchored to the sea-bed. He did make a note of an unusual configuration near Scalpay on the second day, with two people dancing on the walkways as if out of tobacco, but we put that down to Hearach idiosyncracy.

At the moment of going to press we are, as they say, neither here nor there. But the leader excused himself and left us to it, saying he had important work to do in Bangladesh before the floods. The time has come, I think, to call in the Barvas Navigator. I will report progress next week, *D.V.*

FRIDAY, 12 JUNE 1992

OF MEN AND MIDGES

The weather is a subject that has always interested me a great deal, although I've managed to keep it to myself. One's relationship with the weather is, and always should remain, a private matter. Sadly, very many people will not accept this.

Almost everybody I know, except for a few Americans, will insist on sharing their observations on the weather with me. Even those nearest and dearest to me can attain the superbore level when it comes to weather – although they are well aware of my aversion to public discussion of personal emotion.

All this is bad enough in winter. In the icy grip of March you can almost forgive a comment on the cold, the bitter cold, the freezing cold or the cold rain. You might not have noticed these harsh conditions as you dash from pub to pub in a desperate effort to spend as little time as possible out in the open, and you don't mind the amateur climatologists so long as they follow up with 'Are you coming in for one?'

However, there are some unfortunate souls who have to take the weather in with them – for that is all they have – which is why you have to keep running for fresh shelter (at this game there is always the danger you could end up trapped by the fiend who tells jokes, but that is another story for another day).

The foul-weather man is tolerable because he merely wants to share his misery with you. And you can sometimes shock him, if he listens, with the honest rejoinder that you happen to like wind, rain and hailstones. If you are very quick and he cannot see through his glasses for the driving drizzle, you can bamboozle him with a loud 'Nice day' as you run by. Sometimes, if your victim has had a few, he might take up your cry and go around town shouting 'Nice day' until he gets arrested.

But that was then. You can imagine the depth of my despair since the Scandinavian High took root about a month ago. Even the five intelligent people I knew before the heatwave, men and women renowned for their scintillating conversation, are reduced to constant jabbering about the weather. Total strangers, for some reason, feel it incumbent upon them to draw my attention to the 'Wonderful spell, what!'

As a matter of fact, I had noticed, and I happen to think there is nothing wonderful about it. The white glare hurts my eyes and colours them pink. The tip of my snout, which is longer than the longest peaked cap, turns red – leading strangers to think it could be a whisky nose, as if a doctor would have such a thing. Moreover, the slightest hint of sun and sea air cause my herpes to bloom. You bet I'd noticed.

Much more seriously, though, remember there is a hole in the ozone layer the size of Wales. Yet this doesn't stop young *and old* from exposing the flesh. Flesh, I may add, that would be better hidden, ultra-violet rays or not. Flesh very often freckled and wrinkled between large moles just waiting to spread. But they will not listen.

Women especially will fry themselves at every opportunity, hoping they will look better when brown and that their husbands will stop switching the light off. But there is a terrible price to pay. I have gazed upon old colonial women who stayed too long in the sun and they all had faces like dried dates, and breasts to match. So take heed. Look at Barbara Cartland, white at 90 but without a blemish.

Men are no better – ageing men especially, who fancied themselves to be a bit sporty in their youth. Nothing will do for them but to get the old National Service shorts out for the golf. 'Isn't this marvellous,' they beam, pulling the gut in. 'Give me more of this.' How, pray tell, is one supposed to concentrate on the 'game' while counting Iain Macritchie's varicose veins? Eddie Mackenzie one doesn't mind so much because he is young and looks quite pretty since he shaved the beard off. Still, this weather cannot last. Can it?

On an even more serious note, has anyone noticed the midges this year? This is worse than the weather and even more boringly obvious, I hear you say. But wait a minute. There is a good chance that many of you have not noticed. My own wife with her leathery sun-cured hide isn't bothered by this devilish insect and can mow the lawn while I, with my smooth lily-white skin, daren't venture outside.

Very soon, though, she will know all about them. You will all know. This unnatural weather is to blame for the midges' early arrival, but *not for their size*. An important and alarming upheaval has taken place in the genetic structure of the midge. In fact, it will have to be given a more appropriate name, for it is no longer a midge.

It used to be that the midge would not leave the heather in bright sunlight nor if the wind was stronger than four knots. This is no longer the case.

The new tenacious giant midge thrives on ultra-violet and can tack against a near-gale. Its bite leaves a lump like a tomato – a very ripe tomato containing God only knows what manner of radioactive poison. Whether this dreadful plague is a result of Chernobyl or Dounreay we have not been told, but very soon it will distract from the obsession with the weather.

Only yesterday in one's 'club' I found Sylvia – that fair daughter of Albion who looks after us so well – chasing what she imagined to be a wasp. Naturally, I knew it was no wasp; the wasps haven't arrived yet. When they do I fully expect to see people chasing strange-looking blackbirds with rolled-up newspapers.

A few inches ago I mentioned some Americans I had to deal with recently. I had hoped to get back to their new extended farewell – '*You have a nice day now*' – which has nothing to do with the weather. However, you must excuse me because I'm working to rule and it's such a fine day.

FRIDAY, 17 JULY 1992

Don't get me wrong, life has been quite good to me. Along the way she has dealt me some savage blows but every time, so far, I have managed to dust myself down and strike back. Alas, I fear my resilience is crumbling. The feeble body and the little brain can take no more.

And please don't think I ever asked for or expected too much, because nothing could be further from the truth. I blossomed in poverty and thrived on puritan self-denial in times of temporary affluence. Now let me tell you the desperate state of affairs to which I have sunk.

Exactly 12 months ago I was loafing around the East Indies with dusky maidens in limitless number competing with each other to apply soothing balm to my tortured back. That was fine, but it took this year's 'holiday' to shake off the enormous burden of guilt. This year's relief from toil amounted to three days of penance in the City of Glasgow being led around on a noose through modern wonders of the world like Marks & Spencer and What Every Woman Wants.

But we'll get back to them later. Put your feet up just now and I'll start at the beginning of the voyage at five o'clock in the morning on the ferry called MV *Suilven*.

Before I get to this trip's complaint I would like to thank whoever runs the company for having stopped the violent videos. These, presumably American, movies were bloodthirsty and extremely noisy. The children loved them.

The problem now is what to do with the same children. In the absence of gore on the wall what plans do you have, Mr MacBrayne, to entertain them? Sleep for them is naturally out of the question, but we would like to, having had to get up at the ungodly hour of four in the night. I see no reason why these delightful little boys and girls shouldn't be allowed up on deck to play in the lifeboats.

Although I have to admit, even without the squealing of the young, sleep on one of the *Suilven*'s 12-inch benches is nigh impossible unless one is heavily drugged. And if you did manage to pass into a coma with the aid of Trawler Rum, pneumonia is almost certain in the icy blast of air maliciously directed at paying customers through the 'heaters'.

There was nothing for it but to pass some of the time with one of Roddy the Cook's breakfasts. Poor Roddy, it's not his fault. It is difficult to find decent sausage these days on either side of the Minch. The contents of the sausage are so finely ground now that you cannot detect the ears, tails and scrotums, but rest assured they are in there.

Could I perhaps be so bold as to suggest an alternative in Charley Barley's black puddings. On a heavy sea they are easier to bring up than the modern sausage.

While we are still at breakfast it would be unfair not to mention Roddy's fried eggs. This humble sliver of nourishment is not as easily prepared as many people suppose, but for Roddy's fried eggs it is almost worth the four-hour voyage. On the other hand, perhaps we were lucky and Thursday morning is when he makes a batch for the week.

On to Inverness and through as quickly as possible, for it is not a place where you would want to eat or sleep if half of what we hear is true. Every second morning the wireless issues tales of rape, murder and arson, so it is best to take a chance on Glasgow, where the weight of numbers lengthens the odds against serious injury.

True, one has to risk the infamous A9, about which we also hear as many sad stories. They usually blame speed, but I cannot believe this is the main cause. South of Perth the average speed increases by at least 10mph to 85 but the driving seems safer. I blame the hordes of English people who plague the Highlands towing their homes behind them – probably with enough sandwiches for the fortnight.

Be all that as it may, on Friday I took my place in Glasgow University for my Honorary Doctorate in Lettuce. As most readers will be aware, the University was founded in 1451 by Pope Nicholas V, but do you know what I'm going to tell you, the influence of Rome is as strong as ever it was. The whole dashed ceremony was in Latin. Fine by me, of course, but my poor wife, you know . . . terribly weak in the Classics.

With the little chores out of the way, we were free to concentrate on the important business – but I'm sure you're not really interested in What Every Woman Wants. Unless perhaps the Millionaire Cobbler might be pleased to hear I purchased a fine pair of shoes for a tenner.

But just one word of warning. While wandering around the department of delicate undergarments, you try to keep your eyes on your toes lest anyone thinks there is something peculiar in your personality. As luck would have it, with my gaze fixed on the floor, I 'lost' the wife, which might have led people to suspect I was in there on my own. Desperate to prove my innocence, I thought I'd try on one of my new shoes again, only to stumble and bring down a suspender stand. At this stage what else could I do but buy some of the gear and start waving in the general direction of a strange group of women shouting 'Wait for me'. Still, to avoid being arrested is the main thing.

For some strange reason, the next day she said: you go out with the boys, and I'll go shopping on my own. I managed to track down Alec, the last remaining member of the Byres Road Gang of the Sixties. We had a nice sad time talking of how things were and what we are reduced to now. In my state of profound melancholy I became very emotional and caused further embarrassment to my friends, embarrassment of such intensity that I cannot bear to think of it, far less repeat it here.

Perhaps next week, if my strength returns in some small measure.

Friday, 24 July 1992

(With apologies to John MacLeod, for whom I have the deepest respect)
Unimaginative? Boring? Perhaps! I too could have gone to Mallorca. But I didn't. From my Granny's attic window in Stornoway I stare across a smelly oil-slicked harbour at the once-majestic Castle Grounds. Gloriously green Castle Grounds. Then.

Now? Sycamores, beeches and scattered sturdy oaks, some older than myself, are singed brown and yellow, autumnised before their time by gangs of lager-crazed arsonists in Levi jeans and gaudy imported trainers.

Where did we lose our way, I ask myself on this Sabbath eve. I retreat from this window on the world, as it is, and withdraw to the security I increasingly can find only within the four walls of my own mind. I ponder on imponderables. Spiritual contemplation is rudely interrupted by wheeling, screeching herring gulls unaware or uncaring that this is the seventh day of the week. They shatter my peace and spatter the pavements as if it were Wednesday. Are these Scottish seagulls, I ask no one in particular. No one answers, for there is no one there. I prefer to be on my own.

Unable to think with the abominable roar of motor-bikes, I steel myself for another look down on the street. Yes, *the street* is still there. Two young men, clutching cans, stagger aimlessly towards oblivion. Their destination to them unknown: to me a certainty. They both have the cadaverous appearance of those chosen by the Almighty for His latest experiment in population control. I feel no compassion. Why?

Read the Gospels.

Along a garbage-strewn pier several young women stroll, perilously close to the edge . . . laughing. Laughing at what, I wonder. From my vantage point in the sky I can see quite clearly that their legs are shaven . . . shaved with ladies' Philishaves manufactured in once-Calvinist Holland. Skimpy blouses cover what are very likely see-through brassieres, wired to hoist temptation further into view. The two emaciated young men are attracted by the laughing maidens but continue on their sad way.

I decide to have a shower. Where the once-clean water from the well? Is this the sum total of 35 years of Labour rule . . . a piped trickle of brown–black sludge with gobs of peat and heather?

> " 'S math dhan àl
> nach eil an Gràs
> cho loma-làn
> de riasg
> ri bùrn
> Loch Mòr a' Stàrr."

Where *are* you now, Duncan? I thought.

Must find a place of worship to cleanse the soul this Sabbath evening. To Kenneth Street Free Church? No, I think not. Martin's Memorial, perhaps? Yes, why not! Professor Pater might not approve, but I seek . . . I seek relentlessly . . . not only truth, but copy.

Martin's, the quintessence of established theological conformity. A quick run through ritual, a quick pint in the County and perhaps a quick round of golf? Not quite yet. Stornoway Trust still have the keys to the Golf Club and to the children's swings. Musical instruments in the church, though . . . And who have we here . . . a visiting preacher . . . Lamont of the *Herald*, my goodness. Must be careful this doesn't degenerate to the farcical.

It strikes me as I listen that we are not all that far removed from the malevolent gaze of Our-Lady-On-The-Hill in Barra. Elders' seats are filled with expensively-tailored bums. Upwardly-static exploiters from the Thatcherite years, 'needled' by the only Biblical threat they can remember, who couldn't bring themselves to forsake the pleasures of the flesh and so seek this Half-Way-House between hedonism and salvation – the Church of Scotland.

Is this our Scotland? It is certainly not mine. I dash up to Scotland Street in time to catch the fourth service of the day in the Free Presbyterian Church, to which I am more and more attracted. On the way I encounter further manifestations of depravity that can only be accounted for by present attitudes adopted by certain Free Church theologians. Out of our Free Church pour bunless women and men without hats. And, as if my trials and tribulations had been unto the day insufficient, a minister without a collar! I am reminded of the famous North Lochs sage who said 'Collar not your dog, lest he should one day collar you', and I am consoled.

Once inside, I listen. I am not alone. I look around and notice that all are listening. Listening for the trumpet's summons to that great pseud's corner in the sky. I don't go forward. I cannot. I am not worthy. I leave alone but not well.

Aware that despite my devotions I lack the consistency in style that makes for greatness, I walk alone along the shaded lanes of Matheson's grand plantation. The bikers have gone to bed, the arsonists have burnt their fingers. The Castle Grounds are ominously quiet. A lonely owl hoots.

Suddenly the tinkling sound of girlish laughter reverberates twixt drooping branch and Castle wall and sweetens the aroma of the silver birch. 'Are you alone?' quoth she. 'Am I alone? Am I alone? Has ever one been more alone?' quoth I. But dash it all, this life is too short; I don't want to end up like Jack MacLean. Yes, I was alone, I admitted.

'But that was then and this is now, and if you like I'll show you how to milk the muse of love and rhyme, but steady, you must take your time. Take off your hat, your braces too, but if you like leave on one shoe, embrace me now and live a while, as writers must who aim for style.'

Gosh! I'm quite looking forward to getting back to Glasgow. No adventure? Moi?

(Eachainn is the Old Journalist of the Decade)

FRIDAY, 31 JULY 1992

Many people have drawn my attention to a piece written by some rodent called Nicolson in the *Sunday Times*. Why Highland gentlemen and women should be bothered by anything written in the *Sunday Times* or its sister the *Sun* I cannot imagine. The sort of people who read these 'papers' are not our sort of people and so can be instantly dismissed.

However, I am a wee bit concerned. Some quite innocent readers might on occasion pick up a Murdoch organ when there is nothing else to hand and they could very well belong to that diminishing group that believes what it reads. We must assume Mr Nicolson, when quoting Preston-Smith, chose a typical immigrant, in which case we have to be wary. We have to believe hers is a typical view of the indig, so we must guard our backs against colleagues who have dropped the hyphen. We must treat with even greater suspicion those who changed their names to Macdonald in a desperate move to be accepted into civilised society.

As for Preston-Smith herself, who often got stoned in Harris . . . well, what did she expect? Only a very foolish immigrant would go and live in a glass house in Harris. And, having had to flee from Harris, to then go and settle in Point smacks of the exceedingly foolhardy. One thing that is not made clear in this latter-day Boswell's account is what happened to the poor original owner of the hyphen in Preston-Smith. We are told his heart was broken in Harris and that he 'sped back to London'. I suspect investigations will reveal *she* ate him with a knife and fork.

That is another thing I find mildly irritating. For years now I have been sharing some of my traditional recipes with readers of our learned journal, only to learn from hyphenated anaesthetes like Preston-Smith my instructions are being ignored. Preston-Smith says: 'These people are like animals, they eat with their hands.'

If there is one ingredient essential to the appreciation of the full flavour of my wonderful creations, that is the finger or, sometimes, the whole hand. Yet it seems some of these ignorant refugees from the industrial south have so little taste they would corrupt the divine with cold Sheffield steel. That 'these people' could bring themselves to pollute a delicate venison chop or a fresh herring with stainless steel is beyond belief. They are possibly closely related to the man who invented condoms. We must try to understand, for it is not their fault. I cannot remember who said it, nor in which context, but: 'Let twenty pass and stone the twenty-first.'

Enough of 'these people', for we have more important matters to talk about. Once again I have fallen out with the *Stornoway Gazette* – the second best newspaper in the world. They refuse to accept the Golf Notes.

Fair enough. We have a solution. We are going to bring out our very own paper – *The Bayhead Bugle*. In the *Bugle* you will meet characters who would never make it to the family newspapers (the decency laws, you understand). Colour photographs and Page Three boys every week, with an in-depth profile of Captain Stewart in the first issue. The Bugle will also have a special 'Dominoes Supplement' – another first, we believe. But there will be strictly no gossip unless the Editor decides something is rated really juicy.

Because the 'paper' is non profit-making we will allow a special column for golf bores. Under the headline 'Did You See Me On The Tenth?' everyone will get his turn. With a little luck this will mean we won't have to listen to them in the clubhouse. Order your copy now – ten pee wholesale or one pound thirty from Dr Gordon Davies.

Gordon wasn't the first club professional to realise the Game is rife with snobbery. A certain Scottish pro discovered the secret of success as long ago as the 1920s.

This smart boy was in the south of England. He employed a team of spies to go round the neighbouring clubs checking on their prices. Whatever *their* mark, the bold Scotsman doubled it. In short time golfers from near and far came to buy their gear from your man so they could boast how much it cost. Gordon, being a Yorkshire man, has taken to multiplying the going rate by four. Very soon he should be able to retire to a safe offshore tax haven, but never mind as long as he pays for advertising space in *Bugle*.

If there is one activity that is a greater waste of time than golf, it is the sheepdog trial.

While every other nation in the universe was girding its loins in Barcelona last Saturday, the able-bodied crofters of Lewis were gathered on the Crossbost Common Grazing tormenting their dogs. There is a fair amount of snobbery attached to this game also. They tell me a thousand pounds is not considered a lot to pay for a promising puppy nowadays. For this you could almost buy Dr Murdo Vishu's clubs.

Five days of the week these poor souls chase sheep up and down mountains, whistling, cursing and sweating. On the sixth day they do the same on the flat for fun. In the absence of natural obstacles they erect false gates to confuse both sheep and dog. The animals are further confused because the normal cursing that constitutes 90 per cent of the commands is banned or at least toned down. To add to the chaos, the sheep used were the wild, unfed Crossbost variety, and not the tame beasts you see on television.

I had entered the spaniel Smut for all the competitions this year but the snob who runs things wouldn't have him. 'It could lead to total anarchy,' he muttered. The faithful springer perhaps lacks a little discipline, but I don't see that he could be any more disruptive than some of the prize collies they worship. It seemed a good idea to let him loose on the common at the right moment, but Maggie wouldn't have it.

So, for badness, I crept down to the Crossbost shelter-belt with a high-pitched whistle; and, boy, did I whistle. I whistled till the dogs were as crazy as their masters and the sheep were jumping non-existent gates. I cannot remember when I had so much fun. The demented shepherds have gone home to rethink their retraining. They suspect they have the trials equivalent of the golf disease called shanking. But not a word, now.

Of the many visitors we get at this time of year I shall miss Calum Iain the most when he goes back to Oban. He brings order and sanity to our end of the village.

Sgiobair nan Eathraichean Loibht, as we used to call him, tidies his own croft – and neighbouring ones. He mends fences and shears sheep and then he takes me for a pint. He generally calms me down and leaves me in a state of some tranquillity, unlike the Garrabost Historian, who always leaves me in pain.

Friday, 28 August 1992

I'm told by the people who use such places that the Cleitear Hotel will soon be open again.

Cleitear was never used very much by men from the North side of the Loch for the simple reason that it is situated on the South side. If we in the North learned anything in this life, that was to avoid people from the South when in drink. Some of them didn't even need drink as an excuse: they were known to go over the top from the trenches without the aid of rum. Very handy folk to have around in times of war, but they are permanently frustrated in peacetime. They carry guns, these wild hairy men, and they're forever shooting things. I've seen more than one of these guys, having drink taken, go several rounds with their reflection in a clear pool.

Don't let me put you off the Cleitear, but be warned. The violent nature of the natives was not the only reason we stayed away. Mine hosts have not always been what you might call jolly types. As a matter of fact, the last lot didn't smile much at all.

Also, there has been and still is the problem of Stornoway. Stornoway is where young men want to go on a Saturday night because Stornoway is where the young women are. Sure, there are women in South Lochs, many with big red legs, but there aren't enough of these girls to go round.

However, having said all that, I understand the new owner of the Cleitear, Roddy Dan, has solved some of the problem. In a noble attempt to soften the collective image of his clientele, he plans to bus some gentlemen over from Ranish and Leurbost. Their influence on the wild ones from the South can only be good in the long term.

The only problem I foresee with this modern 'Bus a' Phloy' is how to get past Crossbost without picking *them* up. Perhaps a few of the older chappies like Dòmhnall Ruadh could be encouraged, but we must remember it is not very long since they arrived from the South when our dear Landlords were doing some ethnic cleansing over there. Many of the Crossbost mob are not sufficiently far removed from Orasay to be of any help in the civilising of the Cleitear. As for the folk who live in Balallan itself, the least said the better. Sociologists long ago decided there was nothing could be done. So it is down to us in Ranish and Leurbost.

A much more difficult problem facing Roddy Dan and all of us who are concerned is, having enticed youngsters away from Stornoway to

South Lochs, how to keep them there. If I may make so bold as to offer a few suggestions.

The whole world knows now that the youth of Lewis are afflicted with a desperate compulsion to congregate in the Narrows of Cromwell Street and Point Street. So, the first item on the agenda must be the building of the new Narrows in Habost. This need not be a costly exercise, for all that matters is that the imitation Narrows look roughly like the Town Centre. Cardboard frontages would do just so long as there are some windows to break.

Another ingredient that is absolutely essential for the full enjoyment of a Saturday night is the fish supper wrapping. Again, there is no need to go to the bother of supplying fish and chips. All that is required is white greasy paper to be discarded on the street at midnight.

Then, of course, there has to be a little fighting. This should need very little organisation over on the South Side.

The idea of a free bus on Saturdays is fine, but I think on Fridays I will chug in the Loch in my small boat. Perhaps I'll do a little fishing and anchor at the Cleitear for a bite to eat and a pint. What could be more civilised?

Alas, I see opposition from the wee wife here. North Lochs wives will never let us forget the day of the sponsored row to the Star Inn and back – and what a row that was. The main thing is we didn't lose anyone. However, I must insist that anyone who wants to come along to the Cleitear by boat must be able to swim.

One hates to burden readers with personal problems, but I must, for I'm having a terrible summer.

The first blow was the loss of my galvanised everlasting spade. Thirty-seven pounds out of the Crofters it cost her, but it's not the money. This implement was of great sentimental value, although very heavy, and I would quite like to have it back.

I hardly recovered from that blow when my low-mileage golf shoes took a walk from one's clubhouse. What grieves me most about the shoes

– apart from the obvious deduction that there is someone, possibly an Englishperson, who thinks he can fill them – is that I have not finished paying for them yet. And of course, even if they mysteriously turned up, I could never wear them again. Although I am not without my own private little peculiarities, other people's toes do not appeal to me. As a matter of fact, chiropody is what I would call the last shift, which is why I cannot understand Mellor or that Ferguson woman. So whoever has my shoes, please keep them but give me the money.

My boat, rod and reel I would like back very much. A substantial reward is offered for information leading to etc. Why, for goodness's sake, if people must steal don't they go for my wife's car. Incidentally, that is for sale, if no one wants to steal it.

FRIDAY, 4 SEPTEMBER 1992

WHY I AM SO WISE AND CLEVER
Give me a new roll of linoleum and a sharp Stanley knife and normally I'm a happy man. But bring me the same roll when I have just given up smoking and I get frustrated and eventually so agitated my nose bleeds. My wee wife means well. She encourages me to stop smoking that I may live longer, and then she brings me lino. She doesn't understand that I have only so many lino-laying days left in me until the solution called suicide becomes irresistible.

I am not sure why I should have mentioned lino-laying as the reformed drug addict's purgatory. Perhaps it just happened too soon after withdrawal, and it is a devilish task for tightly strung nerves. Yet there are many other irritations almost as bad. 'Other people' have to rank next to lino-laying in the league of unbearable burdens.

Other people with their all-too-exposed corruption were probably the reason I dimmed the view with drugs as long ago as 1950. 'Empty your pockets,' Miss Dolina Montgomery would say every morning. 'You should be ashamed of yourself picking douts off the school bus floor at the age of five.' 'Please, Miss, I was hungry,' I would plead. And that was easy to believe, because with all the smoking my ribs could be seen through the flour-bag shirt. So you see it has been quite a while.

Speaking as my own doctor, it is probably not advisable to stop suddenly after all this time, and I only chucked the habit so *she* could sleep at night and especially in the mornings. The noises in my bronchial tubes had reached such a pitch that guests in the spare bedroom often woke up in the early hours thinking somebody was playing a concertina on the dormer roof.

In the midst of pain there has been some consolation and a few surprising discoveries. The most startling of these was the realisation in the autumn of my 47th year that I am the reincarnation of the great German philosopher Friedrich Wilhelm Nietzsche. This awesome, dreadful certainty struck me like a blow from an oar in the middle of a cold sober night. At the moment of my rebirth, as it were, I had been brooding on the problems of halitosis among my non-smoking friends (we'll come back to this one in a minute or two).

Frightened but exhilarated, I rushed down to my library to see what I'd written in the last century. Sure enough, there it was in *Ecce Homo* as I'd half-remembered: 'I possess a perfectly uncanny sensitivity of the instinct of cleanliness, so that I perceive physiologically – *smell* – the proximity or – what am I saying – the innermost parts, the entrails of every soul . . . I have this sensitive psychological antennae with which I touch and take hold of every secret: all the concealed dirt at the bottom of many a nature, perhaps conditioned by bad blood but whitewashed by education, is known to me almost on first contact . . . If I have observed correctly, such natures unendurable to my sense of cleanliness for their part also sense the caution of my disgust: they do not thereby become any sweeter smelling . . .'

You see how little changes. I don't suppose Old Fred had only the bad breath of non-smokers in mind when he (I) wrote that, but I have no doubt *they* were high on his list of unendurables. That abstainers from nicotine, whisky and other alleged poisons exhale noxious fumes is not in doubt. It is not their fault . . .

Why should this son of a Christian church minister, this pampered professor, make his comeback in the black-house of a crofter? I made too many simple mistakes, that's why. Of Polish ancestry, I despised the simple German but admired the ruthless Frenchman. I (we) even confessed a French writer beat us into print with the best joke of the century: 'God's only excuse is that He does not exist.' That was a bad move. We should have kept an open mind. Even before I knew who I had been, I tried hard to search for the soul, or certainly not to deny it, in case next time I come back as a smoked farmed salmon.

Many of my friends scoff at the idea of reincarnation but it always seemed to me, long before I had this proof, easier to accept than most of the other nonsensical gillieorms built into their organised superstition.

I would like youall to read Old Fred, even the cousins in South Lochs. We are very easy to read, but it is only fair to remind you that he was not a well man. As I lie here on the kitchen floor gouging the new lino with my Stanley, I hope and pray the sins of this particular father will not be visited on the sons. I am severely tempted to have a smoke to douse the renewed flame of . . . but never mind that. In the time of his greatest creativity – the years of his delusion of omniscience – before he succumbed to the general paralysis of the insane, he probably never imagined he would one day be reduced to laying lino in a crofter's kitchen.

P.S. Following my plea of last week, I am pleased to report I have news of my boat-rod. Thank you.

Still no one comes to buy Maggie's old Volvo. This is a car well-suited to church-going because you can get in with your hat on. It is also very handy for bringing spuds up from the croft. Ideal third car. One new tyre.

FRIDAY, 9 OCTOBER 1992

Some readers of our paper, obviously new recruits, have written to ask for an explanation of my recent reference to the wife's fancy man, Marshall Ward. There is very little I can add because I don't know much about him except that evidently he has very expensive tastes.

Many men, on the final steep slope towards the tropopause, are too proud to accept their wives' need to keep a robust 'boy' about the croft. I would never have known about young Marshall had she thought to use another name on the cheques, but there you are. In any case, it all started during the summer I discovered I could no longer throw a full bag of peat onto a tractor, so I didn't mind too much. I thought perhaps I'd better get my money's worth out of the lad pushing a wheelbarrow or cutting the grass. In the event, at least as far as I'm concerned, Marshall Ward has proved a poor investment. My guess is she might have done better to hire a young Journalist of the Year.

Not long after this man Ward came into our lives the Royal Bank stopped sending back used cheques, so I sort of forgot about him, until, just recently, I made enquiries about the tragic state of my economic affairs and learned I am now supporting a whole team of them. Marshall Ward, D Campbell, some guy called Grattan and half a dozen others whose names I cannot remember. It is probably too late to stop this business once I've implied approval, but I must try.

A strange coincidence, but it so happens I too have a friend and patient called D Campbell, who expects a lion's share of my weekly pocket money.

I didn't mind too much when we both used to frequent the change-houses because then I occasionally got some back. But now he has signed the pledge and I find I do all the giving, much the same as I do at home. I see no solution but to join him in the Temperance Society.

He took this drastic step after he unwisely sought a second opinion about his perforated inner tube. After 20 years in my care he went and consulted another eminent colleague – obviously a quack – who suggested a change of diet. His new man told him hot curries six nights of the week washed down with whisky was not ideal fare for a man in his condition.

His condition, by the way, is serious and painful. I'm not sure how best to explain it to the squeamish unless you try to imagine yourselves carrying in the belly part, instead of the normal smooth and well-oiled piping, 27 miles of old rusty chain.

When the ideas of the second 'doctor' had no immediate effect, as we knew they wouldn't, he took to reading the bogus medicine-men who have to earn a living writing for the tabloids. The sooner these guys are exposed and shot the better. One of them hinted, and Donald latched on as desperate men do, that tobacco was the answer. He suddenly remembered that all his problems started when he stopped smoking 10 years ago and quickly secured a repeat prescription on the NHS for twenty Capstan Full Strength a day. Two chemists, alleged friends and both addicted to that deadly narcotic, thought there might be 'something in it'.

Fortunately, word got back to me before too much damage was done. Now, I think I have him back on as even a keel as anyone carrying that cargo can be. As soon as he gets out of hospital I plan to introduce him to what I call the last-ditch diet – a mixture of lentils and mashed ling's liver. If that doesn't clean the tubes I'll eat my Tenby slip for next year's Derby.

The time has come once again to gird up our loins for a hard winter in the Castle Grounds.

Having severed connections with the O'Brien family forever, I expect to win everything this year. To say my new partner, Dr Taylor, is competitive does not do him justice. He's a demon with a club in his hand. At the moment he's on 10 steroids a day and expects to build up to 15 by Saturday morning. Our plan is to establish a 20-point lead immediately and take it easy coming up to New Year.

But first things first. The main thing we have to ensure is that our feet stay dry. This unfortunately means a costly visit to the Yorkshire fellow's shop. Compared to Davies the Millionaire Cobbler is the soul of generosity. You've probably never come across many Yorkshire persons because they don't travel much. Travel costs money. But you will have heard about them, and whatever you've heard is true.

I foolishly asked for a pair of new cheap shoes to be left behind the bar. The cunning fellow did this and I wore them for a day in the mud. I expect I'll have to pay for them now even if he says they cost more than 10 quid. And I'm not sure if the terms we used to call never-never are still obtainable. However, that doesn't matter much because we will no doubt collect the sweep money most Saturdays.

I should have been in Skye last week for Angus Peter's coming-out party, but I'm sorry, Angus – the pressure of work and play. You remember how that was.

Naturally, I have not been able to stretch to the seven pounds the poetry book costs, and in any case I wouldn't like the bhoys to think I'm the sort of wimp who reads poetry. But I must, for my friends were tearful in their praise. And of course, after Sorley's appreciation, I must try to write a review the simpletons in the Golf Club can understand. Despite the aid of several dictionaries, I still don't know what to make of Sorley's evaluation of the technicalities. I hope the poems are easier to understand than your man's prose.

When Johnny Walker and I progressed from Ranish School or, should I say, were uprooted to the Nicolson Institute, we were ill-prepared.

Like the rest of the country Maws, we were not at ease with townies who had the confidence to speak to teachers. We were absolutely terrified of Alec Urquhart, who constantly stalked the corridors and toilets with a clenched fist. He could read smoke signals like an Apache brave.

We weren't quite sure what to make of Niall Cheòis. Although he was only about four years older than us, he was very big even then and could have been a teacher. We were certainly a wee bit scared but we weren't up to making enquiries in *that* language. Niall would sneak up behind us and bellow, 'Report to my office'. But we soon got to know his weakness. He was no Uggy. He could never resist a smile at the success of his joke. Thirty-odd years later I could still see them coming through the smile, as he set me up, but he still got the better of me at every encounter.

I will miss him very much.

Friday, 13 November 1992

MONDAY The standard of driving in Stornoway has reached the abysmal level at which I have to say something. I feel sure it is not the fault of Stornowegians themselves. They are townies born and bred, accustomed to traffic since the days of the gig. The trouble is that the people of Harris, Ness and darker places come in once a week to stock up with sherry and create disturbances.

These drivers, often cailleachs in new Renaults, are accustomed to wide open spaces and are unsuited to town driving. They seldom exceed 10 miles an hour, which is fine in mid-morning when most of us are at work; but in the middle of the day they are the major cause of congestion – especially when they circumnavigate puddles to keep the Renaults clean. (Where do all these Renaults come from? Has some church elder got the franchise, perhaps?)

Yet these older women are not the worst. The most boorish hoods are usually men – men who will not under any circumstance allow you back into the stream of traffic if you are foolish enough to stop for a paper.

The most difficult place to escape from is the car park on South Beach. Despite the fact that traffic often has to stop at the lights, our fine old Highland gentlemen will break the speed limit to close a gap on someone trying to 'get out'. While I waited behind a poor woman poised at the exit the other day, I managed to eat my fish supper. And all the time her boorish neighbours sped past unseeing or uncaring of her desperation. What could I do but offer a chip.

The strange thing is that on foot these guys are courteous as you'd like. Only behind the wheel does the beast come out in them.

About night driving I can no longer comment because I don't risk it. Only a fool ventures onto the road after dark when the name of the game is still 'Blind the oncoming driver'.

TUESDAY Is it any wonder one has taken to the skies where one feels so much safer?'

I swore after Korea, where I had so many narrow escapes, that I would hang up my flying jacket. But what could I do when my friend the Lawyer begged me on his knees. 'I really need someone of your experience in these conditions,' he pleaded.

The weather was lousy, but with Gus Matheson (Wing Commander, Retired) in the back seat I felt quite secure. Unfortunately one cannot believe the Met Office these days. They rely too much on technology now and hardly any of them are aware of subtle changes in feelings in the water.

Nevertheless, we set off for that peculiar destination called 'wherever there's a break in the cloud'. Unluckily, there was no break. Somewhere in the middle of the Minch when we passed between the masts of a fishing boat we concluded the cloud base might be a little lower than we had been promised. ('S fhada bho bha fios a'm gu robh Leslie a' feuchainn ri cur às dhomh.) There was nothing for it but to follow the *Suilven* back to base. With a strong headwind Kenneth's 'new' aeroplane can just keep up with the ferry.

Still, he wants to try again this week, but I doubt if Gus will come along because he was giving off an unpleasant smell when we flew under a low cliff in Point.

WEDNESDAY I like whenever possible to mix with youngsters and keep up to date with fashion. And, if I may say so, I feel *they* draw some comfort from my presence.

Just occasionally I have to take them to task for their use of language. Not so long ago I partied with a younger generation in Glasgow and some of the company belonged to that hardy, cliche-ridden breed collectively known as the media.

The word in vogue then, or one of the words, was 'tremendously'. Another was 'right'. Every time I addressed someone they always responded with 'Right'.

I was never sure what to make of this quirky uninvited addendum to my every comment but eventually I became oblivious. The word 'right' became so diluted it went unnoticed. No sooner have I blotted 'right' out than my young colleagues have introduced a new one to confuse me.

The very latest seems to be 'This is true'. Whatever I say I am told 'This is true'. Well, now, what do you make of that? Did I ever say anything that wasn't true? Are they hinting that I did or are they merely stalling, unwilling to admit they do not grasp my complex thought-process? I rather think it's the latter.

THURSDAY Last night I had to attend a meeting where men of varying rank had gathered to be addressed by a person of some importance. A most interesting and illuminating experience. I was so engrossed with audience reaction I have completely forgotten what the man had to say. The important point is that I have learned how to behave as a listener.

When you must listen to a person-of-some-importance-that-you-would-like-to-impress you have a difficult problem. Obviously you cannot interrupt, so how do you convey your obsequiousness?

The answer is in the laugh. It comes into the category called the approving chuckle. You must be very careful that it does not come out as a mirthless guffaw. The last thing you want the person of some importance to think is that you are laughing at him.

The approving chuckle implies that you, and only you, have grasped the deep significance and wisdom of the words uttered. You must, however, be on your guard lest the important person make a joke. As these are usually not very funny, they are easily missed. A dreadful faux pas is when you've been chuckling all night and then sit there trying to look sour and intelligent when TPOSI expects a laugh. Above all avoid the nervous titter.

Oh, dear, life is so complex.

FRIDAY, 27 NOVEMBER 1992

For a long time now she has been at me to take a fortnight's holiday and attend to these little jobs about the home that could be done by anyone and are clearly not a priority. It stands to reason that a simple repair job postponed for eighteen months didn't need doing in the first place.

However, just to keep the little woman happy, I arranged two weeks' break from the surgery to be like these other men who are constantly being held up as an example.

November is perhaps not the best time to plan these tasks but what could I do? Cllr Macdonald must have the whole summer off and most of the autumn, so the rest of the eminent colleagues have to fight over November and December. We don't mind because the big man has important work to do, and no one seems inclined to argue with him. This is why I find myself with two clear weeks in November, and even now I had to give him a prize ram to get the second week.

The first week has not been as productive as she would have wished. On Monday, naturally, I had to unwind. I unwound so successfully that it took till late Tuesday morning to stoke the fires of creativity. On my way to get a new leg for the head of my pick I discovered, unfortunately, the wee Nissan had let me down for the first time. This necessitated a lift to Stornoway in search of a spare part.

As luck would have it, I arrive in the Metropolis when all the shops closed for one hour. A fierce southerly gale and driving rain forced me to take shelter in the Criterion, when I found several fellow crofters had also come in to the warmth. I accepted a few wee ones and joined in polite conversation until two o'clock. At two a very wet stranger blew into the bar and said, 'Only a fool would go out on a day like this'. By this time the dirty subject of politics had come up and, although we were all pulling in different directions, we agreed unanimously with the stranger.

At three o'clock a volunteer who had ventured out to study the weather came back with a blade of grass in his beak, but, although the waters had subsided, he claimed it was already nearly dark and there was very little one could do now anyway. Ah, when I consider how my life is spent. About five in the late afternoon or the early evening, depending on how you view these things, the Grazings Committee decided to aim for the six o'clock bus.

By this time ancient, beautiful Gaelic words were being spoken and all sense of time had flown. *'Chuir thu an latha tromach-air-shearrach orm'*, said one old fellow. The youngsters present hadn't heard the expression so it had to be analysed until long after the bus had gone. There is no record of the rest of Tuesday.

On Wednesday morning a touch of flu kept me in bed until the early afternoon, when it was once again time to go looking for the leg of a pick, a starter motor and a tool for the hole in the roof. A long, fruitless search lasted until three o'clock, which was the time for my four-yearly appointment with Mr Doig the optician.

Robert was astonished at the wonderful state of my blood vessels. 'You have the arteries of a much younger man,' he said. I had given my age as sixty-eight but nevertheless I felt sufficiently uplifted by his diagnosis to call in the Criterion for a celebratory dram and a smoke.

The spelling and meaning of 'tromach-air-shearrach' is still uncertain, although we worried away at it for several hours. It was agreed that a certain party would go to the library and steal a Dwelly's and that we should convene again on Thursday afternoon to resume our scholarly studies.

On Thursday, for some strange reason, I was unwell and not able to attend the University. Miraculously, I find I am in possession of a leg for the pick but unluckily it has now started to snow and the ground is frozen. I have to postpone my drainage project and it is too slippery to climb on the roof.

On my way to the Criterion I am apprehended by the wife and forced to go to the County for a bar lunch. I consider this a wild unnecessary extravagance when I have already purchased a salted rib of beef in Bobby Bhragaidh's. Never mind, to keep the peace, I endure the funereal atmosphere and swallow some gruel surrounded by people in suits.

Friday is, of course, the weekend and time to socialise and relax. After a tough week I find the Criterion is the only place to switch off. A little drop of Trawler Rum on a Friday afternoon never did anyone any harm. One is, after all, on holiday.

On Saturday morning I am desperately eager for hard toil but the ground is still frozen. Still, I persevered. After two violent swings the head flew off the new leg. What could I do but go and see what was the crack in the Crit.

Sunday brings a little twinge of guilt and remorse. This, I find, can be kept at bay by making plans for the next week. The hole in the roof is on the agenda for Monday morning.

While we were listening to *Songs of Praise* a ferocious gale and heavy rain commenced. The steady drip into the bucket in the attic increased in volume and tempo. This meant the alarm had to be set so the bucket could be emptied several times in the night. Served her right because, if I've told her once, I've told her a thousand times to deal with problems as they arise.

Please don't worry, I assure her. First thing in the morning I'll get Kenny the Plumber to have a look at the lead. 'You get Kenny first or second thing on Monday and I'm on the ferry and I'm not coming back.' Can anyone tell me what is the matter with this woman?

1993

FRIDAY, 29 JANUARY 1993

Have you ever, in your centrally-heated office, come across one of those romantic bluntheads who comes out with statements like: 'How I envy people who work in the open air. If you ever hear any of your hothouse philosopher colleagues 'at it', do me a favour and pour a bucket of icy water on his blunt head.

For a wee while now I have been close, at a safe distance, to someone who tries to earn a living from the sea. There are probably short periods now and again when his job seems easy or even enjoyable, especially to those who set sail in July of every year, come what may. But when the family fodder depends on sailing daily in this particularly unfriendly winter, the quarry-face is a preferable alternative; unluckily, quarry-faces are now few and far between and the competition for any dry-land job is fierce. There is nothing for it but the sea – when you can, if you can. Since Christmas, you might have managed two days if you were foolhardy or three if you were crazy.

This is all bad enough, but now I read in the news that to be crazy is not enough; you must have a licence. Joseph Heller could not have dreamed a better catch.

To get a licence you must have earned last year, in your registered boat, a certain sum of money. If you were lucky enough to secure a few trips to the North Sea oil-rigs when crabs were scarce or non-existent, well, that's tough. You should have hung around and subsisted on seaweed.

If you were a Member of Parliament with a dozen other pokers in the fire, you're OK. If you were what used to be called a crofter/fisherman, you can score out the fisherman part.

Now, where were our Members when this sly piece of legislation was being hatched by the big greedy owners? Where was Charlie? Where was

Calum? Not, I sincerely hope, hiding in a Buckie, nor even – may the saints look down on us with compassion – in a Bernera pocket (I can guess where Alex Salmond was).

I excuse Cunninghame North this time because, frankly, what goes on in the Highlands is none of his business. Let him play with his trains. I would also excuse the bigger-boat boys of Stornoway. They couldn't possibly have any interest in attacking the part-timers who guddle about inside the three-mile common grazing zone. *(Surely not: Ed.)*

This particular piece of useless, but painful, legislation cannot now be undone, but I wouldn't like to be the first Fishery Officer to arrest my 83-year-old father when he sets his lobster creels in the summer.

As for the rest of us, the implications are horrendous. How long now until I, and my eminent colleagues, are prevented by law from writing our lucrative drivel on PMT and hysterectomies in the *Sunday Mail* and other women's journals. Never mind television. One naturally assumes our learned friends in the House will continue to quadruple their meagre salaries on TV, in between their foreign travel and commitment to the big floppy papers.

I am reliably informed, and have no reason to doubt, that many of our local councillors, some of them crofter/xxxxxxmen, were totally ignorant of higher authority's plans to castrate them. And yet we expected them to have understood the complex financial shenanigans played by BCCI and the Bank of England.

There is so much work to be done in there I'm not so sure I should stand at the next election.

It is really quite cosy here in the little shed where I do my scribbling. With my feet on Smut the spaniel's back and my Tilley lamp and the paraffin heater, I couldn't wish for more.

I gave up on the devilish computer early in December. Just when I thought I was getting the hang of it the powercuts started. Every time I reached the five hundred word mark the lights went out. Now that I am back on the biro I'm doing much better, and I have the all-powerful National Grid to thank. Thank you, Hydro Board.

When we relied on the boys in the local generating station we lost the power maybe once or twice a year – usually on New Year's Eve when nobody cared. And then we didn't have to wait long to be reconnected. The hard men who are lucky enough to work in the open air seldom wasted much time.

One of the side-effects of being on the National Grid, and a great blessing, is that we are now spared much of the drivel being fired at us from the television screen. The ratio of rubbish to what is worthwhile is now almost a whole number, and I'm doubly grateful for the power cuts.

It naturally follows that I listen a lot more to my little battery wireless. An entire news broadcast on the BBC World Service didn't once mention taped telephone calls or anything at all about the games enjoyed by fairytale princesses. Unluckily, I have to listen to a lot of cricket news, but that is a small price to pay for the privacy of my shed.

Right now I hear big Dan Murray talking to two Lewismen and one Lewiswoman on the weighty subject of predestination. The old geezer reckons that if he dies at 72 of lung cancer instead of 92, the good Lord must have meant him to smoke two ounces of Golden Virginia every day. Who is to say he's not right.

I thought I'd cleared up this small matter of predestination for youse all long ago, but it seems not. It is a little late on the page to take it up this week. However, we'll come back to it next week, *DV*.

I'm pleased to see young Torc back with us as a TV critic, but I'm afraid he's not punishing himself sufficiently. He should really watch a lot more and not be so selective (this is what happens when one no longer needs the money).

The TV critic I remember best, and one Torc should study, was Benny Green. For 10 or 20 years he wrote every week in *Punch*, before that magazine became a children's comic, and in all that time he never saw a programme he liked. Now there was a man who took his duties seriously.

> *'Just be thankful you're not cooped up in a stuffy office somewhere with the central heating up full blast!'*

FRIDAY, 19 FEBRUARY 1993

When a man gets very old and the fingers get too stiff and sore to roll tobacco, he needs a rest. When he can no longer go fishing nor do any useful work, it becomes difficult to find the will to battle on.

When the contemporaries are gone, loneliness sets in. Even if he sees people every day, these are generally younger people in a hurry. After a short period of savouring the satisfaction of having outlived all the old friends, he soon gets tired, and it's not the sort of tiredness that disappears with a night's rest.

Still, Eachainn Mòr had the last laugh on the chiropodist. He will not keep tomorrow's appointment. He liked to laugh. It was nothing personal with chiropodists, it was just that one of them hurt him once. She, or he, drew blood. And anyway it was all becoming too much of a hassle.

It was a long, tough life. Yet, somehow, I had a sneaking suspicion he would have like to have outlasted Dòmhnall Beag, although Dòmhnall Beag is much younger. The oldest man in the village is now Murdo Mackenzie, and he is not really very old.

In the meantime we are all chasing the title.

When the wee paper appeared last week with the North Lochs column missing I had several phone calls 'wondering'.

'Was everything all right? It's just that we heard . . .' When I thought about their messages afterwards I realised some of them were a trifle ambiguous. Were they disappointed that the column was missing, or did they mean they were sorry I was still alive?

Who can tell in these fiercely competitive times with so many desperate for lucrative posts such as this one? Although I had decided some time ago to make room for a younger man, I was astonished at the speed with which a moonlighting minister slipped into my seat. I suppose if anyone needs the money, they do.

The Professor's piece seemed to be well received. 'A refreshing alternative,' some readers said, and that is fine. But I'm afraid his practical solutions to political problems do not have the depth and scope of mine. This has made me determined to carry on.

Still, I see no reason why space cannot be found for both of us, just as long as I remain at the top of the page. A question of seniority, you must understand. Nothing personal.

Sad occasions sometimes bring about happy reunions.

I was pleased to see Coinneach, who had been missing for about 40 years or so. Although I see Rhoda quite often, I don't get much chance to harangue her because we don't go to the same places of worship. When I had both Coinneach and Rhoda cornered late at night, I was able to berate them for having blighted my early life.

It is not often you get a chance to preach at teaching types, and after all it was my house.

I followed Coinneach to Ranish School, where I was incessantly told how clever and good he was. I followed Rhoda to Leurbost, where they told me how good and clever and well-behaved she was. Then I followed her to Stornoway, where they said she was a saint. Coinneach, as a student, came back in the summer with leather patches on his elbows, for goodness's sake. What a cissy!

So, you see, it was their fault I became a delinquent. I didn't confess I was happy with my delinquency because I wanted to make them feel guilty, and I think they did because they're so good.

'*Na falbh ri fèith Faoillich*,' the old ones used to say. Never put to sea during a February calm because it cannot last.

Coinneach was uneasy about our fishing trip of last week because he listened to the old ones and he always obeyed. Most of the time the wise ones were right, but they didn't have the 48-hour forecast chart in these days. Nowadays we know better than they did, let who will argue.

After one hour's steaming (I cannot tell where or else the place will be hoaching tomorrow with all these sanctimonious prats with their licences) we hit fishing such as I haven't seen for 20 years. For a couple of hours we hauled in at will large fish of a valuable species, keeping the *saoidhean* for the liver.

We retreated for a while and watched a school of dolphins that came especially to entertain us, jumping 10 feet out of the water, and laughing, presumably at the poor man from Back who was wasting his time well off the mark.

We would have caught a lot more, because it is difficult to stop, but the long-lost accident-prone cousin yelped in pain. I didn't pay much attention because I remembered the last time he made a fuss, about 45 years ago. He was carried screaming from the potato field, speared through the foot with a well-manured *gràp*.

Iodine and bandages were found and the wellie cut off, for it to be discovered only that the fork had passed between his unmarked toes. He was severely beaten for having spoiled the wellies, but I learned to ignore his cries of pain.

This time, though, we couldn't doubt the evidence of the hook in his hand, barb an' all. He is still, however, a bit of a cissy and wouldn't let us tackle the job with a rusty hacksaw. There was nothing for it but to leave all that fish and head for the Ospadal. You would think in a new £40m Ospadal they could have saved the hook.

I'm not sure what we're going to do if this good fishing continues. Traditionally, when local needs were satisfied it was all right to sell fish to the people of Stornoway, but now with the threat of heavy fines this could be too risky. I'm afraid the thought of giving it away to them is too painful.

I've never been very much into the reminiscence industry, but there are times . . .

Last week I spent a while looking through old letters – some sad, and some pathetic war-time missives that were intensely infuriating. But I had to smile at the beautifully humorous letter from the lady from Shawbost who bought our last milking cow.

One thing that I am very annoyed about is that I still have not learned how to splice rope.

FRIDAY, 19 MARCH 1993

Well, now, are you a C, a D or an E, or are you one of the lucky As? I'm told by a nosey friend I'm a D, but I'm not having it – not when Leslie is a C.

I stepped out the perimeter of his house while he slept and I measured the height of his gable-end. Unless I made an error in the dark, the dimensions of our humble homes are the same. My flimsy furniture is out of MFI while his is handcrafted by the finest joiners in Point.

So how is it done? How did he manage to keep the tax collectors at bay? Why have they not noted the solid gold taps in the bathrooms and the ancient and priceless French tapestries in the oak-lined hall? Is it the beard and the bohemian appearance? Has he perhaps crossed some greasy paw with silver?

Nothing so crude, my friends. When our greedy assessors made the rounds they didn't bother to knock on his door. They might have slowed down a little as they passed, but why stop at a house with a battered Lada parked outside.

We don't know for sure how much of this goes on, but look closely at the homes of any people you know with Ladas. Look closer still if the driver has a hole in the seat of his army-surplus trousers. All that time we imagined Ladas at the doors of the fairly well-off signified sympathy with the old Soviet Union, but now we know they were looking to a future roof tax. Perhaps anyone who is shameless enough to embarrass his family with a Lada deserves to escape the full roof tax.

Like all stories, this latest form of extortion has another side to it. Certain ladies in the town, or so they say, are unhappy with their local taxation band because it is too low. The Fs have taken it on the snout because others at their sherry mornings are Hs. Come to think of it, I'm not sure the longstanding relationship with my sporting partner has not come to an end over this classification nonsense. Will he want to associate with a D when he's an E?

I see nothing but trouble ahead.

Not so long ago the mark of civilisation was water running through taps inside the house. The owners barely gave you time to finish your cup of tea when you were asked: '*Bheil do dhileag agad?*' Then they would follow you into the new bathroom in case you weren't sure where to do it. When you finished, if you could – for it wasn't easy to make water on a guided tour – you had to express delight with the decor and satisfaction with the plumbing, although, had you been honest, you might have preferred to go outside.

Nowadays, in the 'Lada homes' you will still have to go outside because they'd rather your bladder burst than admit to having a bathroom. On the other hand, if you mix with the Es, who would like to be Fs, they will give you a choice and probably call the bog a lavatory. They'll show you the bidet in case you want to wash your feet. And all this they do in the hope you will report their three bathrooms in your appeal.

Of the one hundred or so home-owners I've canvassed, 80 say they intend to appeal because they are being asked to pay too much and the others are probably in the bidet category and want to pay more. The latter tend to belong to the travelling class and need a high valuation for the estate agent's advert: the sort who tend to sell houses and look on them as assets rather than homes. I would let them pay as much as they wish.

The water rate is a different kettle of peat altogether. The gungy liquid that sometimes trickles through our taps wouldn't be worth a brown farthing in Ethiopia, never mind Shawbost. The poor urchins of Tunisia wouldn't use this residue of drowned sheep and seagulls' droppings to brush their teeth, yet our leaders have the audacity to value it at £184. For this sort of money we should have beer flowing through our taps.

Of course, we all know the reason for the ludicrous cost of our water: as a commodity it must be made worthwhile for the privateers. It is difficult to believe that even our councillors imagine some entrepreneur is going to buy the water from Loch Orasaigh. It would cost £184 a gallon to bring it up to EEC standards. Very likely it would prove cheaper, in these islands where the rain never ceases, to ship clean water in from Kent (better furry kettles than furry arteries).

Some years ago inspectors from Consumer Protection, or some such body, insisted salmon-packers should have a certificate from the appropriate authority to prove their ice was made from EEC standard water. For some reason, and we should certainly be told this one, it was not sufficient to show that it was the same water we drank and put in our whisky. I'm afraid the only way we'll ever be able to sell our water is if we can fool some buyer into believing it is Guinness. But, ah, but, we must remember the privateers would be buying to sell on and not to drink. Would they care much about the worms at the bottom of your glass or mine?

Don't worry, boys, I have the answer. Not an easy solution, for it involves work, but at least we'll save some money. It so happens that on the hill behind my house there is an old deep well that once served the Church of Scotland manse. Holy water, you could almost say, clear as gin and full of minerals. Unfortunately the supply pipe was made of lead, which probably accounts for the poor health suffered by the ministers of long ago. We would have to dig up the old pipe and replace it with plastic, and here we come to the difficult bit – money.

There should be enough water to supply three or four of my neighbours' houses, and the well is, after all, on my croft. The landlords will probably have to be bought, and there could be a legal battle with the Council. However, I expect to provide this first and most basic necessity of life for around £170 per year, with generous discounts for pensioners. The only snag I foresee at this stage is that the superior quality of my water could bring those lucky enough to be on my well into band F. Still, the Koran says: 'It is no sin for you that you seek the bounty of your Lord.'

There is still much of the fine detail to be worked out, but I expect to have my 'great water plan' completed by the time I return from the Pyramids. To ensure the smooth and trouble-free implementation of my scheme I have enlisted Russel Consultants of Ranish.

Although it is never mentioned by travel agents, it seems sensible to study Koran instruction for those undertaking pilgrimage. I'm not too keen on 'fasting for three days during and seven days after the pilgrimage'.

Still, it does say 'The pilgrim should take whatever offering is easy to obtain'. And *nowhere* does it mention you shouldn't drink the water.

I'll see you in three weeks' time, Insh Allah.

FRIDAY, 9 APRIL 1993

How little did we imagine three weeks ago when I, flippantly, foretold trouble for Maggie at the Wailing Wall it would all come to pass. To tell the truth, I'm in always wary of the Middle East because you never know when the Children of Israel might take it into their heads to do some smiting. But more of that later when we get our breath back. To begin at the beginning, as we always should, the problems started with Caledonian MacBrayne himself. One eagle-eyed employee of that company, probably a Sgiathanach, spotted, without the aid of glasses, in the dark, at five in the morning, our 'return ticket' was several days 'out of date'.

So there we were halfway down the ramp with our tyres still on the native sod and she's already into the travellers' cheques. A lean fortnight loomed but I need not have worried. My friend Roddy the chef passed a few sausages out through the porthole in the crew's quarters and a small saving was made on the first lap.

As it happened, my fear of starvation through lack of shekels was based on ignorance of the countries we planned to visit. The bountiful wind of providence, in Cyprus and Israel, shakes so much life-sustaining fruit off the bough it is not necessary to buy. Not necessary, but it is still easier to buy a bag of oranges for fifty pee than to bend down and pick them. As for potatoes, don't mention them because I'm embarrassed: I was the only person stopped at Customs on the 'sheer bulk' principle. They couldn't accept anyone was trying to smuggle potatoes. But there you are.

Talking of bulk, you should see these German girls. *(Sorry, I must take the red pen to this stuff: Ed.)* OK, we'll keep it clean. My experiences of entering former colonies have not always been happy. Usually a little baksheesh is required and immigration officers generally don't bother to hide their contempt for the old enemy. Cyprus is different. At Paphos I encountered for the first time an immigration person who smiled.

All Cypriots tend to smile a lot, although they've seen some hard times and despite continuing difficulties with boorish, ignorant tourists. These tend to fall into two main categories. There are those who come from Coronation Street, Geordieland or Glasgow in small noisy groups, and there are the lonely ones who are eager to make friends. Then there is the tiny unsociable minority to which I belong: those who came away for a little peace. Peace is not so easy to find but the Gaelic language helps. If you're heard talking this strange tongue, it lends some credibility to your claim 'not to speak the English'. You must certainly ignore the plea on your hotel noticeboard from Mr Smith in room 501 looking for bridge players because you've paid to get away from all that.

Limassol is a bit of a Blackpool nowadays but an ideal central spot in which to set up camp. You must, of course, hire a four-wheel-drive vehicle for the assault on Mount Olympus. The advertised snow is not a tourist con: it is deep and real and only two hours' drive from the warm ocean. (Nam faiceadh tu Maggie a' dèanamh duine mòr dhith fhèin le Mitsubishi Pajero duine eile.) I must admit I didn't see all that much of the mountains; I could never spare more than one eye for the terrifying gorges under every hairpin bend but it sure does work up a thirst.

The local brew, Keo, is one of the very best at a pound a litre. Along with ouzo and brandy at £1.50 a bottle, it is all too easy to neglect the solids. Oranges are fine for a couple of days but you must search for the best kebabs and meze. You have to build up your strength for the pilgrimage to Jerusalem and Cairo yet beware of the touts claiming 'Mama and Papa in the kitchen'. The product tends to be greasy and based on pork. After a few days spent hardening the moles to the ultra violet, you are ready for the cruise.

Before we go any further I must warn any readers who might have contemplated this commando course you must be fit. On the first of Jerusalem's hills we nearly lost an old guy very early in the day. We had to pack this unfortunate pilgrim in a taxi and promise to see him at the

Wailing Wall. Later on, in the Church of the Holy Sepulchre, when an old lady couldn't manage the steps, I heard herself shout, 'Let my husband through, he's a doctor' but I pretended not to hear. One was, after all, on holiday.

I wouldn't recommend Cyprus as a base from which to rush around Israel and Egypt unless the bodily parts are in good working order. By the time we reached the Fourteenth Station of the Cross I wouldn't have bet on half of them lasting all the way to Cairo. It occurred to me that perhaps some of them came with the intention of pegging out in Jerusalem, which must naturally be close to heaven. Why so many Arabs then, you are bound to ask.

But you need not enquire, because your guide will tell you all. The tour bus with its captive audience is heaven-sent for Zionist propaganda. For three hours, after you leave your boat in Haifa, you will learn a lot about the bad Arabs. You will be shown the squalor in which they choose to live and invited to make comparison with the cleanliness of the Christian and Jewish Quarters. The history of the Jews from Moses up to 1948 is covered in ten minutes and from '48 to '93 in two hours.

It was a relief to escape our guide's lopsided view of the world and to stroll through the teeming bazaars. At the Wall I thought I would don a skullcap and touch the holy stones for luck, before the casino, and this is where Maggie nearly caused what is usually referred to as an international incident.

She was so mesmerised by the number of people carrying guns she didn't notice the Bible-black bearded Jew bearing down on her. I missed the opening shots but I did catch this exchange.

Maggie: I'm sorry if I offend you.

Moses: Not just me, madam: you are offending everyone here. Cover yourself up.

The is very strange, *arsa mise rium fhìn*, for her dress reaches her ankles, but by this time her temper was up.

Maggie: Offending you, indeed. I'll have you know *you* are offending *me* and you are wasting your time wailing because the Messiah has been and gone and is the mainstay of your balance of payments. Unless you believe in the Lord Jesus Christ as your Saviour you are doomed to eternal wailing.

Moses, who looked so much like our own Seceders, was speechless. I thought I'd drag her quickly towards the bus for Bethlehem, where there are no arm fetishists. At least they didn't complain about her wantonly exposed elbows, probably because they were too busy selling beads and holy water. Business is business, said the Jew, bare arms or no.

Until I've recovered from jet lag and studied her notes, I cannot tell you how we got on in the casino or amongst the Bedouin, but I suspect not all that well. Anyway, I'll let you know next week.

Friday, 16 April 1993

When I left you last week in Bethlehem . . . Gosh, that sounds good. Reminds me of the opening line in Alec Mackay's novel: 'When I went to sleep last night in Damascus . . .' Alec was so pleased with this first line he made no further progress. But who knows, now that he's retired.

Anyway, I seem to remember we left Jerusalem, when Maggie insulted Moses, and were heading north for Haifa. On the way we were shown the blighted banana harvest. A sharp frost had destroyed the entire year's crop, which means, of course, an enormous loss of revenue. This is the trouble with touring rather than travelling. The tourist can never escape the host's propaganda and appeals for sympathy, whereas the traveller can choose to avoid banana fields if they give him indigestion. Travelling unfortunately costs a lot more.

One would be tempted to contribute a few shekels to this brave, hard-working little nation's coffers if one knew how the shekels were going to be spent. With only six million of them surrounded by 50 million hostile Arabs, there is no doubt they need a defence. But when it costs over 70 per cent of the nation's wealth, and a fair proportion of America's, is it worth the gamble? Perhaps with their history it is, but it seems to me they are too willing to smite little Arab children.

We leave the birthplace of the world's religions from Haifa and the last sight of the Holy Land is the Bahá'í Temple. I know nothing of the Baha'í faith except that theirs seems a gentle creed. They have not yet caused any wars and don't seem to crave power or want to dominate their fellow man. When I get a little older I may give it a bash.

From what I've heard from old sailors, Port Said doesn't seem to have changed much in 50 years. Norrie Macgregor of Stornoway asked me to look out for his cousin Jimmy, and sure enough, he's still there. 'A wee deoch an dorais, Jimmy, buy three for a pound,' he shouts in a Glasgow accent. It's always three of whatever it is for a pound and Jimmy must have learned the 'canny' and romantic Scots cannot resist three of anything for a pound. (There must be some truth in what we always thought was a vile English slander.)

The English themselves make a fascinating subject for study on board ship. Part of the cost of the cruise was an 'English' breakfast, and they're going to have it if it means staying up all night. This seems very odd behaviour from a race that exists at home on Marmite and toast. I cannot help thinking that were it not for their passion for saving they would be fatter and unhealthier than the Scots.

Our 'guide' in Egypt was an interesting mini-skirted feminist from the University of Alexandria who seemed as much at home in English and French as she presumably was in Arabic. While we drove along the Suez Canal and through the Eastern Desert, this raven-haired Cleopatra entertained and educated us without one mention of the enemy, Israel. And all the while the middle-aged Grangemouth couple in front of me slept soundly.

A strange thing about the British, Highlanders excepted of course, is their pride in stupidity. Far from being ashamed of their total lack of knowledge of foreign tongues and customs, they are proud of their ignorance and wear it like a badge of honour. This will no longer do, I'm afraid. The 'Jimmy Macgregors' of the world would prefer Deutschmarks and we cannot nowadays send a gunboat to change their minds.

Talking of guns, we lost our armoured escort (a Nissan pick-up with a few boy soldiers) in Cairo, but it didn't matter much because our bus couldn't keep up with them on the open road. Not that there is any great danger in any case because, as always in alleged trouble spots, your chances of meeting bandits are slim.

Not so in America, though. The poor man who got murdered in New Orleans this week had apparently cancelled a planned holiday in Egypt because of the troubles. The trouble in Egypt, as is the case everywhere, is caused by a few religious fanatics who want women to cover their faces. They have shot a tourist or two but, by and large, you are more likely to be killed in downtown Stornoway on a Saturday night or at a protest meeting in the Town Hall.

My Grangemouth cailleach soon woke up in Cairo, though. Not many could sleep in that chaos. It was a Moslem holiday, and with Ramadan just over, every man, wife and granny was out on the streets. Estimates of the population range from 12 to 15 million but I don't suppose anyone really knows. The city is mercifully free of traffic laws or rules of any sort. Still, the river of steel and smoking exhausts keeps moving, which is more than can be said for the M25. They ride happily five to a motorbike and spit where they like, much to the amusement of the Grangemouths.

In Cairo it is difficult to know whether you are at any moment in a shanty town or 'up market'. Modern apartments, surrounded by rubble, stand side by side with tumbledown shacks. Half-built houses could be on the way up or falling down. Near the occasional oasis of affluence you sometimes see folk searching among the garbage for titbits, much as they do now in British cities, but in Cairo the hungry look healthier.

At the Pyramids and the Sphinx, Bedouin on camel or horseback will offer you a ride and they have been known to disappear over the sand dunes with fair-skinned maidens. This seems a grand opportunity to get rid of the wife, but, alas, I was not made an offer. After three days in the sun Maggie looks pretty much like one of their own.

Even in the 'cool' air of late, late March, the temperature as measured in the shade at Cairo Airport gives no hint of what to expect in the desert. The heat reflected from the Pyramids shrivels the eyeballs and makes the Sphinx turn her back to them. These are places for the traveller rather than the tourist. As a tourist among hundreds of other tourists, you feel more like an extra in a Hollywood epic.

And the same goes for the Museum of Antiquities. Tutenkhamun's worldly treasures and his provisions of the journey through eternity are wonders to contemplate on your own. I wonder what happened to the meat they packed for their dead king's voyages?

I would have liked to take you on the Nile with me, but sadly I am called back home urgently to deal with problems arising from our new water rates. There was only just time to dip Maggie quickly in Aphrodite's bath. She arose naked from the waves, a glorious vision of pre-Hellenic beauty, and for two weeks now I have awaited developments. Today, as I make these entries in my diaries, she is running a temperature of 106. I think perhaps something went wrong along the way.

Friday, 23 April 1993

GAELIC AND RELATED MATTERS
The question is, what is Prime Time?

When the miraculous windfall for Gaelic television was announced, we were promised Prime Time viewing, but when exactly is the Gaelic viewer in his prime? Certainly not at twenty past six in the evening.

At 1820, as they call it, the Gaelic viewer, far from being in his prime, is probably at his lowest ebb. After a fierce day in the Harris Tweed mill, the potential Gaelic viewer is naturally in the Criterion unwinding his bodily bobbin with a small aperitif. And the same goes for other people still in gainful employment.

Even those who happen to be at home at this hour – like the wife frying the fish – tend to forget, having been accustomed to Gaelic programmes in the middle of the night. And if she does suddenly remember in time to catch the second half of a programme, the poor man comes home from his day's toil to burnt fish.

Children's programmes should naturally go out early, and for *siabann* it doesn't matter much; but serious programmes should revert to 2300 or thereabouts when man is approaching something like his prime. Sìm, *Aig Baile*, at 1930 has some chance and the same goes for Karen NicMhathain. As for Karen, I suspect transmission time wouldn't matter too much, for most people would risk the sack and leave work early. *Ainm a' Ghàidheil* (1820) is, I'm afraid, still somewhere in my *bhidio*, if that devilish machine worked. Judging from talk on the street, *Ainm a' Ghàidheil* sounds promising. I only hope there is no significance in its going out at *Machair* time.

Most of *Machair* is also somewhere in my machine to be viewed on *Latha Buidhe Bealltainn* – the traditional day for Gaelic sacrifice. Apparently the *Machair* team 'start a hectic 10-day shoot' this week, although who is to be shot and who spared is not yet clear. But I cannot say too much because I still have some hope of being the 'extra in the pub' (one presumes the stuff in the glasses is real). Like Alasdair a' Bhocsair, I'm in danger of being accused of sour grapes (they don't grow in the Gàidhealtachd) but I am disappointed they're not going to use the bedroom scene I wrote for Maggie. I like to think it was all my fault and not to do with the shape of her body.

When they start shooting this time they should line up against the wall all those in the 'team' who didn't seem to realise that *farmad* (envy) is not the same as *iadach* (sexual jealousy). Can you imagine the love-struck boy who stumbles on his girl in the arms of another screaming: 'Dash it, how I envy you'. Envy in either language might be classed as a sin, but, unlike sexual jealousy, it doesn't usually lead to murder and gory melodrama. The sub-title viewers were spared that particular embarrassment – but then, they are in the majority.

If you will permit me, Dear Ed, a wee diversion from visual tree-spreading: can I mention the BBC rodeo. The mass exodus of free-lancurshs to TV has left a wee opening for Seonag Monk. A serious consequence of her programme at dinner-time, Saturday, is that the Clerk of the Grazings Comedy and the Golfers cannot be got out on time, for listening to the Gaelic language as it used to be.

Apart from *Machair* the first year's output, so far, looks very much like the same old thing. A song or two round the peat-fire flame, a nostalgic glimpse of the old black-house and the exile's inevitable return to the 'wee bit hill an' glen'. All safe stuff, and always looking back, but what is the way forward?

Don't worry, I wouldn't ask the question if I didn't have the answer. Sadly, it seems *siabann* was born when soaps generally are in viewing decline. Given the sheer volume of mindless drivel beamed at the addicted, it is inevitable that all will suffer. Such is the deluge at present that even for those with several videos it would be impossible to keep up. So soap has had its day.

The scene to be in now is gardening or cookery programmes – or, better still, a mixture of both. And the prime time of eight o'clock is guaranteed. The vast majority of viewers cannot cook very well and cannot get much to grow, so, naturally, they are intrigued by those who can. *Beechgrove* and similar programmes were very popular but harboured some envy (*farmad*) for the cooks. The resulting ludicrous situation we find now is that halfway through every gardening programme some delicacy is plucked from some garden and rushed to some chef's kitchen.

There seems no reason why Gaeldom, while it has the resources, shouldn't carry this madness to its logical conclusion.

A third type of programme that is very popular is the 'Wish you were here' type with golden girls on sandy beaches washed by crystal-clear silvery seas. Voila! Seileabost!

I understand there is a man down there in Harris not far from Seileabost who has, despite Atlantic storms, managed to grow something. Whatever it is, we pluck it and run to the edge of the world where some dusky Hearach mermaid happens to be stoking the barbecue. 'How very fortunate,' cries the mermaid (dare I suggest the curvacious Rhoda herself), 'that you should happen along with these delicious organically grown vegetables while I was here on my cheap-days (sub-title: Holiday).'

I cannot help thinking this idea for a programme will be number wan. Wait till I tell you the best bit – the fourth dimension. So far we have gardening, cooking and sandy beaches, but remember we are back to Gaelic prime time – 2300 GMT. We can have a sprinkling of sex if we like.

As always, we can rely on South Lochs for this sort of thing. We must suppose that Rhoda is willing and sufficiently versatile to play the part of the mermaid the late Eachainn met on an early morning sail from Marvig. Eachainn managed to make it ashore in a somewhat breathless condition, to be met by one of the boys, probably Seaman Robert *nach maireann*. 'So you met a mermaid, so what,' says Rob.

'This,' *arsa Eachainn*, 'was no ordinary mermaid – the top half was the fish.'

Casting could be a problem with this one. Who wants to play opposite the fish? We'll have to buy the copyright from Eachainn's daughter Morag. And perhaps we'll get transmitted at the old time of 2300 – Gaelic Prime Time (GPT).

FRIDAY, 4 JUNE 1993

'There is a type of person,' said Marcus Aurelius, 'who, if he renders you a service, has no hesitation in claiming credit for it. Another, though not prepared to go so far as that, will nevertheless secretly regard you as in his debt and be fully conscious of what he has done. But there is also the man who, one might almost say, has no consciousness at all of what he has done, like the vine which produces a cluster of grapes and then, having yielded its rightful fruit, looks for no more thanks than a horse that has run his race, a hound that has tracked his quarry, or a bee that has hived her honey. Like them, the man who has done one good action does not cry it aloud, but passes straight on to a second, as the vine passes on to the bearing of another summer's grapes.'

A wee bit strong, perhaps! I'm not sure. I only knew Willie Burns for about 25 years. When the door blew off my Austin in a snowstorm and all the garages refused the challenge because it seemed impossible, Willie said: 'Leave it with me.'

He made a ballpoint note on the back of his greasy hand and promptly forgot about my Austin when someone presented a more interesting engineering crossword. When he finally got round to it, late in the night, he concocted some sort of hinge that lasted the car's lifetime.

I was pleased with the job, but not as pleased as Willie was. In the fulness of time he accepted ten bob. Many years later, when I brought up the subject of the flying door, he had completely forgotten. I was only one of many 'ten-bob' high-tech jobs he enjoyed. He was lucky to have lived his life doing work he not only enjoyed but embraced passionately. He was also the worst businessman I ever met.

As a businessman Willie was never in it, and he got worse with the introduction of the computer. He liked the idea of any kind of new machine and he lovingly latched onto the computer with both horny hands. As he became familiar with the workings of these devilish inventions, he would stay up all night and show you marvellous things like spreadsheets and theoretical cashflows. Whether or not the large figures at the bottom were red or black was of little interest. The technology was all.

For some strange reason Willie got some added satisfaction from tackling a dirty, difficult job when wearing a clean white shirt. But perhaps I've gone on too much. Your man might not have approved. We'll all miss him.

'If a god were to tell you, "Tomorrow, or at best the day after, you will be dead," you would not, unless the most abject of men, be greatly solicitous whether it was to be the later day rather than the morrow – for what is the difference between them? In the same way, do not reckon it of great moment whether it will come years hence, or tomorrow . . . Philosophy aside, an effectual help towards disregarding death is to think of those who clung greedily to their lives. What advantage have they over those who died young? In every case, in some place at some time, the earth now covers them all.' Thus spake Aurelius. 'All of us are creatures of a day; the rememberer and the remembered alike.'

I read in the Stornoway Greysheet a letter from my friend, the Stoic Willie Fulton. Apparently after a football match in Harris Willie discovered two of his tyres slashed. Is Harris no better than Ibrox these days?

This seems a very odd thing to happen to an art teacher. A maths teacher you could understand, because their message is so unpalatable, but a poor artist! I cannot understand this mindless act of violence, but what amused me was Willie's reaction. Any normal Hearach victim would go looking for the culprit and hit him over the head with a shovel. This we might forgive, but Willie asks to seek the culprit and counsel him. I wonder if he too has been reading Marcus Aurelius, who said: 'Be generous and liberal in your attitude to irrational creatures and to the generality of material things, for you have reason and they have none.'

This is what the Christians who adopted Stoic philosophy would call turning the other cheek, but they cheated – took the easy road – when they invoked divinity. It's a great pity our own northern Christians didn't take the Ancients' advice on length of prayer: 'The Athenians pray, "Rain, rain, dear Zeus, upon the fields and plains of Athens." Prayers should either not be offered at all, or else be as simple and ingenuous as this.'

Old Aurelius might have been a bit of a windbag in some ways but somehow, since I discovered him, I find I'm much more comfortable flying around in low cloud with Ken Macdonald in his little aeroplane.

Much has been written and spoken about the new BBC under Mr Boyle.

The Lowland Mafia have supported that other windbag Jimmy Macgregor to a man – and woman. Even the normally sane Joyce McMillan has cried what a shame and has even suggested Macgregor's replacement Ms Nicolson is not up to the job. (You would think, if you didn't know better, they were Gaels writing about other. Gaels.) The truth is, Nancy Nicolson is a much better presenter. She gives her guests a chance to talk, and her choice of music is excellent. *Seo a-nis*. I'm available any day, Nancy.

About Art Sutter, though, it's a great shame. His programme was good and my own Maggie was very friendly with him, and if they had something going that is no business of Boyle's or anyone else. I think perhaps the sooner this Boyle fellow goes back to prison the better for us all.

*   *   *

P.S. Dear Jackson, how are things in Dubai? We're all fine here. I hate to admit, after our 30-year dispute, you were right about Leslie. Love, Eachainn.

FRIDAY, 18 JUNE 1993

Older readers will probably remember the time I accidentally shot a nature conservationist I mistook for a corncrake. The foolish boy was hiding in long grass, in the fading light of a summer's evening, making corncrake noises, when I opened up with both barrels. The matter was hushed up at considerable cost and I'm pleased to say all charges were dropped. (Justice can always be had if you can afford it.)

At that time I was not so concerned with the survival of the corncrake as I am now. I refused to believe the corncrake was an endangered species because, whenever and wherever I laid me down to sleep, that elusive pest would start its nocturnal croaking. And so it was, in my fortieth sleepless summer, I took up the gun.

These were desperate times that required desperate measures. With age and wisdom attitudes change. Our Heritage Mob, as they are now called, will be relieved to hear that, like many crofters, I have hung up my guns. As a matter of record I have now joined that zealous little band called POTCAAC – Protectors Of The Corncrake At Any Cost. We are not a body to be trifled with.

By strange coincidence, our movement was formed, and the constitution formally adopted, only two days before our Heritage boyos announced the Corncrake Grant. Fifty pounds an acre they have offered not to cut any grass earlier than August. Earlier than August indeed! What do they take us for?

Many of our members in POTCAAC are very unhappy with the 'August Clause' and would like this changed to December. As a matter of fact, a conscientious element in our movement, the founding fathers, stopped cutting grass long ago – purely in the interests of the corncrake. It is no mere chance that my own wee croft has been entirely under rushes for many years. Yet never once did I expect any fallowing money.

There is no doubt the Heritage Mob meant well, but money is not the answer. No sooner was filthy lucre mentioned than the wide boys moved in.

Now we have on our hands a corncrake war that could quickly lead to the demise of the 'harmless croaker'.

The hitherto peaceful meadow surrounding my own surgery has always been a haven for corncrakes. They learned to trust my eminent colleagues and would even come up to the windows to 'look' at us. In the space of a few years they came forth and multiplied. Earlier this month we had as many as six within croaking distance. Six may not seem a lot, but in the corncrake world six is a flock. Or, if you like, a fortune.

On the very first night after the 'fifty-quid' offer a Melbost crofter, disguised as a bird watcher, was seen crawling on all fours in the grass – with a net on a pole. I understand the scam is to tether the bird at a safe distance 'down the croft' and invite a corncrake inspector to come and listen. Once the fifty is in the pooch the poor bird is passed on to the next croft for a small consideration.

As you might have expected, the squabbling has commenced, with violent argument about whose 'turn' it is to have the bird tonight. We can safely assume the corncrake itself is very unhappy about being passed from horny hand to horny hand in an onion bag. It wouldn't surprise me if it soon croaks its last.

We in POTCAAC must turn our attention immediately to these most despicable of the poaching classes. Do not hesitate to let them have it where it hurts. Although they imagine they look the part, they are easily distinguished from real birdwatchers. They carry the 'glasses' and wear barber jackets and green wellies but they often forget themselves and turn the wellies down. This is a sure sign.

Rest assured you will hear more of POTCAAC in weeks to come. Already our nightly patrols have been reported on Rodeo Alba as UFOs. What a laugh.

Our traditional lack of sympathy for the humble corncrake was very likely the fault of the ancient Gaelic poets. Like all men of the soil, they were at one with nature and wrote with great feeling for all the birds of the air and even those that couldn't fly. Many fathoms of verse were devoted to the thrush, the blackbird and the lark. Songs of praise were lovingly composed for the ugly cuckoo – yes, and even for the scavenging seagull – but never a mention of the *traon*. Let us hope we are not too late to make amends. I have several hundred songs ready for print, in the style of Fair Duncan, the moment I am elected President of POTCAAC.

Almost by accident I have stumbled upon one of the great discoveries of our time, or anyone else's.

Last year, or thereabouts, I was made an offer by *Reader's Digest* I couldn't refuse – the promise of a huge sum of money and many little presents to be going on with. One of the offers I thought I had refused, but it seems I put my cross in the wrong place; so now, every month and forever more, I will be sent a condensed novel.

I wish I'd thought of that one. Twenty years I've slaved away at the great Gaelic novel when I might have been tending my sheep. Had I known about this wonderful process, I could have squeezed my life's work into a nice little pocketbook – more or less as a dairy cow's yield is condensed into a can of Nestlé.

Yet the time spent at the typewriter was nothing compared with the years wasted on reading – from *Treasure Island* to *Lolita*, not to mention the whole Book from Adam to Paul. Can you imagine the number of Tilley mantles burnt and the strain of people walking between one and the light, when all this could have been condensed. I'll tell you this, if we'd had *Reader's Digest* then, we would have been as educated as the next person.

FRIDAY, 25 JUNE 1993

The story I am about to relate to you now is unequalled in the annals of heinous crime. We'll begin at the beginning, for that is always the best place to start.

It was purely by accident I learned herring was available in the town. We had called on Seonaidh Spleen to see how he was settling in his new home and found him pleasantly fat and contented. The heavenly aroma of fried herring hung heavily in the kitchen air and he had a wide smile on his face. A hospitable man, Seonaidh: he offered us a piece of this and a bit of that, but no mention was made of herring. Although I was desperate enough to have rummaged in his bin, some things are sacred, so naturally I didn't ask (didn't want to attract the attention of the Customs swoop squad).

With the smell still in my nostrils, I headed immediately for the most likely source of the staff of life. Neilly was very cagey when I approached him but after I pinned him to his kipper house floor he admitted a few were to be had between 0800 and 0805 most mornings – but for 'certain people' only. I made the signs and got my name on the books for the following day. Twelve fat ones were to be kept in the chiller until 1405.

I could scarcely concentrate on my prescriptions that morning. Dripping saliva, with small intestines oscillating in anticipation, I may possibly have poisoned a cailleach or two. I wired ahead to the ranch to clear the kitchen and asked for six special Golden Wonders to be unpacked from the store (a sand box kept at a constant 3.5 deg C). At 1405 sharp I entered the aforementioned shop and found a new man at the counter. 'My herring,' I screamed, unable to contain myself, 'bring me my herring.' The new man disappeared into the back premises, where a long discussion took place to the accompaniment of my rumbling stomach.

Management and staff finally emerged to explain and apologise. Seemingly a stranger had presented himself earlier in the day, demanded herring and given my name. Without as much as asking him to show a passport, the new man in the shop handed over my precious cargo.

Now, I've had terrible things done to me in my time. Cheque cards and cars stolen, but what is that compared with loss of herring? In the investigation that immediately commenced, and the inevitable dispute, various solicitors' names came. But, anxious to keep out of court where he couldn't possibly win, Neilly parted with 10 exceptional herring he had kept for his own tea.

Perhaps I gained at the end of the day, but it's the principle of the matter, you understand. What low example of our own species would swindle a man out of his herring? I think we can be certain in view of the description – a short, swarthy East Coast type with treacherous eyes. It was none other than Alex Salmond. If there was ever any doubt, his days are now numbered.

Personally, I have never understood nor had much interest in politics, and I'm constantly astonished at people who can get passionate on that score. I cannot help noticing, though, that the present Government seems to be rather unpopular with many people.

Last Saturday I had a visit from one of my last remaining elderly cousins, Nora. Nobody knows how old she is and it's none of our business, yet she dropped a clue when she said that after 82 years a member she had left the Tory Party. What level of corruption and skullduggery has forced this woman to withdraw from the fold?

Nora came from a long line of tough people, and none so tough as the Da – Ruairidh a' Chuain. Ruairidh sailed the seven seas in search of herring long before the days of Decca and Loran. How he managed these wide open spaces between the Faroes and Norway, late last century, is difficult for us to understand. Aye, Ruairidh was a hard man – as hard as any East Coaster, they used to say. We shouldn't be surprised that he bred tough Tories.

So here we have Nora at her great age spitting fire at the Tories. And not only that, but saying nice things about certain Labour MPs. I discovered in the course of a long Saturday afternoon that some friend of hers passed through the hands of Sam (the Skullsplitter) Galbraith and survived. I don't know who the lady is who was scalped by Sam but no praise is too high for the boy now. It naturally follows he should be the man to run what is left of the National Health Service.

Yet Sam was not alone in bringing about Nora's conversion. I like to drop names occasionally, even common ones like John Smith. I had that

John Smith in the back of my boat once, I let dab. 'Now there is a man for you,' said the old dear. It turns out she knew his grandfather, who was not only just a Christian but a Free Church Christian. Would anyone now dare to question that this is the only man for Prime Minister?

The latest news on the corncrake is not so good. Sure enough, they are more plentiful than ever, and there is at least one on every croft; but both we in POTCAAC and the grant-giving boys have arrived at what can only be classed a corncrake crisis.

As every bird man knows, the starling is a great mimic. Many a starling had never heard a corncrake until the bird came to be passed around the crofts, but now they've learned the 'tune' we have five million corncrakes perched on telephone wires. The cost will be astronomical.

FRIDAY, 2 JULY 1993

Nearly 40 years have now passed since Leurbost School admitted the first wave of barbarians from Balallan and beyond. It was a traumatic time for the gentle children of North Lochs. Some of us never fully recovered from the shock.

Perhaps we were overprotected from the horrors of the world to the south and west: we were certainly innocent in comparison with the invaders. Some of our girls ran home and refused to come back to school, and who could blame them.

Picture us if you can, sheltering from the wind in the headmaster's willows, reading poetry to each other, when they descended upon us like Vikings from a longship. When I say we were innocent, I mean we had begun to discuss blushingly with the girls how babies were made. We had only just commenced nature studies at an elementary level. Some of the bearded louts who came down from the End of The Loch were already being hounded for maintenance money. They looked old enough to have absconded from the Navy and they thought Shakespeare was a breed of ram.

I was reminded of these painful times this evening when the Chairman of Leurbost School Board slipped a newsletter under my front door. The contents of the letter are so outrageous I would have paid no further attention had it been April 1st. But it is not, so we must take the letter seriously.

Leurbost School, it seems, like Keose and Ranish, is scheduled to be turned into a pottery shop for tourists. Not long ago we fought hard to keep the little schools open, but now the parents of the moment have been persuaded these schools are obsolete. 'You must have a new plastic school specially designed for the computer age,' they were told, and they believed this. From what I've seen of modern schools, I doubt if one built now would last until my grandchildren come on stream (look at the Nicolson Institute).

But it is too late for this argument. The decision to build a new school has been taken at a high level and never mind the cost. There is a comic aspect to this doubtful enterprise and, don't worry, I'll get round to it in time. First, let me lament a little for old Gunn's willows under which, from now on, some misplaced refugee will knit tartan dolls for the towrists.

To get back to the invasion of 40 years ago, the initial impact of integration was harsh but short-lived. Those who ran home screaming eventually returned and in the fullness of time came to accept the intruder. Children are tough, especially girl children. Who could ever have foreseen that one day some of our girls would grow up to marry into the End of The Loch.

The civilising process was slow but certain. Many a rough diamond from Up Country became, in time, smooth enough to take up positions of responsibility in public life. Some prospered in commerce and a few even turned to the Church. All this they owe to their brief sojourn in Leurbost School, and they should give thanks to the far-seeing man who brought them out of their misery and into North Lochs.

Now how about this for gratitude? According to the aforementioned letter from the Chairman, there are moves afoot, where else, to have the new school built at the End of The Loch. The sheer effrontery leaves me breathless and reaching for a small rum. No doubt present day parents 'up there' are too young to appreciate the sweet irony of our predicament, but surely they cannot possibly hope to win this battle.

The obvious site for the new school, and the one put forward years ago by that man of vision DHM himself, is the Common Grazing at the west end of Leurbost. If we forget the history of education in these parts and concentrate on the obvious, Cameron Terrace is the only logical site.

I refuse to waste time on banal geographical argument. Just look at the map. As a matter of fact, I refuse to take seriously the notion that 'our' school should be built on someone's private land in the back of beyond. Let us hear no more of this ludicrous proposal and consider the matter closed.

Memories of school, no doubt kindled by last night's newsletter, caused me a very restless night. Disturbed dreams combined with flashes of accurate recollection dragged me back into the past and left me so weak I have to finish this in bed.

Perhaps a letter from the Rev Macdonald in Uig – who used to be Hero, our humorous history teacher – didn't help. Also, some colleague left the complete works of Somerset Maugham in the surgery, which made me dream of Lofty, our English teacher. Possibly all these recent events fused to aggravate the slumbering brain.

Lofty, *nach maireann* and who wasn't the worst, I will always associate with Maugham. And unfortunately Shakespeare. Unbeknown to him, Lofty ruined my career on the stage. Southerly audiences simply would not tolerate my delivery in a Garrabost accent. Still, your man did his best within the guidelines of his day.

I cannot remember much from the history class except dates of the deaths of kings and the introduction of something called current affairs. 'Do you ever see a newspaper at all?' Hero would ask. Still, he sometimes made jokes and even treated us like adults. I wonder what happened to him? What sort of dreadful experience can lead a man to become a Free

Presbyterian minister when he could have joined the Free Church or even remained a history teacher?

Nothing very much stuck in the cells, through no fault of the teachers, but I remember some boys who retained even less. For some reason, during history exams (possibly because dates were easy to crib) we had to mix with a class downstairs for whom there was no hope at all.

One year, after two hours in the torture chamber, my new deskmate, a Stornoway boy, showed me his paper. The result of his two-hour sweat read: 'Thon John Baliol was a hell of a man.' Perhaps this was what drove your man to the Church.

There can be no doubt that we would all, including the Stornoway boys, have fared better in Leurbost. Now that the Nicolson has all but collapsed, let's invite them all to the new six-year secondary at Cameron Terrace.

FRIDAY, 23 JULY 1993

DANCING WITH NUNS

Getting to the country dancing was always a problem, what with finding a man with a car who was reasonably sober, but the dance in Dungloe was a special problem. From Leurbost to Donegal is not far as the crow flies, but then, as the other fellow said, I am not a crow: I thought this time I would try public transport while it still exists.

Once again at five in the morning delivered myself into the care of Caledonian MacBrayne – a fine man in his day, but these days are long gone.

Conditions seemed ideal for a crossing. The wind was calm and the temperature outside was about 50: inside it was pushing 90 and climbing. Several well-built women, including my own wee wife, had stripped almost to the point of indecency. Yet by the time we came abreast of Bayble Island they couldn't take the heat. One brave woman had the audacity to complain to a man in uniform, who said: 'If it was cold you'd still be complaining.'

What could she say when confronted with this sort of solid logic. She came back to nurse her dog, a hairy little Scottie that must have thought he was being prepared for a barbecue. By the time we reached the middle of the Minch the poor terrier was almost done. Children, always the last to succumb, tried to cool the poor animal down by pouring their luke-warm drinks on his flapping tongue.

Matters reached the stage, as they often do, when I had to say something myself. I was uneasy from the start of the voyage when I saw Tormod Cromarty was not on duty. Still, I found another decent man, who said he would like to help but couldn't. 'It all depends who the Chief Engineer of the day is. This is a bad day and his door is locked. The thermostat has only two positions – on or off – and, it being midsummer, naturally it's on.'

Of course we all know what's going on. They are trying to make conditions unbearable now so that when privatisation happens it will not seem so bad. While we were being roasted alive, two bodachs, possibly from Uig, were dozing peacefully in heavy pullovers and winter anoraks. They were of the generation who never complained and would consider any crossing uneventful as long as they weren't torpedoed.

Between Ullapool and Inverness we were well looked after by an old Rapson man, but the day deteriorated as we fell deeper into the Lowlands. In Perth we were herded onto a clapped-out Citylink bus without as much as a pee. Halfway to Stirling the bus broke down and all 60 of us were deposited on the roadside while the driver went and pleaded with his masters at Citylink to send another bus. It was a great relief for the mind and and the bladder when we finally reached Glasgow, the capital of Donegal.

A quick feed at Mrs Wong's, the best Chinese restaurant in this country, and we were all in better humour. I would have had a decent night's rest but for the owl in Cunninghame North's attic. Permanent residents never hear the owl but it always wakens me at four in the morning. Still, this meant we were in plenty time for Tony Gallagher's bus to Gort an Choirce.

Although I suppose this too is private, there is a minimum of bureaucracy and no hard-and-fast rules nor timetables. I was pleased to see that smoking is not only permitted, it seems to be compulsory. No tickets are issued and when I wrote a cheque for the fare and started fumbling for the card people worry about over here, your man said: 'Don't bother about that, sure you'll be wanting to come back.'

We'll skip the P&O ferry between Cairnryan and Larne, for the least said the better. Perhaps just a brief message for Roddy, the *Suilven* cook: P&O could somehow offer a variety of fresh fish. Isn't that wonderful.

Gallagher's driver on the Larne to Donegal stretch was one of us, a real Maw. We can always tell one another abroad. 'You'll be going to the Macafferty wedding, I suppose,' says he.

Through the cold North as quickly as possible and then a civilised stop in Letterkenny for the bladder and refreshment. 'How long are you stopping?' *arsa mise.* 'For as long as it takes,' says he. Public transport was beginning to appeal again. Several hours later we were dropped, in the old-fashioned way, at the host's door.

People came and went and came back again. I estimated about 20 of us were expecting to be put up for the night. The house was big but not that big, so I wondered where we were all going to sleep. But after a while I didn't worry too much. Some of them evidently had no intention of sleeping at all.

At one in the morning when we had done a lot of talking, Gerry the Dubliner harnessed himself to an accordion, Pat from Cork hauled in his keyboard and Sean took out his bodhrán. The Dubliner was a terrible blasphemer. Both the nun and I had to have a word with him, but he didn't seem to understand that if he comes to Lewis he'll have to stop taking the Lord's name in vain. There seems to be a nun in every family, by the way, much as we have cùramachs. It occurs to me now that the Dubliner was a very religious man and perhaps this is why he calls on Jesus with every breath.

The wedding service in Eaglais Cholm Cille on Cnoc Fola was a cheerful Gaelic affair. Although the priest could be serious when he had to, he still found time to remind God that Donegal were playing Derry that afternoon and to root for the good guys. In the event there must have been a more potent prayer transmitted from Derry in English. His ways are indeed mysterious.

The wedding feast itself was a grand affair in the strangely named Dungloe. Strangely named in English because the town is properly called An Clochán Liath. I guess whoever built the fort must have had difficulty with the Gaelic name, the way his type still do.

Around 300 of us sat down to eat – maybe more, because no one seems concerned with numbers – and judging by the portions, there must be a fierce beef surplus in Ireland. I know some hotels not far away who could have fed five thousand with that amount.

The festivities proper got under way with very little delay. There doesn't seem to be the same suicidal rush for strong drink to which we are accustomed, perhaps because they are not ruled by the clock. However, some of us are too set in our ways, which is perhaps why I got into a bit of trouble with a tall slender nun from Doire Beag. Maybe I was holding her a wee bit tighter than necessary, but I managed to persuade her my balance was gone and the close grip had nothing to do with passion. They are a very tolerant and understanding people. Even when I fell on top of her she just laughed.

For some reason Irish musicians are very much into Scottish music these days. I'm afraid I got into a fight with Big Pat from Cork over this, but I see my bus is here . . . If they don't set the priests on me I'll see you next week.

FRIDAY, 13 AUGUST 1993

Having had to write, for a later edition of this paper, a few words in praise of a book published by the *Stornoway Gazette,* I feel a desperate need to lash out at something. Don't want the bhoys to think I've gone soft. It is almost as if I'd been caught in some sort of cissy act like hanging out the washing, drying dishes or reading poetry.

Now I have to prove I'm tough. Who can I go for? Big Fred perhaps, or Macgregor! Nothing personal, you understand; it's that company they work for called British Telecom. Three days now I've been without a telephone. The weekend, you see. BT will not call their poverty-stricken engineers out at weekends nowadays for religious reasons. This has nothing to do with overtime payments and the need to amass millions for their Chief Executive: telephones lie unrepaired purely out of respect for the Sabbath, and we should applaud that respect.

With Muslims to cater for on Fridays, Jews on Saturdays, Presbyterians on Sundays, Catholics on 165 Holidays of Obligation and I don't know who else, we will soon be restricted to the occasional Wednesday morning for call-outs.

Not that it bothers me, but think of my poor patients and the wee wife. Also, and this is really serious, I had invited Cunninghame North and his Lady for a herring party at the weekend. Could he last several hours without a phone? We doubted it.

Maggie thought of going next door to borrow a little girl's toy telephone. We hoped this would do North if withdrawal symptoms became unbearable.

While I conjured up a culinary miracle to titillate the jaded palate of any sybarite, North stalked up and down the kitchen floor clearly ill at ease. Now and again he would glance furtively at the dead instrument on the wall willing it to ring. He struggled manfully through the starter, but we all know most of it stuck in his craw. 'Could I be missing a call to yet another TV interview?' we could see him thinking.

Suddenly, unable to endure the torture for another moment, he made a dash for the front door. We had forgotten he had a phone in the car. For the rest of the afternoon he sat quite happily by the car-phone while the servant passed herring and other titbits through the open window. It is really very sad.

Why the unhealthy spite for grass and rain? This is the question I ask myself as I lie here on my bunk watching a magnificent ivory cumulus develop over Cromore. In a few minutes it will rain heavily and tomorrow the knee-high grass that surrounds us would be even higher – given a chance.

For some strange reason this regular, over-generous 'blessing' with life-sustaining rain does not please everyone. My wife is one of them; but I suppose she is to be excused, having been brought up in the semi-tropical paradise called Partick. No that the indig are any better. All around me they complain about the weather as if in another life they had been accustomed to something different and better. And they all hate grass. They just will not leave it alone.

I cannot understand this obsession with grass-cutting and see no reason for it unless it is to be used for winter fodder. Mowers, and even noisier strimmers, never stop in what used to be my quiet corner of the world. If I liked noise I would have lived in a city and never mind the corncrake. Why don't these people go and live in Saudia Arabia, where rain never falls and grass never grows? Or, better still, let them spend a summer in Bangladesh. That would shut them up.

Talking of Bangladesh, I see much has been written about Ali's Curry Shop in recent weeks. We must be careful here. When you only have one of anything you cannot knock it.

But, ah, but, there are things that have to be said. Some time ago, when rumours of Sunday opening reached the pubs, I thought it might be wise to start frequenting Ali's during the week. It wouldn't do to just suddenly be seen going on Sundays.

Fortunately, the Lawyer needs me desperately since he started flying and he shows his appreciation with the occasional lavish treat. In Ali's we tasted a bit of everything, and we rated it seven out of ten. (This, is of course, by UK standards. Since I was spoiled in my youth by Ceylonese cooks, no other curry will ever compare.)

So Ali's was fine, that first time. We ate well and retired to dance it off in the Golf Club, where some terribly outspoken types passed comment on our appearance. Granted that we might have been messy eaters, it doesn't explain the hideous yellow colour of our hands and faces. A yellow that grew yellower as the night wore on and wouldn't wash off. My wife, who is particular about these things, looked as if she'd done her hair in a Tikka oven.

I don't know what sort of colourful new spice Ali has imported but we got over that and there was no trouble with the intestines.

Yet think of the future and Sunday opening. There can be no sneaky curries before the evening service. The man in the pulpit will be able to identify the spice-eaters from their jaundiced appearance. Yes, even those who lurk in the back pews. Just the other day I called back in Ali's for a takeaway. I'm sorry, Ali, but the truth must be told. That sort of stuff may be very well for the *Machair* cast and other luvvies of little taste, but it simply will not do for the regulars in the Criterion, who often reminisce about nights on Bugis Street.

Dash it all, I'm beginning to feel so much better I may get up if she calls me once more. On the back cover of the book I mentioned earlier I've discovered the following legend in bold black print: *Designed, Typeset and Printed by the Stornoway Gazettte Ltd.*

I'm glad some things never change. I will definitely get up now and call our Dear Ed if the phone works.

FRIDAY, 20 AUGUST 1993

Sin agad e. The last of the very old-timers has gone from Ranish. Rathanais, Raernis or, as the Comhairle would have it, Ranais. Spell it how you will, what mattered to those who came to the funeral of Seonaidh Beag am Balachan was the unique cut of it.

Some of them hadn't been for a long time and had forgotten there was nowhere quite like the east end of Ranish for scenic extravagance. Even now, despite its ugly new white houses, Ranish retains its magic. Lemreway and Orinsay are fine, in their own way, but I'll bet if Calum Kennedy had had his own way he would have been born in Ranish. Those of us who were born there have never been in any doubt that God created Ranish on the first day and then shaped the rest of the world with the leftover clay. Parts of Crossbost were lucky, but by the time He reached Leurbost He was tired and scattering carelessly.

So was I. And I blame Seonaidh Beag. His son Coinneach and I were more than happy down in the glen but then Seonaidh built a house in Druim an Aoil. A home in Druim an Aoil is not to be scorned if you're homeless; but when you already have a home in paradise, even a crowded home, Druim an Aoil has all the attraction of Mongolia in the days of Ghengis Khan.

Seonaidh, an industrious man, was doing what he thought was best. As the senior man on the fishing boat *Proceed*, and an ex-Naval officer, he was not without influence. Not long after his move my own father followed him on the self-improving trail, uprooted us, and trekked to Leurbost. Now, if Druim an Aoil was desolate, Leurbost was absolute Hell. We had scary rhymes about these people.

Despite the closeness of fine old gentlemen neighbours like Daniel, I couldn't take Leurbost. Leurbost was the singular traumatic experience of my long life. (People thought it odd because I was 11 at the time. Late developer, you understand.)

Like Coinneach earlier in Druim an Aoil, I escaped to Paradise at every opportunity and I still do. Today at Seonaidh's funeral I looked down at the Minch and reconstructed those early years in my own wee mind, the way elderly folk do. The continuous line of herring boat lights still seemed real enough and the hill where we tried to kill my brother is still there.

Please don't think this was premeditated homicide: it was just that Coinneach had a new tricycle and the brother was old enough to walk and had started following us. Sunday night, with the old folk in church, seemed as good a time as any to test the bike. We placed the brother in the saddle and launched him from the top of the hill. The old byre wall where he stopped the bike with his head is also still there.

But we were not without compassion. The basinful of water we used to clean him up was completely red by the time they came from church. Naturally, my mother thought we had killed him, so she tried to kill me, although till this day I don't see what good that would have done her. I guess even then I secretly envied Coinneach because his mother never tried to kill him – maybe because he was an only child.

Although we didn't realise it then, even before we left Paradise, a recession of sorts had hit us. For a few years after the war the fishing must have been good. I remember 'old women's talk', like 'I don't care if they do drink it, it's better that they are here.'

Perhaps that had something to do with relief that they had survived. I don't know: I cannot remember everything. Anyway, the price of fish fell and the old boys left for the Hydro. We didn't know where the Hydro was but it was a great place for presents. Boy, did we get presents. The most beautiful presents anybody ever saw. Two colours of plastic coated wire in brilliant red or yellow. You could use them to decorate the National-Dried-Milk-tin boats or just look at them in their gaudy coats.

Whatever happened to Lochluichart and places like that – we had learned some geography by this time – the Hydro also went down the tubes. However, the Harris Tweed mills saved our bacon, or at least our fried bread. Seonaidh was one of the first to get established, and gradually others from North Lochs snuck in to the warmth of the warp.

I'm told that at meetings not even my neighbour Doilidh nor even Arthur Scargill could out-talk Seonaidh Beag am Balachan. I wouldn't know about that but what I do know is that a greater storyteller was never born. (Yes, I was going to record, but, as always, too late.)

Even telling them second-hand he could make me smell the trenches of the First World War. What should have been an uneventful tale of a walk to Cùl a' Ghàrraidh with the cow he could weave into a fascinating adventure. (I understand Alasdair Neileag has some interesting tapes if we can prise them out from under his bed.)

I wouldn't like the Rev Alec Murdo to think I recalled all of these early moments while he was praying; but I must confess to some of them, if he'll hear my confession.

Oh, aye, and a few more alarming thoughts such as who is left now. The next batch of senior citizens to go – that crowd includes Alasdair Neileag, Alec Dan, Dixie, Atch, Aonghas Beag and Robbie – what stories do they have to tell? A few years at the whalers or skiving on the railways! What use that! And then after that there is only us.

Friday, 17 September 1993

The time has come for me to venture over the Harris Hills to call on John MacLeod, who is no longer Young. This brave man thinks he can fight the Philistines on his own, but I fear they are too many. I hope he is not too proud to accept my strong right arm in friendship. Perhaps together we can conquer the universe.

I am not about to suggest he join us in the Lodge, for he does not strike me as the sort who approves of gangs, but surely he will allow a few of us to take his side against the Hun.

The Hun in John's case is the reader with the literal mind. There is, unfortunately, nothing that can be done to stop this unhappy species from reading. Their sort probably make up the majority of readers and they are doomed to spend their tormented, humourless lives swimming in the shallow end. Like the poor, they will always be with us.

Only when these blighted people become publishers are they a serious menace to civilisation 'as we know it'. When Mr MacLeod writes, in the self-mocking mode, that he intends to wield his column to his greater dream of conquering the universe, his publishers and many of his readers miss the comic stroke: they say he is 'barking mad'. Believe me, John, I know the pain, but you should never give them the satisfaction of a response.

My excuse for not having made the literary pilgrimage to Harris long ago is fear. I have heard too many stories about the lonely hills and glens, and much as I admire those who seek isolation to write, I suspect they don't know what they have let themselves in for.

I knew a dedicated poet once who imagined his creativity was stifled in the throbbing metropolis of Stornoway. Unable to bear 'other people', he found himself a lonely little bothan in the hills to the south and settled down to reshape the universe.

After several weeks on the lunar hills of Harris, during which he had not seen another living soul, he began to hanker for human contact. His output until his move to the wilderness had not amounted to much, but nevertheless it had been regular. Too late he discovered his inspiration had been the pubs and the crowds. Yet he was a stubborn cratur and not the type to admit he'd made a mistake. He would stick it out, he thought, no matter what.

Then one day – one of many lonely days – he saw a stranger coming over the hills from the direction of Uig. A huge hairman with dangling arms and very little forehead. 'Good day,' said the poet, 'I'm very glad to see you.'

'And I'm pleased to see you,' said the hairy one. 'I'm your nearest neighbour and I'd like to welcome you over at my place. We'll have a wee party in your honour.'

'This is very kind of you,' said the poet. 'What sort of party had you in mind?'

'Och, you know,' said the stranger. 'Plenty of booze, sex and maybe some fighting.'

'Great stuff,' said the poet. 'I'll bring a bottle. Will there be many there?'

The hairy stranger's wet lips drew back in a hideous grin, revealing several green stumps where his teeth had been. 'Just you and me, boy, just you and me.'

No doubt John MacLeod will have heard some of these stories by now, which is why I'm reluctant to make the journey. I wouldn't like him to run for the ferry when he sees me approach.

I am not a deeply religious person, but I'm very uneasy about much of what I see on television.

The other night I switched on in time to catch a programme on genetic engineering. The scenery was startling. A hillside somewhere with a flock of sheep outlined against the setting sun. 'These are no ordinary sheep,' said an American professor's voice. 'They are part sheep, part man.'

Didn't I tell you it would come to this. For 20 years I've been warning them, but they wouldn't listen, and for many a long day I've suspected the sheep in North Lochs were not what they seemed. Often when I've driven too close to a roadside ewe I've looked in the rear-view mirror and seen her shaking her 'fist'. I'm pleased that, at last, we can discuss this business openly.

Much will depend on whose genes they transfer to the lower animals. If some sheep, instead of shaking her 'fist', stops you the next time you pass and says, 'Do you mind', you may be certain she is part polite Englishman. Where will it all stop. Will you soon go into your barber's to find a couple of rams ahead of you in the queue? The next time the good wife dishes up the lamb chops, can you be certain you're not eating a friend?

Of course, this funny business is not restricted to sheep. They've also been tampering with pigs and bulls. I know the Good Book has given us dominion over the creatures, but when is a creature not a creature?

The daughter in the city tries to keep me informed about what goes on away from civilisation, and it seems there are some very peculiar things indeed going on at present.

For a few years now people who have to travel from the Western Isles have been reluctant to admit their place of birth. They claim to come from the Long Island or try to confuse by being over-specific with Geocrab or Carloway – anything but the Western Isles. Whether this denial by a once proud people is a result of BCCI or STV I cannot say, but it has been evident and noted by sociologists 'from away'.

Now the daughter tells of an incident that may herald a reversal of the trend.

When out on the town last week, somewhere in the centre of Glasgow, a 'gentleman' in a pub took a notion for her and, when sufficiently primed, made his move. He was dressed to kill. A bobbin *geansaidh* tucked in the trousers, a gap in his teeth and a half-bottle on the hip. Clearly one of ours.

'How you must miss your island home,' was his line, with much more of the same. She thought from his accent he must have been in the city for a long time. However, it transpired as the drink wore on that he had never been north of Maryhill except for a brief visit to Tiree. 'As if we didn't,' says she, 'have enough sad cases of our own.'

It occurs to me he could have been an out-of-work actor with an eye on *Machair*.

FRIDAY, 29 OCTOBER 1993

I can hardly believe the husband-swapping season is already upon us. Only yesterday, it seems, we frolicked and gambolled in the sun-kissed heather of the long summer evenings. *(What? Where? Ed.)* A short holiday, one hour lost on the clock, a blaw of snow from the north and we are into winter sports.

The great problem with our winter sports, in the cold Calvinistic north, is the lack of guilt. Common knowledge has it that we are driven by the need to work. This notion works well in the long sunlit days of summer when neighbourly Christians, sharpening shears and peat-cutting tools, cast damning glances at the frivolous tools of dilettanti and mutter: *'B' e caitheamh an latha fhoghair e.'* With the memory of that damning phrase we can all do suitable penance at childish caman or at card play. We can hate ourselves, in summer, for our idleness. But in winter, well, what else can we do but play games.

This leaves us in a terrible void, with nothing to contemplate but our own mortality. In the absence of guilt about work neglected, we naturally begin to think about what we are about. What are we doing here? Children, in their idle pursuits, kicking balls and throwing stones, are forgiven. But we adults, should we be wasting time?

A terrible waste of time is something we have heard a lot about in our churchgoing days. Time is short. Time to prepare, that is. Moments wasted in the short run up to the long jump into time everlasting.

How do we overcome this dreadful inculcation, even in winter, when we have cleaned the chimneys on a Saturday morning as Dixie had?

I asked Robbie. 'Ask your partner Dr Taylor,' says Robbie. 'We're supposed to be playing him at 1.30 but he won't be there. He might turn up at 2.30. As a matter of fact, 1.30 is the same as 2.30 to Donald. There isn't much difference.'

I hadn't perhaps given as much time as I should have done to my friend Dr Donald's philosophy. I should be thankful to people like Robbie and Dixie, who, in their worldly humour, drew my attention to the good Doctor's awareness of infinity and eternity. Robbie was being smart but not as smart as Donald, because Donald knows there is no difference, in the grand scheme of things, between 1.30 and 2.30 and regulates his life accordingly.

Unfortunately, lesser mortals than Donald, in which category I must include myself, have not yet embraced his comforting approach to and disregard for the generation-in-a-hurry. When he turns up, in the fullness of time, his good-natured chuckle, often taken as an apology by those who don't know him, sticks in my throat. When I take him to task for being late, he turns on me and with the gentlest thrust asks why I was early. I have no answer, for the moment, but I'm working at it.

Anyway, that is only golf, a daytime pursuit. On Tuesday it's card play, an activity more suited to the hours of darkness and preferred by the black archangel and by Donald. I turned up at seven as instructed, with my fingertips powdered and my intellect as finely honed as ever was any soap writer's. No sign of Dr T, of course, but nevertheless I was able to renew my acquaintance with some other old friends, also lost in time.

Mr Whiteford and Nina, nighthawks both, I hadn't seen since early March. 'Where hast thou been?' quoth Nina, for that is how we spake. Ye before I could respake she began to unburden her troubles with your man, the husband. Before she could unload too much, I mentioned that I'd seen poor ADW at the funeral of our old friend Dugald. I was in the company of D Campbell, Turf Accountant, at the time, and to be honest, I confessed, although we argued about a very short price, the Bookie accepted my wager on Allan getting within 30 years of Dugald. 'I wouldn't mind a share,' said the loyal wife (and nobody can dispute that). 'But I'm not so well myself.'

This mysterious remark, tossed off by a woman who appears to be as healthy as anyone in early retirement can be, I stored, but didn't forget, while I mixed with some other elderly people.

We talked about ADW and the way he drags that painful hip around when he could get a private plastic one, instead of waiting for the NHS like the good socialist he is. But then someone volunteered a theory that makes sense when you come to think of it. 'He's punishing himself. Oh, yes, it's all deliberate. Too young for the war, and then such an easy life, as the best Rector we never had. A bit like Denis Healy – life has been good to him . . . no major responsibility . . . now he is devoured by guilt.'

Like the good friend I am, I went over immediately to tell him what his colleagues had been saying. Naturally, he assumed I meant Nina. 'Did you hear about our overnight train journey?' says he, forgetting to mention whether or not it was the Orient Express. 'She climbed into the top bunk although I protested. I could have managed the ascent despite my condition. She awoke, no doubt to her own snoring, before dawn, forgot she was resting at some altitude and rolled out of bed. I heard a scream and caught a glimpse of a naked body flashing past my pillow.'

'You didn't,' *arsa mise*, 'try to catch her?'

'What,' *ars esan*, 'the way she bids?'

The outcome of it all, not yet known to Allan, is that if he doesn't come out of the 'hip anaesthetic' I am going to play with Nina. And if he does, she says, he has to play with Donald. That's what friends are for.

THE SIARACH DRONNAG

The importance of diet at this time of year cannot be overestimated. At the risk of incurring the wrath of my medical colleagues, I would suggest there is nothing better in the winter months than to be a little overweight. You only have to look at the Eskimo, Siarach women and the grey seal: a good layer of padding never did them any harm.

This year especially, with a biting easterly air stream coming at us from Vladivostok carrying all manner of virulent invaders, a few inches of healthy fat is the first line of defence. Our West Side ladies didn't get where they are today through self-starvation or by posing in gymnasiums with weight-lifting equipment. Look at any native woman from the Butt to Mangersta, preferably from behind, and you'll see what God intended for this climate. Not too tall but well braced. They have no fear of winds from Peking or anywhere else.

It is no secret that the women of these parts generally outlive their skinny imported husbands by 20 years or more. In anticipation of letters asking, 'How can we get to look like Siarach Woman?', I'll give a few hints now to save time and stamps.

A great deal of it is in the genes, of course, but genes have to be fed. And fed properly. Many allegedly expert dieticians (consultants, mind you) earn their living through false pretences: they practise starvation rather than nutrition. Men and women who've suffered at their hands in the name of fashion look as if they're on their way out with some wasting disease. These poor deluded people have no protection at all against winds from Siberia.

Forget all that nonsense and listen to me. And remember, what works for women usually works for men.

As recently as three weeks ago a sickly individual of my acquaintance approached me in my Point St office and asked for help, 'if it isn't too late'. He thought he had flu. He was probably right, and no wonder. Ribs almost visible through his Arnish jacket, and no belly to speak of. 'Look at these gentlemen at the bar,' I said, pointing at some 17-stone regulars. 'Did you ever see them with a runny nose, never mind flu?'

The gaunt one was too far gone to start him off with ling liver. I ordered him down to Neilly's with a prescription for a huge coalfish. The old and healthy will recognise now that I had gone for the last resort that seldom fails: '*Ucas air a phronnadh na shalchar*'. For the benefit of those without the language, this is a simple but very powerful dish.

Take a good size of coaly with plenty liver and boil the fish and liver together for 20 minutes or until a raw egg in the shell won't sink through the soup. Have as many Kerr's Pink as you like ready on the side. There are two roads you can take from there, I told him. Start by mashing the whitefish, liver and potatoes together, and eat while washing down with the *sùgh*. Or mix in the liquid and 'drink' as a *stapag*.

After two weeks on this medication the patient and I were once again together in the office when someone said he hadn't seen the man with the sunken cheeks for some time and wondered if he'd pulled through. I didn't let on that your man, the same one, had just bought the round. To tell the truth, I hardly recognised him myself.

Some Siarach lady will no doubt write to correct me, claiming the *biorach* (tope) was the traditional base for this life-saver, and their African *dronnags*, but the *ucas* is the mainline. Not only is it stronger, one big *ucas* is a fortnight's course of treatment. Taken in the *stapag* form, it needs no reheating. It can be ate cold, morning and night. But a word of warning for the 'paper stomachs'. Do not, if you are unaccustomed to proper food, start with more than one full bowl. You cannot become a Siarach overnight.

The daughter came home with a young man this week and I'm not quite sure how to handle the situation. I mean, what do you do with these city types on a sunny November morning?

After a long walk in my garden during which he showed little interest in my trees, I let him dig the last row of late potatoes. This he finds amusing and comments on the wonder of it all. 'Gosh,' he says, 'aren't they dirty . . . not at all like Presto's.'

Luckily I remember Coinneach telling me a whale has come to live its last days in Loch Grimsiadar. This is not the sort of thing they often see at Ibrox. Well, not recently.

As it happens, the Minke has adopted for its last playground the deep pool at the bottom of Torcuil's croft. When we abandoned the oar halfway through Grim Shader, the 'young man' says what now – I see no whales. We have to walk to the shore, bloody fool, says I, and we have to climb this fence. Not that way, I scream, you don't climb. For God's sake, you lift your leg over. Look, even my wee wife can do it.

All the time I had an eye out for Torcuil. He writes Gaelic poetry. He can be very unpredictable and might easily let loose with a shotgun if he doesn't like the sound of us. I couldn't see him, although I suspected he might have been hiding in the rushes. Speak Gaelic. Speak Gaelic at the top of your voices, I urged them, and keep walking. They tried, although it sounded to me like Gordon Jackson's attempt at German in *The Great Escape*.

Nevertheless we reached the shore unscathed and for 20 minutes the whale performed its sad ritual for us. The 'young man' was impressed and so was I. He seems far from being as anaesthetised as the average Rangers supporter. I thought it better not to mention I'd caught a glint, in the low afternoon sun, from what might have been a firearm on the Ranish side of the Loch.

On the way back, Torcuil – who must have decided we were all right – came out of hiding to tell us a yarn. Remember Jonah, he started, for he knows his Bible, well, he went on . . . But to cut his story short, apparently a certain gentleman went missing after a small '*buaireadh*' at the bush end of Grimsiadar in an age when whales were common. 'I'm not saying anything about this whale, mind you,' he said, saying it.

I wasted no time at all in the circumnavigation of the Loch. Much to the horror of my passengers, I took terrible chances on the narrow bends towards Ranish. Thankfully, I made it just in time. Coinneach and the old whaler, Kenny The Plumber, were taking aim with a polished harpoon when I stopped then. 'Hold your fire,' I pleaded. 'There could be a very old man from Grimsiadar in there.'

'What a great pity,' *arsa Coinneach*. 'What a waste . . . can you imagine the size of liver in that beast?'

FRIDAY, 17 DECEMBER 1993

About this time of year, not long of the war, Dòmhnall Chailein, Aonghas Sheonaidh and others with South Lochs connections used to shoot and melt down a grey seal for the boys. Fish were not scarce, after the long rest, but December gales often meant the usual breakfast chaser – cod liver oil – was in short supply.

Unfortunately for us, there was no shortage of seals. I'll never forgive your old man, Alec. Even after you had learned to block the sinuses and swallow without tasting, much as we do with whisky now, seal oil would often work its way to the surface of the brose on the bumpy Arnish Moor – aye, and sometimes would erupt in mid-morning during double maths.

There is no doubt seal blubber was a useful boost in the lean winter months for both young and old. It kept out the cold and alleviated rheumatic pains, it was thought to delay the onset of menopausal wrinkles and work wonders for the libido, and it was a well-known cure for dandruff.

Quite apart from its medicinal qualities, you could use it in the sump of an old engine, you could burn it or oil hinges with it. But it has to be admitted it was not easy to swallow.

Whether or not it did us any good in the long term it is too soon to say. After all, we have only reached the half-century, and it is possible that without the grey seal we might not have made 40. The one thing we know for certain is that it ruined many an early romance.

I think it was Jackie Macaskill's class . . . at a certain point in `The Miller's Tale', emboldened by Jackie's delivery of ribald language, I leaned forward to nibble the earlobe of the innocent Matheson Road girl in front. I took a deep breath to whisper sweet words of poetry, but, alas, the seal oil and the brose had reached a crucial stage of fermentation. A huge bubble of gas escaped, causing those four seats in front to all but faint.

Being banished from the class was nothing compared with having lost her love forever. I thought I might have won her back with Bristol Tipped and Cadbury Wholenut. But no, it was not meant to be.

From that day on the only glance she ever cast in my direction was down a sniffy nose, and she went on to marry a butcher. I cannot say I blame her. *(What's with this reminiscing? Ed.)*

Sorry, Sir, it was the Loch Grimsiadar whale, with all that blubber, that brought it back – and, of course, the time of year.

Five weeks now since the Minke took up residence in North Lochs. Channel Four had it last night, and any week now the Stornoway Greysheet will make it front page 'news'.

Television coverage has come late, but better late than never because the resulting tourist activity has already reached alarming proportions. Torcuil's croft, as was regrettably reported here a long time ago, offers the best access to the whale. Although the hordes are welcome – for some of them might buy a half-pint and a pickled onion in the town – the damage to grazing on the croft will far outweigh the meagre bonus to the publicans.

Surprisingly, Torcuil has not yet erected a turnstile. Although he is not a seeker after wealth, I thought perhaps he might have exacted a small toll by way of compensation. When I tackled him on this matter he was a trifle secretive but admitted he was merely biding his moment. Until now the whale has been making conventional noises when it surfaces. But at the dead of night your man has been nesting in the seaweed encouraging the beast to belch in 'Gaelic'. When the blowing in Gaelic is perfected – with appropriate subtitles – said Torcuil, 'The world's my oyster.'

The Gaelic Television Committee (Committee Television na Gaelic) has apparently already approached him about renting the croft, and have even hinted that the standard of the Gaelic 'blowing' is not too important. After all, they said, 'she' is only a learner, and the scenery is nice.

While all this brews my friend Stewart Angus in Nature Conservancy has not been idle. At least in the last fortnight he hasn't. In the early days of the whale I could tell from the smirk on his face he hoped 'she' had come in to eat the salmon farm. Small matter, he hinted.

However, with increasing public attention, something had to be done. Booker McConnell, eager as always for a good press, have now agreed to move their valuable broodstock from Loch Grimshader. This exercise is not only costly, it is a total waste of time. As often as not the Minke surfaces seaward of the cages and could leave if it wanted to, which it obviously doesn't. As all old whale-watchers know, 'she' has chosen Loch Grimshader as her place to die.

If and when the salmon cages are removed next week and the whale leaves the Loch of its own accord, I will go down there to the shore and eat my sou'wester. Not a tasty bite, but when I think of what we would have to swallow if the old ones were alive, the sou'wester is no challenge.

By the time you read this certain people over in Skye will be building up towards a huge hooley on Saturday night – all on the gross and obscene profit made by this paper.

Of all the rotten tricks ever played by the Sgiathanach, this is the lowest. They knew well Saturday was impossible for those of us who toil in Lewis. Quite apart from the transportation problem, we wouldn't dream of dancing into the small hours of the Sabbath.

Never mind . . . Cunninghame North and I will take a picnic down to Grimshader and watch the whale.

IN SEARCH OF SOUTH LOCHS NUMBER WAN: A CHRISTMAS TALE

Although it would not be beyond me to make up a little yarn for Christmas, as I have often done in the past, this year I would like to tell a true story as it happened in South Lochs nearly one hundred and fifty years ago.

We have long known that the gentleman known as the Millionaire Cobbler (Smith) is only twice removed from South Lochs: he still walks like a Maw and can speak Gaelic. His friend Fred of British Telecom (MacLennan) defies any sort of ethnic identification. He has the wild appearance of a Hearach, the height of a Niseach; he dallies with the dilettanti of Matheson Road, and speaks only the modern languages. Yet, for but a stroke of fortune, Fred might very well have been the Millionaire, and the Cobbler might this day have been climbing poles.

But let us begin at the beginning, which was the middle of last century. There happened to be in Marvig, at that time, a lassie of uncommon beauty. Her skin was so soft and her locks so fair that the young bards of Gravir, lacking the courage to approach her, wrote epic poetry in her praise. She was thought at the time, or so the old-timers wrote, to be not of this world. Or certainly not of that world where the women tended to be dark and squat.

However, one bold Smith of Marvig, a fierce but handsome lad in whom the Viking blood still ran strong, had the confidence to look her in the eye. He lay in wait for her at milking time, sat behind her in church and carried her pails from the well. Each and every springtime he made her a present of a young lamb and a newborn calf, until at last her father had to take him aside and say: 'Young man, your presents are eating me out of house and fodder; what's your game, cove?'

'My game, Sir, is no game,' quoth the boy Smith (for that is how they spoke then). 'I believe your daughter to be the only woman on earth for me, and unless I am much mistaken I am the only man for her.'

The old fellow was deeply touched by this but he was also a true Marvig lobsterman and a cynic to boot. 'My dear boy,' he said, 'put your hand on my chest. Feel that. Yes, it pounds within. I have a heart and your romantic notions make it flutter. But what, pray tell me, are your prospects? List for me your assets in the way of cash and collateral?'

The young boy Smith was not to be discouraged. He numbered his sheep, his pig and his three cows, but, alas, there was no subsidy then, so the old fellow just laughed. 'Be gone, you fool,' he sneered. 'But by all means come back when you have something to offer my daughter.'

The stalwart Smith swore that he would indeed go. He would go and not come back until he was worthy of Mary with the golden locks. He would work his fingers to the bone. He would follow the herring to Iceland and further if necessary. He sold his pig, bought a pair of fine seaboots and a ticket to the Broch. For three long years no more was heard of him.

Needless to say, Mary took it badly. Had there been a convent in South Lochs at the time she would very likely have joined, but there wasn't.

As so often happens in these cases, there was a bachelor in the village eager to console. In this case his name was MacLennan, and although he was not without a few bob, Mary would not be consoled. She carried her own water from the well and refused all pet lambs. She sent MacLennan's

Valentines back unopened and stopped going to church because he insisted on sitting behind her singing his lungs out.

For nearly three years MacLennan besieged her with every weapon in his seductive armoury, and yet she held out. We must remember that in those days baubles with which to bribe and corrupt were scarce. But every woman has her price. When MacLennan presented her with a pair of the very latest in high heels from Paris, she weakened and declared her love for the the boy Smith was not the raging fire it once was.

The old fellow reckoned if MacLennan could furnish his beloved daughter with fancy footwear from a foreign land it must be love. In no time at all a wedding was announced. Sheep were slaughtered and every hen between Orinsay and Cromore was plucked. It was going to be a grand affair. The church in Gravir was decorated for the occasion and boats were hired for guests from the North.

The old fellow, still dazzled by the shoes from Paris, spared no expense. Thrice distilled whisky was brought from every parish by the cartload and a man called Kennedy was engaged at great cost to sing at the wedding.

On the Big Day – they talk of it still – you couldn't have packed another child into the kirk. All went well until the minister reached the crucial moment when he had to ask if anyone present had any cause to object to the union.

'I do,' said a powerful voice from the church door. When the astonished vicar regained his strength, he asked the stranger to step forward. Yes, it was the young man Smith, bearded and bigger but instantly recognised by all.

He strode up to the altar in the most magnificent pair of waders anyone present had ever seen. He stood beside the bride-to-be and said he believed the fair Mary would not wish to marry anyone but him.

'This is surely easily settled,' said the preacher. 'Which of these men do you wish to marry?' he asked the blushing Mary.

'*Gabhaidh mi fear nam bòtannan mòra*,' she is on record as having answered. It is also on record that the grooms were substituted and that the marriage took place there and then.

There is something we don't know for sure but we can guess. 'Fear nam bòtannan mora' would no doubt have learned in time of his Mary's love for fancy shoes, and that was probably the foundation of the Cobbler's dynasty.

1994

FRIDAY, 14 JANUARY 1994

When I told our Dear Ed I planned this week to make a list of my achievements in the year just past, he said, 'Go ahead, dear boy; this should make for a nice short column.' But wait you.

At a quick glance through the year's diary I see the occasional modest success among many failures. Take, for instance, my treatment of the Turf Accountant.

Twelve months ago you wouldn't have taken even money about him surviving the year. His entire corp was perforated and he was fading away like my horses in the final furlong. Some of the best-known doctors in the land had written him off. During that last spell in hospital his 'friend' Kenny Fags had started referring to him in the past tense, and I must admit I had prepared a nasty obituary in anticipation of the worst.

Yet who did I meet running in Lady Lever Park on the 5th of the New Year? Who else but your man, at full gallop although a trifle pale. It seems I got to him with the old-fashioned remedies just in time. But of course he is not happy.

That is the way with hypochondriacs. Take away their one genuine cause for complaint and they quickly find another. Your man rested from his exertions for a moment and pointed towards the general region of his own liver (it could be anywhere now). 'Severe pain,' he said. 'Doubt I've had it.'

Now it is very likely this was no more than a stitch or indigestion, but still it is a great opportunity to whip out his gall bladder; and I'll tell you why I recommended this drastic action.

Eighteen years ago *(That's a long way back for a previous success – Ed.)* I had a similar case in my old colleague Dr Fingalstein. The man was full of bile.

For 40 years he had suffered terribly from the bile bladder. A small glass of whisky and a fried egg and he was sick for days. Into hospital and out with his revolting organ, and we had a new man – a man without bile. He hasn't had a hangover since 1975.

You see why we simply must operate on the Turf Accountant. Can you imagine how much more generous will be his odds when we get rid of all that bile.

Ach, never mind my achievements: we would need a whole newspaper. So let's do something else. (*What about the failures? – Ed.*) OK, so there's a few of them as well. The voodoo hasn't worked on Lilley and Portillo: they're still alive, but give me time.

Normally I never tackle anything that looks as if it could become difficult, which is why my failure rate is so low. However, last summer I talked myself into a task that frightens the stuffing out of me. Nobody is forcing me and no one expects much, but unfortunately I have become obsessed.

In a moment of madness, probably intoxicated by Anne Lorne's nearness, I suggested the Good Soldier Svejk was as Gaelic as they come and should be adapted to our needs in the dramatic form. Life is too short to wait for a native genious to appear, so why not borrow Jaroslav Hasek.

I started out to read Svejk again but found I was reading for enjoyment. On the third round I took some notes and I think the project may be possible, although I will probably have to sub-contract to someone like Tormod Calum (with experience of stagecraft), a big overdraft and time on his hands.

I regret, Marisa, there is little scope for women in Svejk – although perhaps Lieutenant Lucas could be yours if you can grow a moustache. I had better not reveal any more just yet in case some hoodlum like Alasdair a' Bhocsair steals my idea. So, to work. There is not a moment to be lost.

*   *   *

It is Friday the 7th of January as I stroll around Stornoway Harbour on a glorious high.

I am slightly dizzy and I take a minor stagger, so I draw away from the edge in case I fall into a boat. An old man looks at me and I can see he thinks I'm drunk, but I'm not. I smile at a pleasant-looking middle-aged woman but she frowns and hurries away.

What is the matter with these people? I walk through the town shaking hands with friends and strangers, wishing Happy New Years. Friends shake their heads tolerantly and strangers look suspicious. What is wrong with these inhibited creatures in their closed-in world? I'll tell you what's wrong with them. No faith.

On the morning of the 4th I had my greatest success of all time. I woke up with religion. Yes, the cùram. I went to bed a sinner – nay, a drunken sinner with impure thoughts – and I woke up cleansed. Only five days ago I was as most of you are today, but today I am a new person. I wonder if it's still all right to play bridge tonight. Dash it, I think I'll take a chance.

On New Year's night, or it could have been the 2nd or 3rd, our house was again full of joyful youngsters – male and female. A strange thing I noticed among this generation of average age 20 is that the male of the species is more refined in language and gesture, perhaps even in appearance. This has me beat unless it has something to do with the liberalisation of women. If this is the case, the sooner we get them back in the kitchen the better.

Two Donalds, one from Crossbost and the other from Leurbost, gave us two hours of the funniest unscripted entertainment I have experienced since Norman Maclean was a boy. My only hope is that they don't come to rely on alcohol – that the abnormal won't become the norm. But I must start preaching in my fourth day of holiness.

Inevitably we got to talking about the late Niall Cheòis. Everyone between the Butt and Daliburgh knows of his influence on the music world, but he left another little legacy in North Lochs that is not so well known. While young fools everywhere argue about Celtic and Rangers, there is in North Lochs, thanks to Niall, a small band of happy Stenhousemuir supporters.

Let us all now get back to basics, but remember the condoms.

FRIDAY, 11 FEBRUARY 1994

About 40 years ago on the east coast of Lewis, was it? Now that makes sense. This was a time of want and illness for us all, in the aftermath of the Holocaust, but we put it down to the lack of protein and food in general.

Fish were scarce and cockles had all but disappeared. At the time we were totally dependent on what the Granny brought back from the shore. Each morning at eleven she kindled a fire for the potatoes and climbed down the rocks with her rod and line for the rest of our meal. As each day passed she returned with less and less. But she soon died, and we very nearly lost the brother. The hens stopped laying and the sheep on Seumas Cleite lost their wool.

A long damp summer and no shoes meant every youngster on the East Coast suffered from foot-rot and torrential diarrhoea. No one could spell this desperate affliction. Every waif in the long pathetic queue for the headmaster's belt had the same excuse-me note – 'Please excuse Iain for the *spùt*.' A more pitiful sight than these half-naked children running between house and byre with their short trousers under their arms you never saw. They knew it was a plague, but didn't suspect it had been deliberately let loose on our shores.

At this time a couple of my young friends were diagnosed 'down with typhoid', undoubtedly by some quack in the pay of the Ministry of War. A suitable old lady with no relatives, Ceit Thorastaigh, was selected and isolated as a carrier and would probably have been put down but for the minister.

Make no mistake, the claim forms now being filled in for our compensation will cause severe turbulence when they reach the bowels of the Treasury, but nowhere near the severity of the demands that will be made from North Tolsta. There is no way the damage done to these poor people can be measured, far less compensated.

Nice to see the girls together again when Number One Daughter blessed us with a brief visit. I'd forgotten what it was like to be kept awake by the hilarious reminiscing of the Art class of '89. It makes them feel so old and me so young. (Check that one, Dear Daughter, for the use of I and Me before you get a job with *The Telegraph*.)

'You must go and see,' they commanded, 'Monsieur Brady's exhibition in the Gallery. He must have paid attention to us when we were mere students.'

Now that they're so old, they feel they can confide as women of the world: they feel they can talk openly about a certain Sixth Year Arts expedition to Edinburgh, as if it had taken place in the last century, when their eyes might have been opened but they kept them closed in fear of what they might see.

But enough of that Edinburgh trip, in case the old rector Eddie Young comes back from the grave. Go and see the present exhibition in the Lanntair that was only made possible through Mellie's insistence, from an early age, that Miss Ritchie and Monsieur Brady were made for each other.

These fantasies of Brady's, reconstructed in old *Sunday Mails*, Archangel Tar and superglue, have captivated visitors to such an extent that purchases have been made. From now on, towards further exhibitions, anxious owners will follow the slick of fish like hungry seals. A smart move, M Brady, to set up a happy fantasy home in what looks at first glance like an exotic Indian Ocean cowrie, but which to the ordinary man on the croft looks all too sadly like a dog-whelk. Sure, that is how we all beguiled them.

Although seriously envious and full of admiration for your man Brady, I have to ask myself: where would I hang any of his fishermen's nightmares? One man's nightmare, I know, is another's great catch, and

I can think of no fisherman who ever caught enough fish to afford a hall big enough to house himself and Miss Ritchie – and one of their papier-mache sharks.

I hear talk, disturbing talk, in my club, that my eldest son has taken to writing for an East Coast paper. What am I supposed to do? I cannot stop him as long as he doesn't violate the sacred vows he swore as a boy when we laid him in the box at his initiation. I hope he values his tongue and his debt to the ancients more than he does to this Aberdonian rag.

In any case, I told him, when dealing with the NorthEastBeEast, be sure to get your money in your hand, before you write a word.

Fair enough, says he, but who's going to write the 'good wans'? They always come out of the Lodge.

OK, *arsa mise*, just this once, tell them about your first night, but let's see it here first.

OK, says he, it's a deal.

I have always, said he, felt the undertakers of any town get a poor press, although they have one hell of a job. The only time they get a mention is in a graveside mumbled obligation. This does not do justice to my friend Brother A. The night they laid me in the coffin when I was accepted unto the Broederbond, they all said I looked fine.

'By God, he does,' said the undertaker. 'What a pity he's not a real corpse.'

I'll let him off with that one for the simple reason that young Al is not on the Square. He merely takes advantage of the parlour's proximity to the Temple and he hopes some night he'll get a bit of overtime. May the Supreme Architect of the Universe forgive us our misuse of the compass.

It behoves us all to exercise the utmost decorum at this time of grief and embarrassment for the Tories. I would like to take this opportunity to plead with our local men in the House not to be cads. If the filthy perverts across the floor want to dress up in women's clothing, then that

is their business. Let the lewd and swinish wallow in their own filth and
. . . (Enough – Ed.)

FRIDAY, 18 FEBRUARY 1994

Whilst dining out in Meall Ros the other night my friend the Councillor
leaned across the table and told me, in strictest confidence, he planned to
renovate several black-houses in Garenin. Like many romantics brought
up in the lap of luxury, he has no idea what the reality was like. Although
perhaps he noticed me moving my half-finished dinner to the side as the
memory of the hen's beak in my porridge came back.

Yet, despite the bubonic memories, I'm tempted to put my name down
for one of the black-houses. Although earwigs and centipedes were our
constant companions, at least we were warm. The thatched roof and the
trapped hot smoke probably helped to keep the temperature up, and the heat
of the animal bodies in the lower end of the house no doubt also helped.

Contrast the relative comfort of those days with my condition today
as I sit at the machine wearing a hat and long-johns for protection
against the Siberian airstream. My home looks fairly similar to many of
the so-called modern homes I see around me, so I can assume I am not
the only man working from home and shivering. The fault must lie with
the design. The cost of building the modern house is nothing compared
to the cost of keeping warm once you're in it.

There's an oil-fired boiler at the back, double glazing, a peat fire in
the living room, a gas fire for emergencies (February) and also electric
storage heaters. Still, every 10 minutes, to keep the circulation going, I
have to stop and chase Maggie round the kitchen. We haven't even got
the consolation of blackbirds' songs from nests in the wall.

When I think of the rules that had to be followed and the hordes who
were paid to enforce them, I cannot begin to understand why I am still
cold. Perhaps the eight holes they insisted I left under the floor for the
gales to blow through were a mistake. Perhaps it is just that the blood is
thin, but it is, after all, the same blood that flowed in the black-house.

The more I think about it the more convinced I am you are right, Alec, to go for thatch and three-foot stone-and-earth walls. However, I see problems ahead with the guys in planning. Apart from fire regulations, a petty preoccupation of theirs, there is the question of windows. They are obsessed with sunlight and always insist on six-by-four windows when all you had in mind was a small porthole. All this means is that wives, as soon as they move in, have to buy bigger curtains to keep the light out.

The tiny two-paned window in the black-house wall allowed a narrow beam of sunlight to penetrate the fog within. If you were prepared to move around the room, this was sufficient to learn to read by. If you were too lazy to read while lying in your Sunday morning bed, you could watch bluebottles dancing and humming round the drying cod hanging in the single blue shaft of light. That was our *Dr Who*.

Go for it, Councillor, but remember we want the real thing. We do not want to live in some sort of sanitised version dreamed of and designed by architects who are too young to remember. If you are looking for a consultant who knows what he is talking about, look no further.

Some years ago I remember tackling a colleague with both feet for wallowing in nostalgia, for his constant decrying of everything modern and his ludicrous belief that things in general, including black-houses, were better in the distant past. Of course, I was younger then, but now I think perhaps he had a good point.

On the subject of books in particular I gradually came to believe my colleague was right. I started a hundred new novels and seldom finished one, preferring to go back to at least a quarter of a century and often farther. (Never quite reached the extreme, though, of a female friend who hasn't yet got over the Reformation.)

The great test of a book's worth is the February test, especially if it's a heavy hardback. When the temperature in the modern home is the same as it is outside, the hand holding the book above the covers quickly goes numb. The temptation to give up and go to sleep is difficult to resist.

One recent exception, in 1980 I think, was *The Year of the French*, by Thomas Flanagan. I fought sleep and cold for half the night, and although it was too long for one 'sitting' I couldn't wait for the morning to start again. Historical novels I cannot normally abide, but *The Year of the French* was sublime.

There have been a few over the years in the not-too-bad class, but only a few. I've had to wait a long time but at last I think I'm on to something special. Number One daughter met me in Glasgow last week and said: 'I have this book you must read, by AL Kennedy. Everybody's talking about it.' Not to me, they're not, because the people I mix with don't read books any more.

To humour her, and because I thought the Kennedy might be a long-lost cousin, I took it. The blurb on the back is made up of a selection of quotes from well-known newspaper critics, but don't let this put you off. These critics are usually friends of the publishers, bought and paid for, but not in this case. AL Kennedy's *Looking for a Possible Dance* stands up well to the February Test – and, what is more astonishing, AL Kennedy is a young woman.

Unlike most modern novels, *Looking for the Possible Dance* seems to have been written to be read rather than with a view to the film. How about this for a neat piece of sedition . . .

'*The Ceilidh: Notes for those new to the country or otherwise uninformed.*

'The purposes of the ceilidh, a uniquely unsullied flowering of Scottish culture, are many. Among these are the taking of spiritous liquors, the singing of songs, the playing of music, dancing, joking, wynching, fighting, greeting, eating stovies and looking at the moon while vomiting or contemplating the certainty of death.'

Some of the Gelic introspection will be too disturbing for many, but I recommend it to my few friends who still read and whose houses are warm enough to manage more than a newspaper column.

FRIDAY, 11 MARCH 1994

The first item on the agenda this week has to be Calum Siarach's 65th birthday. I realise one shouldn't use the press for personal messages but this is too important. Usually, in North Lochs, a man has to die before his 'friends' feel they have to say what a rascal he was, but for once we won't wait for the Grim Reaper.

The celebration will commence in the Criterion around lunchtime (that is dinner-time in Leurbost). Do not worry if the man is not there himself; just order what you like and he will settle the tab later on.

To be honest, and that is what we are about, it is largely due to Calum that neither I nor anyone else in North Lochs who had to work nights will see 65. During his reign as postman he shortened our lives by at least 10 years. They tell me night work reduces life expectancy by 10 years in any case. Add to that, or subtract, the Calum factor, and I guess every year is a bonus now.

Being slightly deaf himself, he probably never realised how loud the horn on a Post Office van was. I could usually hear his tooting when he was halfway through Crossbost. By the time he reached Leurbost it was as well to get up. If he saw curtains still drawn, it brought the seven demons out in him. Why he felt unwanted final demands and *Reader's Digest* prizes should have been heralded by exuberant horn-blowing we shall never know. But that is how it was.

So I would urge you all to drink heavily on Calum's slate.

Some of my comrades in sport would no doubt have been surprised at my behaviour last Saturday. When I thought no one was watching I lured the good Doctor into the woods at the Castle and gave him a hard smack on the head with a nine-iron. But I assure you it was for his own good.

I think it was Tormod a' Bhocsair (*nach maireann*) who first thought of this drastic remedy for people who have led a cerebral sort of life. In the early days of computers your man noticed the storage registers filled up quickly and had to be cleared from time to time. The same treatment must obviously work for the human, or near-human, brain.

The Back Chemist's brain, having spent a life-time immersed in chemical complexity, is now as full as an egg. This is why he can never remember our system or plan, whichever game we play, and why I had to re-boot him with a sharp blow to the head. Now we can start at the beginning again. Expect a remarkable improvement on all fronts.

For all his lapses at the bridge table, my partner keeps up to the minute in the world of medicine. At last he has given me a concoction that works for herpes – Zovirax, I think it's called.

When we were recently blessed with a huge shoal of herring, possibly attracted by the whale, I spent some time at sea – with the inevitable result. There is something about sea-water that invariably reactivates the herpes. Bleeding profusely from the lips, I approached the good Doctor and asked if there was anything new.

There certainly was. Zovirax. My eruptions were reduced in a day and killed off on the second. As always, there is a price to pay. In this case £5.95, but well worth it. But notice how crafty these medicine-men are. 'Apply this,' ars esan, 'five times a day and you'll be fit to kiss in no time.' Of course it doesn't take 'five times a day' or anything like that. But the tube is exceedingly small and if you use it five times a day you'll soon be back for another one. These boys didn't get where they are today through applying costly creams once a day. But the main thing is that it works. I can now look forward to the salmon season for the first time in some years.

I mentioned herring back there but perhaps I shouldn't have done, in case the bad boys of the East Coast get to hear. Not that I grudge them a catch; my concern is for Torcuil's whale. Yes, it is still there and doing well, although I've heard the poachers talking of its being worth £5,000 in Japan.

This would be a great shame because we are all quite attached to the beast now. And naturally it is a powerful attraction for the towrists. They tell me Torcuil is getting rid of his sheep and plans to open a cafe. In the meantime we must protect the herring to protect the whale.

This will not be easy while my friend Coinneach is alive and well. When I called on him recently he was eating herring for the fourth time that day. Diana is very creative, yet she has all but run out of recipes. She had boiled them, fried them, steamed them and salted some, and on the second day was down to herring roe omelette.

A grand thing is the creative wife. Compare Coinneach's situation with my own sad Partick plight. When I came home from a hard day's toil, give her her due, she had attempted to deal with my herring, but what a disaster. She had discarded the roes. 'Sure, that's just guts,' *ars ise*. I had a terrible job retrieving them from the wheely-bin, and now the Lawyer has to defend me on what I understand they call a 'domestic'.

Once again I must address a few harsh words to the Gaelic Television Comedy. On Sunday night BBC1 advertised a Gaelic service, from Dunvegan, at 11.30pm. We were especially interested because the Dunvegan minister is a North Lochs man – but at nearly midnight! Do they not realise some of us have to work?

Bad enough that they should show this type of programme on the Sabbath, but when you consider that most of those who are hooked on religious programmes live in old folks' homes where the lights go out at nine o'clock, it is unforgiveable. I hope you are going to do something about it, Doc.

FRIDAY, 22 APRIL 1994

At six o'clock on Monday evening on the main(!) road between Stornoway and Harris I have the rare privilege of driving my own car. For several miles I've been pushing buttons trying to find some local news to no avail. Gaelic would be fine, English would do, but whatever the boy has done to 'our' radio I am permanently tuned into sounds so modern I cannot believe they are also popular.

On any other escape route from Stornoway but the 'main' one, such as those leading to the West Side or Uig, I might have been able to concentrate on the scanning of obscure frequencies for the elusive native tongue, but on our road you need both eyes and both hands to avoid potholes while maintaining a safe position behind a long convoy of tired nurses doing their customary 20 knots.

Despite my handicap I continued to twiddle, and I heard, as I dropped down to Cameron Terrace, a Scottish female voice, and this is what she said: 'I like to plan ahead, I like to know what I'll be doing in 20 years' time.' With these words the transmission was lost and I turned into North Lochs, where tomorrow, never mind '10 years' time', is far from certain.

I suddenly remembered my narrow escape from death at the same corner only 10 hours earlier. At half-past seven, even on our rocky road, one feels safe, because only the shepherds are up. Yet, remembering the history of Elders' Corner – where several prominent members of the Free Church were nearly written off – one naturally, instinctively, slows down, because if it could happen to them it could happen to lesser immortals.

Co-dhiù, in the early morning, I crawled up to the main drag, paused for a second to fiddle with the radio . . . and it was as well I did. Either to the long-gone Elders, or to popular music, I owe my escape from sudden death. Had I edged out, even slowly, as is my norm, I would have been cut in half by a man in a hurry. I don't for a moment blame the man in a hurry. He too would now be up there with the Elders *nach maireann* and it wouldn't have been his fault.

There is no sign to tell the stranger the people of Sleepy Hollow might have arisen and harnessed their horses. You can hardly blame the stranger – when Comhairle nan Eilean is scarcely aware that we exist. And you can hardly blame Comhairle nan Eilean when the North Lochs component of the Whole has consisted of a long string of the deaf and mute.

But to get back to Elders' Corner: before anyone is killed, I must remind those who are not familiar with the terrain the Council house scheme upstream, Cameron Terrace, should normally have already alerted the speeding stranger. Over the years so many children have been injured at Cameron Terrace that had they been mutilated in a more fashionable location questions would have been asked in the House.

When I say fashionable, don't get me wrong. There was a day. Some of the first of us to see flushing toilets saw them in Cameron Terrace. This very early row of joined-up boxes was once the Beverley Hills of the Lake District, where people were proud to ask you in to do your *dileag*.

But in time all the people by the Loch, with some help from DAFS, acquired their own modern homes and Cameron Terrace became just another housing scheme, different from others only in that it had no speed limit.

Naturally no one cared much what these people wanted, but now things have changed dramatically. Many of the residents of Cameron Terrace have bought their houses. Surely now all these Independent councillors will listen. They must realise they are no longer dealing with mere Council tenants and Council tenants' children. The children of men of property deserve to be looked after.

Perhaps a 20-mile-an-hour speed limit would not be too much to ask for. This would mean that the speeding stranger might slow down to 40, which would give the people of Sleepy Hollow a chance to exit. Mark my words, unless some action is taken one of us is going to find himself very soon back-to-back with *Iain an Tàillear nach maireann*, at the right hand of Malcolm Muggeridge.

Since the foul weather began at the beginning of March my wee wife has been somewhat depressed. She is never at her best while still carrying some condition, and, like younger fillies, she hasn't shed her winter coat yet. She has taken to reading temperatures to me from her daily paper. 'Listen to this,' says she: 'it's over 70 in the Greek Islands.'

After last year's experience with Greek George I cannot let her go on her own. In any case, I keep telling her we cannot afford it. We must think of our old age. You know, a few pennies aside for the rainy day and all that. 'Every *£$*%*&* day is a rainy day in this *£*$£*%*&* place,' she would snarl.

I held out until my narrow escape this morning, after which I thought, *Chan eil a-màireach air a ghealltainn*. Forget the silly woman who likes to know what she will be doing in 20 years' time, let's blow it now.

The main problem for us, when she feels the need for the sun, has always been getting to Glasgow while still retaining some cash for the ouzo. I'm delighted to say this problem no longer exists.

On this day of severe shocks, DR at the BA desk had another in store for me. It doesn't seem so very long since I had to give my daughter a loan of one hundred punds for a single flight to Glasgow. Do you know what I'm going to tell you now: today your man gave me two return tickets for that same price.

For 20 years I've been urging BA and CalMac to slash their prices and fill their seats. I guess it was too obvious. People now cannot afford not to go to Glasgow whether they need to or not. I can see them having to lay on extra flights very soon – *if* we are spared to see anything.

FRIDAY, 20 MAY 1994

Terms like Anatolia and Asia Minor will sound old-fashioned to many of our younger readers. Possibly the names mean nothing at all. But those who had their early schooling in Fidigarry, after the last wan, have good cause to remember.

When the bell rang and the Headmaster's class was released, Mòr would unfurl a huge map of the world and begin an hour-long unpaid geography session. Mòr's special interest in Asia Minor (second only to Palestine) was perhaps fired by the importance of the Bosphorus and the cost of the Dardanelles in the previous war. Whatever inspired her, the result of her enthusiasm is that old codgers like me, who learned little else, at least always know where they are.

When we're in Turkey we know we're not in Spain. This, again, will seem silly to the sophisticated readers of this paper, yet I think I can surprise you. To a great many of those who take advantage of cheap holiday flights, a tan is a tan. Turkey will be remembered as being different to Spain or Orlando only from the regular loud call to prayer. This happy state of ignorance does not only apply to the young. At an adjacent table an elderly lady from Milngavie, discussing the menu with her companion, said, 'They're sort of Jewish, you know.' Oh, aye.

Never mind the old, for they have earned their peace of mind. My quarrel, albeit a friendly one, during these two weeks in Turkey, was with the youngish. They are all quite deaf and will all soon be totally deaf.

This, for the old girl and me, is dangerously close to the summer for a holiday. Usually March is as late as I dare risk 'the package', because any later the sun is too high in the sky and draws the young birds out of their shaded tenement eaves. Yet, I thought, Turkey is not a Costa Disco. It should be safe.

At Dalaman airport at midnight Turkish time we were met by a Thomson rep (for it was indeed Clann Thòmais) who ushered us onto a bus – destination unknown. The fact that it was four hours away was the least of my worries, for I can sleep on a goat's back on any mountain road. The tremor of alarm that prevented sleep was the welcome from our delightful rep, the tiny Eastender Liza. In due course I fell in love with her, but the introduction was terrifying.

She told us we were all headed for various hotels in Bodrum and that we were all wonderful and we were all going to have a fabulous time. 'What are you all going to have?' she asked, and I suddenly realised with a quake in the pancreas she expected a reply as if we were all a playschool audience. Several voices of the Parkhead and Ibrox type, well burred with duty-free, responded in their own inimitable fashion. Liza looked worried and so did I. It was never like this in Spain or Butlins.

When we stopped for the 'half-way-house bus a' phloy' routine, and for the Meze, several young ladies who had obviously not risked Asian Minor lavatories emerged from the wee houses with clenched cheeks and worried eyes, but at least it kept them quiet for two hours. At our hotel we finally collapsed, after a brief visit to European toilets, on clean cool sheets at 4.30 in the morning.

At precisely 5am I levitated and came to, about a foot from the ceiling, convinced the trumpet had sounded. And indeed it had. As it happened, our open window was less than a stone's throw from the loudspeaker of the nearest mosque, and the precentor had a foghorn voice. On the way down I must have disturbed my partner, who asked me to try to stop snoring.

During the next three days I learned to welcome the music from the mosque, for it meant a brief respite from a thumping repetitive dirge called 'Like a Virgin' that seemed to be top of the Turkish hit parade.

Breakfast on the first morning held promise of peace.

The swimming pool seemed unnaturally blue under a clear sky, and despite a sleepless night I began to relax. A few people sat around in silence the way they do in strange surroundings, except Alison and Elaine, our ambassadors from Clydebank. They are stretched out more or less naked in the morning sun unaware they are in a country where women normally cover their heads. And already they are on first-name terms with the manager. 'Genghis, turn the music on, will you,' they command. He seems happy to comply, and unconcerned with their wanton display.

All too often you read old fogies sermonising about noisy youf, but my guess is they don't know what they're talking about; they haven't been incarcerated with them in a small town like Bodrum. Immediately I start to plan my escape.

On my way to the harbour I call in at a music shop, perchance to find some pipe or fiddle music with which to retaliate, but they cater only for the Alisons. Down at the beautiful old harbour that attracted so many artists in happier days my spirits lift a little. A forest of masts as far as the eye can see, and they are all for hire.

Without a moment's hesitation I book a day afloat on a magnificent 40-foot gullet (varnished pine on sturdy oak ribs) and settle down aft to wait for the minimum eight people required to cover the fuel costs. The few people on board seem old enough to be harmless, but then at the last minute Harry Enfield's slobs embark with a noisy uncontrollable brat and a tape recorder the size of a suitcase. For the first time in my life I wish I was back home cutting peat. Had a sudden gale not forced us back early, I would now be doing time in Bodrum Castle Dungeon for the manslaughter of the slobs.

Neither Mòr nor Ataturk could ever have visualised modern Turkey.

*   *   *

Yet it still offers peace for the likes of Neil and Keith, two gay guys from London. They do not get harassed and abused here as they do in most places. Yet to my dismay they too are into modern music that gets louder as it becomes more tuneless. Still, through the numbing effect of raki and lager, I find myself among the last 10 at the bar.

A natural grouping has begun to form and plans for various atrocities are made. As the senior person present, I feel it is my duty to keep an eye on these youngsters. Perhaps it doesn't really matter where you are after all.

For a whole week I write one thousand words of accurate diary each day, but I fear this record of lewd and reckless orgies will not be suitable for our superior paper. Perhaps I'll try it on the *P & J*.

FRIDAY, 27 MAY 1994

Somewhere in the darkest crevices of the Secret Service there is a man employed whose work is to tell the Post Office whenever a resident of this country goes abroad. It is easy to imagine and even easier to understand his coded messages: 'Such and such a house empty, unload now.'

Upon receipt of this joyful news, the Postmaster General who stores bad news until the off – in this case Eddie Mackenzie – calls the boys and asks them if they want some overtime. 'Several bags to be dumped in Leurbost, boys; no rush, you have a fortnight. Use the garage if the lobby overflows. But remember to keep dry all envelopes written in red.'

Well, I have news for you, Eddie: you were wasting your overtime on this occasion, for the house was not empty. I suspect it was constantly far from empty. From the way the furniture was rearranged it looked as if some games had taken place that would have been easier to accommodate in the community hall. And most of the Royal Mail had been shovelled under the stairs so the doors could be opened. Some had probably been used to fire the boiler when conventional fuel had run out, and judging from the lack of official brown envelopes, I suspect these must give off a good heat. In any case, that will be my excuse in the near future for not responding to Final Demands.

What strange rituals took place can only be guessed at from the amphitheatre reconstruction in the 'living room'. As it happened, I had spent some time on holiday studying the Greek and Roman styles and was immediately able to identify the 'living room' as classic Roman. The 180-degree spectator accommodation was focused on the glass-fronted fire through which someone had evidently fallen. I think we can assume the brown-envelope fuel had run out, because we have no reports from the Ospadal or Fire Brigade.

The scene in the garden was partly hidden from the main road by the sudden flowering of shrubs and trees. Nevertheless, the broken hammock was visible on approach, but certain items of discarded clothing, subsequently found in the knee-high grass, are impossible to explain.

While all this – whatever it was – was going on the spaniel Smut was in his element. Every time he emerged from his favourite muddy stream he chose a different bed, obviously delighted with the new world where anarchy reigned and all the subjects were happy. The same happy subjects who made use of the facilities were clearly house-trained to the same level as the spaniel. Smut, whatever else you can accuse him of, doesn't go to bed in his wellies.

But be warned, all ye parents of North Lochs, I have done some useful detective work, and I'm going after the wealthier Daddies. From the small gap in the glass-fronted room heater I can deduce the culprit could not have been Dòmhnall Mòr an Troich nor Big John. This leaves Mac Don Neil and Mac Alec George. As Mac Don Neil is notoriously laid-back, while Mac Alec George is a lively swinger from the chandeliers like his uncle Tabaidh, I must go after the Crossbost Elder.

The Elder has amassed a considerable fortune, but he is a fair man and will not want this dragged through the courts.

If ever we go away again, I think we'll leave the dog on his own and send the boy to the kennels.

Apart from the football dents in the kitchen wall there does not seem to be any serious structural damage, and in time she was able to clear a path through the debris. Among the many letters, we were sorry to find, too late, several invitations. One from the people of Ranish to a wee hooley in honour of the Rev Alec Murdo's elevation to Moderator obviously arrived the day after we left. I understand they had one of the wildest nights since the entire village used to celebrate New Year in Bo's.

Although, normally, it is difficult to choose a gift for a man who has everything, they tell me there was remarkably little argument about what present to give the Reverend. They were unanimous in their choice of a handsome clock. Not to be outdone – they seldom are – the Crossbost congregation collected for a small token of appreciation and, lo and behold, did they not settle for a watch.

What is it with all these timepieces? Here we have a man whose only measure of time is eternity, so they shower him with clocks and watches. Do you suppose they're trying to tell him something?

And all this time there I was trudging in the footsteps of St Paul round the ancient city of Ephesus. I'm sure Alec Murdo will forgive me for missing his party. If I learned nothing else in my travels I can at least now give him the correct pronunciation of Efesos, and he will be pleased to hear I picked up a cheap duty-free watch.

Among the invitations there are, as always, several from thon Gaelic crowd in Stornoway. They have destroyed what little confidence I had. Hardly a month goes past they don't try to get me into one writing school or another. The parallel with Alec Murdo and the timepieces is all too clear. Don't think I am not appreciative of their concern; I can take a hint. But, like most people of my age, I am too busy earning a living to go to school.

In any case, for us, it is all too late. If a man's beard has turned grey and he still hasn't written, it is doubtful if he ever will. Although I cannot see that anyone can be taught to write, as such, those who do try to write need help and encouragement. They should concentrate their resources on the young and hopeful and forget the crumblies. And, of course, there is no encouragement like financial reward.

Even now, as I write – with my other hand – a wee sketch for Marisa, she sends me yet another kind invitation to attend a writing class. How do I know my efforts are not being held up in front of a class as an example of what not to do. I too can be hurt, you know. A more sensitive artist would have, by now, given up in despair. In fact I am kept going only through Saul Bellow's letters of encouragement.

FRIDAY, 3 JUNE 1994

In a world where the pace of change grows ever speedier and more confusing for those of us creeping up in years, it is nice to know some things – or at least some people – never change. We embrace with relief the few remaining certainties, and we cling to them lovingly lest they too become strange and foreign.

Among my small band of close friends very few could still say they are the same men they were 12 years ago. Some have continued the struggle. They've ploughed manfully onwards in the New World, bewildered and immeasurably saddened, and they've let themselves age quite unnecessarily. A few have sensibly withdrawn from the race and become hermits. These few I expect to see re-emerge in 10 years' time fresh-faced and unwrinkled.

I am often asked what happened to those who used to feature in the column regularly – men like the West End Tory and the Barvas Navigator. The West End Tory retired to meditate in solitude when the Thatcher revolution didn't turn out as planned. The Navigator also withdrew. They are the type I expect to see coming out at 60 when the rest of us are worn out.

The Navigator, of course, became a Da and settled down on the Machair. In the days when he used to fly in from distant corners of the earth I would see him every two months or so. Now I don't see him at all, although I hear the occasional report of him walking the shore with the heir.

It has to be admitted the Navigator had more reason than most to retire from the hectic New World to the seclusion of Barvas. In addition to the trauma of a late addition to the family, he suffered a terrible shock on his only venture back to 'life'.

He was persuaded with a huge amount of money to leave the croft for a few weeks and fly to Singapore. All he had to do then was bring a new ship back to Port Said. Not much to ask of an old sea dog, you might think. They hadn't told him the ship was completely computerised, but they had left a user's guide on the bridge.

He never had much time for modern technology. After several days of going round in circles in dull cloudy weather in the Indian Ocean, unable to communicate with the oriental crew, he reached a stage of anxiety where he considered consulting the manual. The sky eventually cleared, the sun and the stars appeared, so he was able to set a course for the Suez Canal.

He never leaves dry soil now unless conditions are suitable for his windsurfer, and even then, they tell me, he carries a compass.

Although these boys have changed, I live in hope they will change back some day. In the meantime we are grateful for stars of the old Diary who never change. One such person is world-famed anthropologist Macpherson. Fresh into London from a recent study of the little people who live around the Bay of Bengal, he asked me to meet him and Moira at 11.26am in Tarbert, Harris.

Why I agreed I'll never understand, because he has caused me more grief than any landlord ever caused the people of Lochs. Anyway, he has a wife who looks better with every passing year, so I made my way to Tarbert.

At 11.26 the boat was still some way off and looking to be at least five minutes late, which I knew would aggravate him considerably. Such lapses would, to him, smack of disorganisation and poor leadership. As soon as the faces on board became discernible I could sense his agitation. He was at the head, naturally, of a group of passengers on the upper deck and visibly writhing with the urge to take command.

Depending on the state of the tide, the gangway will be lowered to the second deck or hoisted to the top, where a huddle of suitcase-carrying voyagers were looking to someone to make a decision much as a flock of sheep look to a shepherd. Sure enough, the old Base Commander led them down below just in time to see the gangway being lifted over his head to the upper deck. There was nothing for it but to steer them all back up again, although it wasn't easy in the narrow alleyways. He doesn't change, you know.

Anyone else would have left it at that and pretended he hadn't seen me pretending I hadn't noticed, but not himself. His early training in psychology has been forgotten or subugated to his need to be in the right all the time. The incident was analysed all the way up the Clisham, down the other side and for another hour until Balallan. The 'unusual' design of the Tarbert pier was brought into the equation, but he eventually came up with the feeble excuse that the lower deck had been painted. Moira and I agreed that must indeed have been the reason for the gangway decision, and I foolishly added that people often made the same mistake.

This didn't please him at all. He asked us not to be so bloody patronising and if we had 'nothing intelligent to contribute' it would be better to keep quiet.

Fortunately, he was distracted by the celebrations at Balallan, which had to be explained in detail. I tried as best I could to tell him about the Park Deer Raid, which interested him a great deal. He didn't actually say 'what they should have done', but I could see him thinking it. For the rest of the afternoon I could tell he was preoccupied with these events of one hundred years ago.

Of course he wasn't satisfied with my version of the raid. He insisted I bring him along to the night's festivities where he could hear and meet Murdanie Mast, Calum Kennedy and other heroes from the South.

At the end of the night he wondered aloud why South Lochs, despite the early hardship, managed to produce so much talent, while the North, well . . . He didn't finish, because he knows the unspoken insult hurts the most.

I look forward to seeing him next year – unchanged.

Something that did change, and for the better: for the first time this century a dance in Balallan Hall did not end with a fight. And something that will never change . . . Where do you suppose certain well-kent faces were while the rest of the population was distracted by the celebrations? Where else!

FRIDAY, 17 JUNE 1994

PHYSICIST, HEAL THYSELF

Until I was recently struck down in the prime of life I had no idea hypertension was the most common ailment in the north and west of Scotland. Unless my friends and patients had the complexion of a cuckoo wrasse I never bothered to gauge their pressure.

Occasionally I felt I had to do something about the sort of large florid lady that used to be so plentiful in Lochs. You know the type with the dangerous rollers, running south from the shoulder-blades, like a bicycle inner tube bulging through the weak wall of a tyre. Naturally, then I took some action, for we know what eventually happens to the inner tube.

'*Cha robh pressure air an latha b' fheàrr a bha e,*' as Cailleach an Dèacoin used to say; and this is the level at which many of us viewed 'the pressure'. Something good for a comic turn and associated with the aged and infirm.

The sad but true story is very different. The young, in enormous numbers – yes, some even younger, paler and thinner than I – are afflicted. I very much regret I did not make a scientific study of this problem long ago. Quite clearly, it is much too important to be left solely in the hands of chemical merchants whose main aim in life is to manufacture cheap concoctions that can be sold at a huge profit.

The solution to hypertension, unless I'm very much mistaken, and we know how unlikely that is, lies with the selfless physicists who seek no more reward for their lives' work than a Nobel Prize.

The nearest thing to a physicist I have to hand at present is Councillor Macdonald. He specialises in thermodynamics, and therein, I suspect, lies the cause of hypertension and the eventual solution. We must bear in mind the average doctor's knowledge of physics does not extend beyond Boyle's Law, while the common chemist has only reached the stage of making gas and plenty of it. Contrast that with the Councillor, who has a grasp of the subject to first year university level and would have gone further had it not got too difficult at a time when he was distracted by spiritual matters. He is very thorough and has agreed to become author-in-chief of our eagerly-awaited paper on pressure.

Once his enthusiasm was fired for our exciting new project, sheep and transportation committees were forgotten. He was very quick to compare and spot the similarities between the bubbling, swirling fluid we call blood and the atmosphere in general with its complex partial pressures. Last week he disappeared into his study with his Venturi Tube, and textbooks so heavy only he could carry. He wasn't seen for two days, after which he appeared sweating, pale and haggard and nearly bald from head-scratching. He quickly swallowed a cup of coffee, muttered something about velocity potential, the importance of 'f' in the vorticity equation, the great height of the people of Finland, and returned to his papers asking not to be disturbed.

For a third day we crept about in silence barely able to contain our excitement. It was too clear the great man was nearing a solution – you could feel it in the air. At the end of day three he appeared before us and threw a sheaf of closely-typed papers on the floor.

'Damn fools,' he cried. 'They've obviously never taken coriolis parameters into consideration. Gravitational forces in our circumstances are very much secondary to the effect of the angular velocity of the earth. Add to that the violence of centripetal force in conjunction with the eightsome reel, and I think we have solved the problem. The answer is, in short,' he said, 'there is no problem. Given our monthly latitude and our habit of walking bent against wind, our blood pressure is fine. Readings of 220 over 110 are as they should be for these parts.' What a man!

We noticed with some alarm he had been working in pounds per square inch but he said this was to make his paper easier to understand for boys who are accustomed to working on tractors. Usually the Councillor is a firm believer in plain speaking and simple language.

'There is nothing so complex,' he often says, 'that it cannot be simplified to a level where it can be understood in Callanish and Portnalong. People don't appreciate the work done by the average Lewis heart until you tell them that miraculous machine, for 70 years or more, pumps out blood at a pressure exactly equivalent to our planet's atmospheric pressure at the top of Mount Everest.'

Of course it will take time for our hero's findings to be accepted. There is nothing quite like the scientific establishment for jealousy and bitchiness. The biochemists will be furious that we physicists have forged ahead of them in the blood pressure business. Quite apart from all the wrangling, we physicists are nothing if not modest. We are always prepared to admit there is a remote chance we may be wrong. For this reason you must continue to believe the average Lewis blood pressure is abnormal and do your best to reduce it.

This is not always easy without drugs. However, I believe I can point you in the right direction – or perhaps I should say two directions.

Take time off the next chance you get to study the man called Callan who owns and works in Marybank Garage. His is the style you want to emulate. He works away steadily from dawn to dusk at a steady pace. He never seems to hurry and he has time to pause and listen to your troubles. Because of the even tenor of his ways, he doesn't have troubles of his own. You will note he whistles tunefully as he wrestles with steel and rubber. Remember the echo of whistling from every hillside among young boys attending cattle when we were young! There was no pressure then and there need not be any pressure now, if you follow Callan's example.

That is one way, but now I'll tell you another. Perhaps you know or have heard of Chris Kelso who does terrible violence to the English language in the Greysheet's 'Golf Notes'.

Although this man is scarlet in eye and cheek, he does not, miraculously, suffer from hypertension. He looks exactly like the sort I would have treated in the old days without bothering with the pressure gauge, yet he is cardiovascularily sound. The reason is simple. He spits out the badness without inhibition. It is almost impossible for your man to pass a fellow human being on street or playing field without a venomous outpouring. A constant stream of abuse directed against one and all leaves his own passages relatively clean and pure.

This second example is not, I realise, a course many would choose. Yet I cannot help thinking, had my own pen been similarly charged with vitriol, I might be a lot healthier today.

FRIDAY, 24 JUNE 1994

All over the world at this moment (in history) people who appreciate the greatest game are laid back on their sofas waiting for the Brazilian footballers to strut their stuff on television. The men and women of the blighted island of Lewis are the exception. We, unfortunately, had a gust of wind over 25 knots this afternoon (Monday). Ever since we had the National Grid (whatever that is) thrust upon us, the light goes out when the wind blows.

It is probably a coincidence that our electricity supply became intermittent and unreliable at about the same time the service was taken away from the people and privatised. When we were dependent on the little powerhouse down by the Sandwick shore we seldom experienced a blackout unless we had northerly hurricane with hail, and even then it was soon fixed. But now that our power is generated in Scotland, we spend much of the time wrapping our frozen foods in newspapers. I understand the captain of this industry gets paid about half a million pounds a year when he should be taken out on the moor, hung from a 30,000 volt wire and thrashed to within an inch of his life.

The sad aspect of this continuing saga is that there is no chance of ever reverting to our safe and reliable source. Even if a referendum was held tomorrow and we were unanimous in our wish to have our power supplied from Battery Road, we wouldn't get our way because we do not live in a democracy, despite their frequent cries to the contrary. Sadly, hardly anything that has been stolen from the people in the last 15 years can be restored, nor can the gravy train for the few be put into reverse. It is doubtful if it can even be stopped no matter who is in power.

To dwell on these matters when we should be watching Brazil is doubly depressing. From Brazil we expect something special. Perhaps we expect too much. As if they didn't have enough to live up to, someone at the BBC had the far from bright idea, a few weeks ago, of showing the magical Brazilian team of 1970. It was bad enough that those of us who remembered them the first time round should have our hopes falsely raised, but now we have a younger generation who have been conned into thinking that is what it might be like.

So much for Brazil. BBC2 has not recovered from the afternoon's powercut, but Grampian has survived to offer us Holland against Saudi Arabia. I can hardly believe this and definitely won't stay up to watch the second half. These big square-headed Dutchmen, like our own spoilt brats, are obviously paid far too much to care about trying very hard. The undernourished desert Bedouin, on the other hand, are giving all they've got and are running rings round the Lowlanders.

The Saudi boys have no doubt been fuelled by an incentive more stimulating than the offer of money – possibly the promise they can keep all their limbs if they score – but that is no excuse for the Dutch performance. Until a few years ago the Saudis hadn't heard of football. Their games were much rougher and played on the backs of their camels, yet here they are a goal up as I prepare for bed. My only consolation is that Scotland were mercifully eliminated in time to avoid humiliation at the feet of some barbaric dictatorship.

My other concern, following the Saudis' gutsy display, is that thon gang of oil-rich Arabs will tire of horse-racing and start buying into football. On other second thoughts, perhaps there might be something to be said for an Arab invasion. If, for instance, they were to buy Hibs or Hearts, perhaps these clubs could afford fresh young legs instead of having to rely on ageing rejects from the Glasgow clubs.

I suspect, though, it is too late for anyone to save Scottish or for that matter English football. Children's football is much too organised from an early age. Leagues and competition when they should be playing all summer from dawn till dusk with 25-a-side and plenty substitutes. (Of course, I forget it is not easy to find 25 these days with that damn pill.)

All of which reminds me of the Irish. Don't let us forget their glorious start against the Italians. I couldn't help wondering which team the Pope would be rooting for in this tricky situation, and I put the question to an Irish girl friend. 'Never mind the Pope,' she says, 'God was on our side.' Jackie Charlton must be doing some marvellous missionary work on that dark island.

We must sadly put the serious business of football aside for a moment to concentrate on another tournament with only three main players – Blair, Prescott and the woman Beckett.

Regrettably, I was not consulted about the runners in this race, otherwise I would have chosen Robin Cook. His racing column in a Lowland paper is most entertaining, but more important, he is the worst tipster at the game. This suggests to me he doesn't waste his time on prolonged study of horseflesh but instead gets on with serious work.

Someone suggested somewhere Mr Cook was not very pretty. Who in the name of God wants a pretty Prime Minister? As a matter of fact, Mr Cook looks distinguished the way a statesman should and does not seem unlike Abraham Lincoln in profile. Still, he seems to have been ill-advised and has not, as they say, 'allowed his name to go forward'.

That leaves us with the aforementioned threesome. Until yesterday I intended to cast my vote for Beckett, but then I saw something on television so disturbing I now intend to go for Prescott. This poor Beckett woman had obviously listened and paid attention to the nasty cracks about Cook's appearance and had taken it to herself. She allowed herself to be dolled up for the cameras as if she was auditioning for Hollywood. A most disgusting spectacle. True, she does not have what is usually regarded as a pretty face; but, in her natural state, I find her interesting and sexy (ah, the beholder's eye), Sadly, the painted version reminds of old colonial women who drank too much and spent too long in the sun.

I had intended going along with Blair but his silence on the rail strike disturbs. He should have encouraged the strikers and offered them some incentive to stop the chief crooks' plans to make the railways a suitable gift for their friends. Also I would have liked to hear Blair threatening to tax the rich. This leaves me with the rough Yorkshireman. Does it matter if he doesn't speak in sentences as long as he frightens those who steal from the poor.

Apologies to the keen scientists who phoned to complain about last week's 'monthly latitude'. The master's handwritten note read 'northerly'. I don't know what a monthly latitude could be unless it's what we take with the bank.

Friday, 15 July 1994

My late father didn't leave much in the way of wealth. Four score and three years of hard labour on this earth and all he left me was one old salmon net. Mind you, he didn't want much, any more than I do. Just enough for a decent burial – a few pennies to clear the slate with Al Crae (what a fine name for an undertaker, I've often thought).

When I say I don't want much I believe that to be true, but I still wouldn't mind the occasional wild salmon to see what all the fuss is about. For 10 years or more I ate only the farmed stuff. I published so much propaganda about farmed salmon I eventually came to believe what I wrote. Not that there is anything wrong with a properly starved farmed fish, yet it has to be admitted it does not compare with the fat fish that has been around a bit and seen the world. But there again, you can get a lean, dry wild salmon in the same way you sometimes get a poor herring.

Anyway, for the first time in 11 years I thought I would dust down the old fellow's net and try my hand in the uncaged ocean. I should have suspected the worst when I couldn't find Ansag's bonnet – the one that brought me so much luck in the old days when we were young and green and swimming in the corn.

To prepare for the wild I had to kit myself out in the Millionaire Cobbler's shop. Probably, like me, there are readers out there who withdrew from the world some time ago and have no idea of the full horror of present-day reality. Did you know, for instance, that a waterproof jacket now costs seventy pounds sterling? I think perhaps we should start calling your man the Billionaire Cobbler.

All that is by the way and doesn't take us any nearer the action, but just hold on. On second thoughts, don't. Perhaps I'll spare you the gory details. Suffice to say that my old man's only treasure is now in the custody of that latter-day pirate the Fishery Protection vessel *Moidart*. For two days the taxpayer's multi-million pound *Moidart* has been on duty between Point and Cromore. I only mention this because the taxpayer has a right to know where his money goes.

But I have news for these boys on the *Moidart*. When my friend Calum Macdonald is Secretary of State for Scotland the *Moidart* will go the same way as the Royal Yacht *Britannia*.

The sad irony of a sad tale is that the sea around Lewis this year is boiling with salmon. Old hands say they have never seen so many, and still they would have us believe the whole lot belongs to three or four faceless foreigners. I am told the well-known Grimersta lackey, Whitehouse, has been trying to prevent the honest men of Carloway from fishing off the rocks with rod and line. It is astonishing that this man has not come to a bad end. Clearly the people of Uig are a gentle race. I would bet your man wouldn't have lasted a season in Balallan.

Now, I realise fish have to be protected, and salmon is no different. I do not suggest for a minute we should have a free-for-all. What would happen then is the wealthy would take over from a different angle. Those who could afford big boats and bigger nets would block off the Atlantic between Rockall and Bernera and the Minch between the Butt and Cape Wrath. There would be little left for 83-year-old crofters like Murdanie Mast.

While we wait for the salmon ranching that can only come after a prolonged spell of decent government, I would like to make a few suggestions on the management of salmon fishing.

As things stand at the moment, the only people who benefit are the manufacturers of monofilament. Fishery Protection vessels that should be at deep sea work hang around estuaries scooping up monofilament nets as fast as they can be produced. The obvious answer is to ban monofilament. This could easily be done at source because we must assume factories are easier to track and nab than alleged poachers.

In any case, fishing with monofilament requires no skill. It is deadly not only for fish but for everything that swims in the sea except the dirty seal. Let us bring this foul method of fishing to an end immediately.

To avoid costly redundancies the crew of the *Moidart* could be retained to police and control salmon fishing with ordinary nylon nets. A fixed number of nets of certain length per licensed boat, and salmon would be, as it should be, just another fish. This, I realise, would be unacceptable to those who are allergic to any sort of work that is legal, but that cannot be helped.

When I tried to contact my friends in the House to instruct them on the subject of salmon, I was told both Calum and Cunninghame North were at the Barra Fèis. I am not sure that what we need are members who seem to have time for enjoyment. The sort of MP who would appeal to older Lewismen would never take a day off to wallow in wordly pleasure – when there is work to be done.

Talking of pleasure, the Open is under way in Stornoway and the strangest things you could have imagined have taken place.

Not only have I not qualified for the later stage of Golf Week, which surprised a great many people, but the Good Doctor Taylor has, which surprised even more.

DT only started playing two years ago, and I am pleased to say I took him under my wing as partner in the Winter League when no one else would have anything to do with him. It is gratifying to see, at last, so much of my hard work being rewarded.

As chance would have it, DT has to play the Lawyer in the semi-final of the over-forty-at-least section. The Lawyer was once a five handicap and has been playing golf since he was four years old. He tells us he has applied for membership in the bowling club, for if Dr Taylor beats him he will never again lift a club in anger. Today (Thursday) is the day, and I am not too proud to offer to caddy for the Good Doctor.

I expect the celebrations will last until very near the Sabbath. Ah, Mary Flora of Auchinloch, if only you knew what things have come to. Have a nice day.

Friday, 22 July 1994

The Garrabost Historian has been complaining in recent years, when he comes home in July, about the lack of insects on the croft – bluebottles especially. I was fairly sure the shortage of bluebottles was caused by too many sheep and the shortage of that other fly by the scarcity of cattle.

Overgrazing by far too many sheep meant the long wet summer grass of old never got a chance. And without cattle to attract their own particular dirty fans with their big beautiful pancakes, it seemed clear why we suffered a shortage of flies. But the Historian would have none of it. He maintained the 10 year herring ban was the cause of all our misfortune, including the lack of insects. No one else I know worried about or complained about the missing bluebottles – they were happy to do without – but then no one else lives so much in the past as the Historian.

Perhaps I should explain for the younger readers the tie between the bluebottle, the common housefly and the herring. In the not so wasteful days before kitchen paper very fresh fish had to be dried in the sun before frying. Most housewives had their drying boards. Only in Point and Lochs were we so poor the herring were draped artistically on the peat stack, where they were lavishly garnished by bluebottles. Not that those who had 'done well' and progressed to the drying boards escaped the flies – they just missed out on subtle flavours imparted by the peat. (With or without a board the additional atraction of herring might have been enough to get Dr Finlay's stack accepted by the Tate.)

But all that is by the way, for the bluebottles are back, and I'll tell you why. They are back because the barbecue brought them back. I don't know for sure why this South African craze started to spread north, but spread it certainly has. I could have understood the braaifisk having spread as far north as the south of England, where the weather is sometimes suitable. Certainly Tiree, from a climatological point of view, would seem the furthest north you would expect to see the braai.

But this is not the case. No croft is right without its braai – as far north as the Butt o' Lewis and, for all we know, as far north as Unst. The Crofter's Store in Stornoway, they tell me, now sells more charcoal than Layers Mash. I often give thanks my granny didn't live to see the day.

The barbecue season in Lewis starts early. It has to because the only dry weather comes in May. Unfortunately, at that same time a cold searing wind from the Siberian Tundra drives across the Baltic and the North Sea all the way to Bernera. Still, to the man with the new braai, the only temperature that matters is that of the charcoal. On go the balaclavas and out come the salmon steaks. A guest list – or hit list – is drawn up for the great outdoor feast. Guests or victims are selected for their hardiness. Unless you are of the blood of those prisoners of war who fought with the Germans on the Eastern Front, you will not last an evening at a Lewis barbecue in May.

At this very moment, it is a safe bet someone in these northerly latitudes is slaving over hot charcoal embers while his unfortunate guests try to keep the circulation going with drink they brought along themselves.

As early as the tenth of May, on a bright sunny day, I was asked to attend the first 'picnic' of the season in a remote village called Miavaig on the west coast of Lewis. Miavaig is a picturesque little township where the Gaelic can sometimes still be heard. Except for the scenery, Miavaig has little going for it. Yet, although it is a full hour's drive from Stornoway and the comforts we associate with the east coast, they still have their barbecues.

As it happened, I was fresh back from Turkey and had grown accustomed to strolling about in the sleeveless pullover. On the day, the north-easterly had a fierce bite to it. To please the hosts, we crouched against the hillside and ate outside, but we suffered for our good manners. My wife soon went down with bronchitis and the chill aggravated my arthritis to such an extent our own blood pressure reached a plateau from which it may never descend.

Before we had fully recovered we were commanded to attend a feast in Tong, where there is evidence of wealth and the barbecue is a permanent fixture. It was a cloudy drizzly night with a wind off Broad Bay, but this didn't put them off. A tent was erected in the garden so that we could be inside while pretending to be outside. To make the situation almost tolerable, the Good Doctor provided an ocean of strong drink and made a bonfire of a neighbour's outhouse, but still my health suffered and the gauge read even higher.

(My only memory of a more ludicrous sight than a man at a braai in cold drizzle is that of late-of-these-parts Macpherson, performing over hot charcoal in a valley between two volcanoes in Java, where he could have fried the steak on the patio.)

I noticed at both the Lewis venues that the households sported dining rooms and tables big enough to do justice to a Free Church Manse, yet there we were eating outside in the cold. I realise it is difficult to avoid the sort of guest who invariably sets the curtains on fire or the one who breaks valuable furniture, but surely there is still no need to drive the majority out on the grass.

The business of eating itself is impossible. If you somehow manage not to burn yourself retrieving a carbonised sausage from the cinders, someone else will probably stab you while he tries to balance his glass of punch on a paper plate. At the same time you must mutter as best you can through chattering teeth how much you are enjoying yourself.

When the weather warms up a little – when the temperature climbs over 50 – then the flies come out. If you managed to avoid being stabbed in the early season, you will now certainly be laid low by insects lured away from the nearest septic tank by the aroma of your barbecued steak. That is unless you were hardened in your youth, like myself and the Historian, on a constant diet of Herring and Bluebottle.

The sooner Environmental Health take a hand and ban these spectacles, the sooner we'll recover a measure of good health.

Friday, 12 August 1994

Twenty-three is a fine age at which to retire, don't you think? You scrimp and save to try and give them a smattering of education, all the while denying yourself the meanest luxury, only to have them tell you, at the fine old age of 23 after one year in work: 'That's it – I've had enough, I'm retiring.'

Right now, as we speak, the daughter is off to New York and she hasn't even got a gun. New York is but the first stop on the way round the world, but it is the only one I worry about. This is probably because I have never been there – fear of our old friend the unknown. Had she said she was going to live rough for a while in Beirut or going camping in the jungles of Borneo, I might have felt a little uneasy, but New York is something else.

If we can believe what we see on TV, the place is full of drug-crazed people with guns. It is even worse, they say, than Glasgow. I will feel happier when she reaches the bush.

I cannot say I'm too happy about these Greyhound buses either. Too often we've seen Charles Bronson and the boys blasting away with pistols much the same as they did in the Wild West. For some reason Greyhound buses often feature. They seem to attract psychopaths. Still, the main thing is they are cheap.

New York's finest, they used to call the police, but I fear this has changed. I have advised the daughter to walk around all the time with her hands up. They tell me if you reach suddenly for a handkerchief New York's finest are likely to shoot you dead. In the land of the free their most treasured freedom is the freedom to shoot their neighbours. Although I have never been a mollycoddling parent, the soonest I hear they've said *soraidh* to New York the better.

Although I said I'd never been to New York, this doesn't mean I don't know it. Of course I do, like the back of my hand. We have all known New York from an early age. We got to know the Bronx and the skyline of Manhattan before we knew the Skyeline of Skye. We saw all these places from the 1/9s in the old cinema.

The best guide of them all was probably Damon Runyon, with whom I passed many an afternoon on the corner of 42nd Street keeping a lookout for Harry the Horse and Bugsy (who minded the baby).

A bit later on in life, I confess to having wasted many a night with Dorothy Parker and Thurber in the Algonquin throwing them back while recording each other's wisecracks. This was what some of us were at while our peers were having Donnchadh Bàn thrashed into them. I'm very much afraid the old town has changed a lot, which is why I worry about the daughter.

When she hits Chicago I'm afraid she is on her own. Al Capone and his gangsters I hardly knew at all, so I cannot help her, but if she makes it to the cold North-West she will remember much of it from our dreams and our early travels with Jack London.

I am only the teeniest bit concerned, yet I cannot help remembering panicky phone calls when she first went to Glasgow. 'Dear Father, which art in Leurbost, help us this day. Liz and I are on Byres Road but we cannot find the University.'

Can you imagine the cost of phone calls from Singapore? 'Dear Da, I cannot find Bugis St. P.S. Everyone looks the same. Ten times I stopped to speak to that man who owned the Chinese resturant in Stornoway but he pretends not to know me.'

Perhaps we were all a bit like that when we first went 'away'. In London at 17 (although of course I hadn't retired) I was shocked on the very first day when an old friend went past me in his grey Austin A60 and didn't stop. But I must have been very quick on the uptake, for it didn't take me very long to learn there were quite a few A60s in London.

The old woman is being a bit of an old woman about the parting. One has to be hard on them at times like this. I've had to say quite fiercely to her 'Stop it, woman', when she makes remarks like: 'That could be her aeroplane going overhead now.' This cannot go on. I mean, will the old one be saying in eight months' time: 'She should be arriving in Surabaya today.'

During the last few weeks my investments have done very badly, which naturally means resources are extremely low. When one's portfolio is top-heavy with a four-legged commodity this is to be expected. The highs can become suddenly very low.

This is why I'm afraid I was not able to help the daughter in the usual way. Not that I would have helped her with hard cash, because that way they don't get to see the world: all they get to know if they have money is the inside of hotels.

After all, Carnegie's old man didn't send him off with many pieces of silver. He went with nothing. You will detect I have not given up on her staying in America to make her fortune so she can send money back home in the old-fashioned way. Even better if she sends an invitation from the beach house in Southern California for the Da to come and spend the autumn of his days in the sun.

In the meantime I'm afraid she'll have to compete with a million other refugees washed up on America's shores for dishwashing jobs to keep body and soul together.

I might have seemed mean to her with money, but I did promise to phone acquaintances in distant corners warning them to look out for her. They cannot miss her in British Columbia coming over the Rockies in long crofting strides carrying some salt herring.

Somehow I think she'll be back. Twenty-three is just a wee bit young to retire to a travelling life, even in this new age.

FRIDAY, 19 AUGUST 1994

For what could very well turn out to be the last time, I crossed the Minch last week in the MV *Suilven*. Not only do I sense, the way ancient boatmen do, the old girl is coming towards the end, I have good reason to suspect I'm not far behind her.

It would be quite fitting that we should give up the struggle together, for haven't we loved and fought this last quarter-century with the passion of a Frenchwoman. Yes, I'm afraid the old girl is beginning to make the sort of creaking noises below the water-line that we all do when we reach a certain age. She is merely saying I am tired and I need a rest.

She does not mean by this she wants a rest when the Summer Isles hove in sight, as her skippers seem to think; she means a proper rest when her day is done. While she is still on the run she would be happier to be run at full steam ahead and never mind the tourists who want to see dolphins. Some of us have work to do.

Until last week I hadn't crossed for a while, yet I knew many things were not right the moment I boarded. At first I suspected they were holding some sort of mariners' convention, for I had never seen so many strange men in uniform. Sensing a story, I went in search of a crew member, but I couldn't find any. It took several nautical miles to dawn on me we had been taken over by aliens, above and below deck.

Quickly I steered Maggie in the direction of the galley, although she protested it was too early to eat – even of Roddy's superlative fare. She need not have worried. Although the soup was cold and grey as ever, it was obviously not Roddy's – nor even Cromarty's, for, if nothing else, these boys could put a good fatty crust on a soup. There was clearly a strange hand on the chopper this day.

Not only was Roddy gone, the entire crew had been replaced with unfamiliar changelings. I retired to the bar to dwell on these matters with a comforter of Guinness, but even this was not as it should be. My barman, although polite and efficient as aliens always are, was for all that still an alien. I could hardly raise a highly confidential subject such as the missing crew with an alien.

As I prowled hither and thither through alleyways and Bosun's stores in search of clues, I finally happened upon an old crew member, Murchadh Shearraidh, who was travelling in disguise with his wife (his wife was the disguise). Obviously a scared man, he whispered quickly: 'They have gone to the Clyde.' And he disappeared quickly into a lifeboat.

Now, then, what we have to find out is why a ship's crew should suddenly, after all this time, desert and head for the Clyde, where I understand conditions are much as they were with the old East India Company. Could it possibly mean they sensed the same as I did? Do they too know the *Suilven* has not long to go? Can they not bear to see the old girl suffer?

Some of us can understand. Men should not be ashamed to weep.

Although I too have been threatened with the scrapyard by my eminent colleagues, I have hopes I might still outlive the *Suilven*. My consultant not only gives me hope of some more time, he promises that if I make some radical changes in my style in 10 years' time I may be able to pass myself off as a man of 70.

I feel good about this. It is nothing to boast about, but I'm the only one among my contemporaries who has a certificate of roadworthiness, never mind the promise of another 10 years. But the comfort I draw I measure carefully, for we have been told all too often, you never know the moment.

In the last two months, since I broke down, I have taken what precautions I can. I've checked the insurance policies and made a new will leaving her everything – including the numbered accounts. There is nothing much else to be done.

As far as the immortal soul is concerned, I like to think I have always been as prepared as the next person. I feel . . . how should I put it . . . my chariot is well-oiled and ready to fly. However, I do not intend to give in easily, and neither does my consultant.

One of the funniest lines I've come across since my engine started to fail was in a little medical book I discovered during one of my short waiting periods. After several simple paragraphs it came to the old diastolic pressure and said something like: 'Don't you worry your pretty little head about this. It is much too complicated, so let your doctor worry for you.'

Well, now, that is a good one. 'Let your doctor worry.' Imagine your doctor after a hard day at the surgery coming home to his dear wife, refusing his tea and toast with the words: 'I couldn't possibly eat a thing, I'm much too worried about your man's pressure.'

One thousand, seven hundred and fifty-nine other patients – some with broken bones and some with broken hearts – he had to turn away from the surgery that day because he was much too worried about my pressure! Don't the people who write these books think we already suffer enough from guilt?

All too clearly I can see my consultant at the top of his backswing saying to his hypertensive partner: 'It is no good, I cannot concentrate for worrying about your diastolic. I concede, here's me pound.'

No wonder people hate to bother their doctors. I was always much happier healing myself, on the quiet, because once the eminents got hold of me they thought I, as a fellow medicine-man, should allow myself to be experimented on. And once they get you wired up you've had it.

In the last two weeks I've seen all my internal organs in much greater detail than I would have wished, and in colour. Although I'm assured the messy-looking lumps they call the kidneys are supposed to look like that, they didn't seem at all appetising – even after a 12-hour fast.

I liked the fancy echo-sounder, though. With that sort of gear you could distinguish between lobster and crab on the ocean floor, and the slightest danger you could sense a mile away. Perhaps for the last few months of her life they should install one in the *Suilven*, for I feel she could not withstand the gentlest scratch on her belly.

FRIDAY, 2 SEPTEMBER 1994

Around this time last week I was on the verge of a bitter complaint about not being able to get petrol on a Sunday in Stornoway, while drugs are freely available. To whom exactly I was going to address my complaint I'm not sure: perhaps the churches! In the event, I suffered a sharp pain in the back of my head, so I decided to hold fire, just in case.

Now that I'm a little better maybe we can risk it, and seek, once again, an explanation for the grand paradox.

Over the years our 'Last Stronghold of the Gospel' has attracted as much attention from the vipers of the low press as the behaviour of the Royal Family. And nothing has been used more as an example of our extremism than the chained-up swings in the children's playground. Who chains them or who gives the orders nobody seems to know. He or she must go out at the dead of night to secure these instruments of the devil, and then presumably he can sleep soundly until Monday morning.

As it happens, I now believe this is a very wise move, not because I would deny the children a swing on the Sabbath but because unchained swings would constitute a grave danger to certain adults.

On any Sunday afternoon during this long fine summer you can see the poor souls rolling out of the pubs, especially along Kenneth Street and out Bayhead. Mark my words, for I know better than most, if these swings were free to swing, they would prove irresistible to drunks. There is always one. You remember all too well from our own 'poor soul' days. 'I bet I could climb that pole,' he would say, barely able to stagger. The result was inevitably intensive care.

This is how it would be with the swings, so they had better remain chained until we tackle the main problem.

Why, we wonder, does the Mother Church turn a blind eye on the sad cases that tumble out of the County Hotel while at the same time showering brimstone on little children? My guess is they secretly do not want these people to get better.

Here, I believe we can draw a parallel with the long-suffering wife whose husband is bad in drink. This type of woman, and there are many of them, thrives on what appears to be a state of misery. She has the constant sympathy of neighbours and is often addicted to pity. When she catches her man in a rare condition of sobriety, she can scream and abuse the poor man until he is eventually driven out in search of the only comfort he knows. Poor woman, they all say.

Poor woman perhaps she is, but what about the poor man? A little understanding would go a long way, but that is unlikely. The woman, you see, has the power, while he is in his useless state. The last thing she wants is a change that might mean his getting better. Her need is not unlike the mother's who doesn't want to see her children grow out of dependency. Remove her perceived burden and she loses her sense of purpose, not to mention the sympathy of a community.

All of which brings us back to Mother Church and the easy road. And what could be easier than the chaining of children's swings. It is certainly easier than attempting to tackle the real problem. Not, of course, that they have any desire to solve the main problem, for they desperately need the enemy. Without the blind drunk groping his way along the wall they are without their most potent weapon, perhaps even without the main reason for their existence.

It is not beyond belief that, with their almost Jesuit cunning, they have thought far into the future to see the chained swings causing enough resentment to drive young people to drink.

There are other reasons why the Church would not want too many to reform all at once, but I'm afraid we must abandon them for another week, for we have several secular problems to address.

Occasionally I meet boys from Harris in my travels, and they keep me informed about the Superquarry. Some of them are not at all happy with what is known as the Quarry Benefit Group. Whose benefit? they ask.

Now it would be impertinent for us in Lewis to get too closely involved with Harris were it not for the fact that we have 1,600 unemployed of our own to add to Harris's 150.

I have always taken the view that Harris has more than enough mountains to spare one. You would think at a glance they have enough rock to do the rest of the world. Just as long as they landscape nicely behind them, by all means let them take one mountain.

But what worries the boys who need work most is that Benefit Groups and the like are almost always made up of retired professional people on fat pensions who can well afford to delay much-needed work. Are they more concerned with development of their own hobby (i.e. talking) than with impact on the community and jobs?

I realise the need for careful future planning, but those who do the planning are invariably in no hurry because they do not have to worry about the groceries. The man with a family, no work and precious little dole just wishes they would hurry up.

Is that Coinneach's boy, I've been asked by some mutual friends? You know, the fellow in the paper with the First Class Honours in Chemistry!

That this boy from the shoulder of Sloc nam Marbh should have a special bent for chemistry should come as no surprise for those who understand such things. It is all in the genes. I know nothing of Diana's Ness ancestry, but on the Ranish side Tabaidh comes from a long line of Alchemists.

This talent reached its cusp in Coinneach himself. Not only was he good at sums, almost everything he ever touched turned to gold. It is little wonder he encouraged the boy to tackle the subject in its modern form.

Quite apart from inherent ability, the boy Tabaidh lived exclusively on fish from the day he was born. There has never been any doubt that fish is good for brains, on top of which we must remember we are talking here of nothing but the best fish. Tabaidh went to school sooking on ling's marags the way other boys sooked on lollipops. There is a younger one coming along with webbed toes who will almost certainly go to the very top.

FRIDAY, 16 SEPTEMBER 1994

There was a strange news item on the Gayltalk this morning – a snippet, I think, that was misunderstood by most of those involved. Apparently shinty referees are no longer prepared to come to Skye unless they have police protection.

This comes as no surprise to the people of Lewis, who have long viewed their cousins across the water with dark suspicion. Even when unarmed and sober, the Skyeman is considered a dangerous enemy; when aroused in battle, with a lethal weapon in his hands, you would as soon tackle the wild men of Borneo.

Back in the Byres Road days, as long ago as '63, I met my first Skyeman and was terribly shocked at the transformation in his personality in the course of a singe day. I assume he was a typical Sgiathanach, although I could be wrong because I never again found the courage to mix with them. You must remember we in Lewis had given up blood sports over a century ago and are altogether a more gentle race.

Anyway, I fell in step with the Skyeman in the early afternoon while he was still docile, like a well-fed lion. As the day wore on the slumbering beast in him began to stir and he seemed to grow bigger. In the early evening a huge polis in uniform came into the Curlers and swaggered around a bit as if marking out his territory. The lawman seemed harmless enough to me, but he triggered some jungle impulses in the Skyeman and he started making low, animal sounds deep into his glass. I should have recognised the signs, but I was fresh to the city and green.

Came the closing hour of ten, as it then was, my companion had grown even bigger and very boisterous. I remembered with grim foreboding the Skyeman in Archie Grant's song. I cannot be sure exactly how it started – one never can. Perhaps someone accidentally bumped into my new friend or merely looked at him in the wrong way. Whatever it was, it got him swinging and blood soon flowed. The earlier polis appeared and was soon dispatched, but reinforcements were quickly on the scene. Although policemen were big in those days, it took several to subdue the boy, but eventually he was bundled into the van. Sadly, I was also thrown in despite my innocence.

It has occurred to me more than once that had the Skyeman taken the right turn in life's forked path he would have made a fine polis himself and would probably by now have been a Superintendent – perhaps even retired and a respectable councillor. Sometimes I picture him and his clan with shinty sticks in their hands. Even in America such weapons would now be difficult to obtain legally.

There will be many listeners to radio and readers of papers 'out there' who still think shinty is a sport almost as harmless as hockey. It is far from it. Not only is it permissible to lift the club above your own head, it is compulsory to bring it down hard and often on the opposition skulls, laying them out cold or even dead. This is a terrifying 'game' wherever it is played, but doubly so in Skye.

In response to this morning's news a police spokesman in Portree protested, as did some other Care in the Community persons, that he could not begin to understand the referees' complaint. He knew of no trouble at shinty games, he said, thus cleverly hinting this was all about crowd behaviour, when it is clear to one and all that the violence takes place on the field. It is long past time this game was outlawed as it was long ago in Lewis about the same time they burned the fiddles.

Regulars will know that I have not been fully fit for some time now and that certain activities are out of bounds.

However, my consultant is a man of compassion and understanding. Once or twice a year he will allow me to lapse provided my nurse is with me. Although my man is not from these parts, he recognises a visit by Aly Bain and his young friend Phil Cunningham is an occasion for a lapse.

There is music to dance to, music to listen to, and perhaps music to eat to, but Aly and Phil play music to drink to. I don't know if they bring about a lapse in all their audiences, but for some reason I have found whenever they come to Lewis many of us are unwell for several days. Perhaps they awaken dormant memories of distant country dances that went on until dawn, or perhaps they disturb something deeper in the psyche that we cannot begin to comprehend.

While dwelling on these things and on the unnecessary whiteness of aspirin once again, I wonder if perhaps the Free Kirk was not right to burn the fiddles. Presumably accordions were not so easy to burn, while fiddles made good firewood, which is why to this day we have many more accordion players than fiddle players. In any case, there is no doubt thon Aly Bain is a devil with the fiddle.

Often at these gigs I have a problem with those seated round about me. Not content to rest and sip, they bob and weave about and generally fidget annoyingly. They are, I now realise, all aspiring accordion players. They must, you understand, worm their way into a position to see Phil Cunningham's right hand, although I'm dashed if I can understand what they hope to learn unless they have the means of replaying the action in slow motion.

Little do they know this is a 'false' hand. The real one is tied behind his back, and the one they see is worked from the guts of the box by an ingenious Chinese computer. I only drop this secret to get a little peace at the next concert.

In a foolhardy attempt to cleanse the soul, I am about to set sail with the Loch Eynort Philosopher for destinations unknown.

The intention is to call at all ports south, but given the lasting north-easterly, Rodel would seem a likely first stop, or perhaps Dunvegan. Eventually, if the wind stays at the same strength from a northerly direction, Killybegs is not ruled out, perhaps with a stop at Laphroaig to see if Tormod has anything on the hip – perchance to pick up a bottle in which to send messages. One should never have any fear of going as far south as the wind will take one, because sooner or later a southerly will spring up.

My only concern is that maybe I should have told my skipper I've never before been in a sailing boat. I guess he must have confidence in the way I walk.

FRIDAY, 23 SEPTEMBER 1994

Last week I signed off in hope of reaching Islay, but it wasn't, as they say, meant to be. When one is at the mercy of the elements one tends to have decisions made for one, and one needs a lot of time. Time and the necessity to work are a thrice-damned curse.

If we should live to retirement age, maybe then we'll have some time on our shaky hands, but what can we do with it at the age of 60 or 65? Sailing in this part of the world would be very difficult or probably impossible because at 60 we will all have become physically useless due to the nature of our day jobs. This is why it would make so much more sense to retire at 40 and go back to work at 65.

Most of the people who are nearest and dearest to me are forced to spend the prime of their lives doing menial, undemanding tasks in order to buy the groceries and pay the mortgage. Any sort of work that can be done sitting down could obviously be easily done by people over 65. It would even be easier for this age group to get up in the early morning because people need less sleep as they get older.

The painful reality is only too well known to us. Physically robust young men and women are chained to desks in the best years of their lives while their bellies fill out and their bums spread. Release these people at 40 and let them go back to 'work' at 60. That is the answer. Give them their gratuities now so they can buy sailing boats.

This morning I am afraid it is easily read that I am very tired. Although I've slept for nearly 24 hours, that wasn't enough. In a sense it was too much because my head has turned to mush and the bones have stiffened up. The muscles along the belly seem to have been twisted like a jib-sheet and my arms are difficult to lift to the height of a keyboard – a keyboard, incidentally, that moves back and fro to meet me although I've been on solid ground for 24 hours.

For all that, I cannot wait for the next time. No croft should be without its yacht – preferably a yacht no smaller than 27 feet. I know people try to cross the Atlantic in smaller boats, but they are types who are tired of life or who have no idea what the sea can be like. A minimum of two tons of deep keel is also desirable because, as I've learned this last week, a lot of time is spent at unusual, unplanned angles to the waves. These are times when a motor boat of similar size would need to be hove-to. But don't let me put you off.

After a comfortable first night moored at the bottom of Stein Inn in Skye, conditions seemed favourable for our sail to Canna. No sooner were we out in the open than the wind took a spite to us. For reasons that need not concern close relatives we decided to put into Lochmaddy two and a half hours later. By strange coincidence the first person I met ashore was the Stornoway accountant Jackie MacKay. I wondered if I owed him any money and if he had flown down to see how we were doing. He seemed pleased enough to see us, but I dare say his presence was pure chance.

The Lochmaddy Hotel, by the way, seems to be a focal point for the huntin' fishin' mob. They were gathered in a semi-circle in the middle of the floor with their loud voices and their half-pints curled into their oxters.

That is, in the well-practised pose they adopt when performing for natives. I noticed one in particular blatantly assessing our apparel, and made a mental note to acquire some suitable yachting clothes for the future. It doesn't do to offend these types with what could be taken for sheep-dipping gear.

On the other foot, I wasn't particularly impressed with their style. There is a common type of trousers you see on these people nowadays as they travel to and from the islands. They come to just below the knee, about plus-four length but tighter, and they are secured above the calf with a buckle. A crude friend in Barra calls them 'jobby-catchers' and this may indeed by the case, but I would doubt there is any need because so much of that flies out the other end.

But that was a by the way. Early next day, not long out of Lochmaddy, the sea and wind again took a dislike to us. The retired gentleman and his wife in the 35-footer moored beside us thought it wiser not to try for Rodel, which proves my argument about retirement.

With wind and sea running together from the north, we had to go halfway to Dunvegan (again) to get a tack on Rubha na h-Òrdaig south of Boisdale. Halfway, though, wasn't enough. There is a nasty shallow gob north of Loch Eynort where wind and tide meet by appointment. Once more we had to head out in the middle, until this time we got a bearing on Barra Head. By now I was becoming very fond of the middle of the Minch, for the middle is as far as you can get away from rocks.

However, while running south-west my Skipper suffered the greatest indignity of his 49 years and it wasn't my fault. For the first time in his long sailing life he was 'pooped', and he still talks of it with great resentment. Being pooped, for the benefit of landlubbers, means taking one over the stern. This particular wave must have come all the way from Cape Wrath to insult him. It came over so quietly into our laps there was no time to do anything but look at each other and laugh.

Sailing into Castlebay on a dark cloudy night is not as easy as it seems from the deck of the *Lord of the Isles*. The navigation lights are somewhat essential and I sincerely hope the man who maintains them isn't colour-blind. It took some time to get the tune into my head, but now that it has lodged it will stay there. If you ask me in 10 years' time, although I might be too old to sail, I can give you a dead-of-night course for any of these anchorages, should you need one.

We gathered strength in the Craigard, the only hotel in Scotland where you can get food at any time of the day or night, and made some more plans. I think it was in the warmth of Craigard that my Skipper started to lose his nerve. Instead of the four-hour dash to Mingulay, he elected to play golf on the new nine-hole course in Barra – although he had never played golf in his life before. In return for this late cautious move we were rewarded with an almost calm moonlight overnight sail to Loch Eynort. It's a great life.

When I said earlier no croft should be without its yacht, I realise it seems a tall order, yet it is not impossible. All it means is you have to wait until the children have flown the nest, then you can sell the house and live in the boat. When I am bitten with a new enthusiasm it is generally a large bite. My wife, who hates the sea, takes some comfort from her knowledge that my enthusiasms are shortlived.

FRIDAY, 18 NOVEMBER 1994

Because the Berlin Wall has come down doesn't mean we no longer have to be on our guard. There are still subversives in our midst who will stop at nothing to bring our country to its knees. Sad to say, some of our own eminent colleagues are numbered among the anarchists.

On this Remembrance Sunday I hear on the news that certain doctors in the south of England are accused of giving far too a high a priority to the needs of patients. Fortunately, there is at least one Health Trust manager, a Mr Lilley, who is not afraid to stand up and say what many of us feel.

'What the public don't seem to realise,' he said, 'is that we are all in this racket together. Domestics, cooks, cleaners, electricians, plumbers and trolley-wheel oilers. We all have to work as one. Our aims are clearly set out and first and foremost we have to be certain we make enough money to pay our managers the sort of salary that will discourage them from leaving the service to set themselves up as second-hand car dealers.

'Unfortunately,' added the spokesperson, 'there are still those among us who do not seem to appreciate the main reason for our existence. These are the doctors and the few qualified nurses left who think all they should do is care for the sick. They still haven't grasped that patients should be managed and not nursed. Make no mistake, these enemies of the state will be weeded out and their names will be made known through the Trust archipelago.'

Thank goodness there are men out there with the courage to speak out. We must all be alert to this poison in the mainstream of health management. I am not sure what exactly the southern doctors who made the headlines on Remembrance Sunday did to upset the profitable organisation of health management. Perhaps they wasted time and money trying to keep some old World War 1 heroes alive. Old codgers in their nineties, and very likely in costly wheelchairs, are a terrible drain on resources. One can hardly claim, with the best will in the world, that these people contribute much for the huge pensions they draw from the taxpayer. Every effort should be made to return them to the community.

Another all too obvious saving could be made on pregnant women. There is no reason why they shouldn't give birth in their own beds as their grandmothers did before them. The saving from every 10 mothers who could be persuaded to do the business at home would mean another manager could be employed. After all, there are very few neighbourhoods without their quota of unemployed midwives. This is what modern health management is all about.

I'm delighted to announce I've been told to expect to see my name in the next Honours list. For my imaginative suggestions, circulated to various health authorities last May, I am told a small gong is on its way. Perhaps an MBE. My plan to introduce gaming machines in every ward was grasped with much enthusiasm. The percentage weighted in favour of the machine should go a long way towards a profitable ward.

In the meantime, keep a wary eye out for any doctor who seems preoccupied with the health of his patients. The system will never run smoothly until these people are driven out of the country. Let them go and do good works in Rwanda.

To the doing of good works there is no end.

With so many people unemployed, I am normally very much against 'working for the glory'. However, when I heard of plans to reshape Stornoway Harbout I felt I had to offer my rough sketches to my old friend Smokey, the Master of the Harbour.

Naturally, I have invited suggestions from my old school buddy, the Lord of the Isles. No doubt Charlie will have his own ideas, but I like to think he has sufficient faith in me not to make any major alterations.

One will, of course, be accused of living in the past; but the past, as can be seen from the accompanying drawing, was much easier on the eye than the present. I feel sure Charles will be with me on this one.

I am sorry, dear Murdoch, but my plan to restore Stornoway to its former glory involves much more knocking down than building. But as nothing worth preserving has been built in the last 200 years, I'm certain my plan will be greeted with great joy by all those who have an eye for beauty.

Clearly, there will be no room for heavy lorries nor any other form of pollution. This will probably alarm our captains of commerce, but there is an easy solution. There is a small port called Tarbert where I guess they would welcome the traffic. If this means a loss of revenue to the Harbour Commission, I am sorry; but I am sure the majority will think it a small price to pay for peace.

FRIDAY, 2 DECEMBER 1994

I swore the day I went back to work I would do no more of these diaries for him, but on this Monday morning I have been backed into a corner. Your man was in his favourite position, on the broad of his back with his weekend comics – *Sporting Life Weekender* and the *News of the World* – when my car wouldn't start.

There was no great urgency, I thought, because I was not due to report for work until 2pm. Unluckily, colleague Flo was having one of her midlife flushes, so I was called in for 10.30am. What seemed to be plenty of time at first was suddenly transformed into one of these moments he is so fond of calling 'not to be wasted'.

After all, I had only probably flooded it, whatever *it* is. If it was really bad I could always call Aonghas Beag. 'Over my dead body,' *ars esan*; 'I am not having one of these Nats tampering with your parts. I'll do it myself.' Had I known then what I know now I would have been quicker and cheaper to call Peter Legg at MacRae and Dick – the only man of 50 I know without high blood pressure.

Very much against natural inclination, he dragged himself downstairs before the black pudding was crisp. 'Show me,' he trumpeted, 'this car that won't start.'

I did. Five minutes later he was back in asking if I had any plasters. I have never understood why, in moments of crisis, he doesn't cover himself in bandages and plasters before he starts. I am not one of those women who is alarmed by or impressed with bleeding knuckles. I've seen too much blood. The men I knew who could accomplish things did so with their knuckles intact. Men like Carrots. Real men.

I could see Charlie next door, at a loose end as it were, looking over anxiously when he saw him in a boilersuit. He probably knew *it* was simplicity itself if only he could get at *it*, but it was more than my life was worth. The master was in control.

At 9.45 he came in looking for a coffee with several dismantled oily bits in his hands and asked if I'd seen the book. Always the book after something has bent or broken. To look in the book beforehand is clearly an affront to manhood. I found the book for him, of course, and headed for the bus. I hoped that dear sweet man Christopher Kelso might happen along in his lorry and give me a lift. Chris knows nothing about engines, but at least he is warm and cuddly. But he didn't, so the bus it had to be.

The rest of my day passed madly as it usually does but not, evidently, as madly as his. When I phoned at midday he thought he had the problem solved, only he'd have to go to town for a part. I checked again at two, only to be told he had to go back for another little part. But don't worry, he added, by nightfall he would have my car restored to its original Nissan perfection or else fall on his sword.

The neighbours told me afterwards he was back and fore so frequently they thought he had started a taxi service, travelling in the late afternoon apparently mob-handed. Who made up the mob I'm not sure, but you can bet they were artists rather than mechanics.

I was reminded of the time the central heating pump broke down and he went for Kenny the Plumber. Three days passed before I got a fire on. Seemingly all these miles of copper piping have to be flushed out with Trawler Rum before the system can be restarted. It is astonishing what you learn when you're married to a handyman.

In the very late afternoon I had a call from home asking me to make an appointment with the Royal Bank with a view to preliminary discussions about a newish car. My own, it seemed, was now beyond repair – but there was no further mention of falling on the sword. Naturally, I refused. If there is begging to be done, let him do it. In any case, I couldn't believe a car that was going fine on Sunday would be 'beyond repair' on Monday.

Fortunately, in the late evening, the brother-in-law was back from work and the master was demoted to what he does best – holding the torch. It took the wee brother a little longer than one would normally expect because he had to take the new parts off and put them on again properly. There was nothing much wrong in the first place, the brother told me quietly. Now the old one is sulking and nursing his bleeding fingers, which is why I have to do the typing this week.

In retrospect, I am not sure I want to drive at this time of year, for there are some jokers going about masquerading as policemen. I was chased and stopped the other night by a young man in what I realise now must have been a borrowed uniform. At the time it all seemed quite realistic. Only later, when I remembered the strange questions, did I become suspicious.

'Your date of birth, please' and 'Is that your husband beside you?' Very flattering, I thought, to appear to be too young to drive. But then I got depressed. I couldn't possibly look that young if he thought the greybeard beside me was my husband. In any case, what a strange question. True, it might not have been my husband; but so what?

Unless there are women going about kidnapping older men, I don't see the relevance. Or could it be these Point Players are out from the Church searching the moors for sporting women travelling with men who are not their husbands? I am all for a clampdown on any kind of dangerous driving, but there is no need to stop every form of fun. Not, of course, that there is much fun in a man with his hand in bandages.

FRIDAY, 23 DECEMBER 1994

With yet another return crossing on the *Suilven* behind me, I feel that is enough. I shall not risk another until the new boat is in service.

I cannot stand the heat. The one redeeming feature of sea travel is that one can venture on to the deck to get cooled down by the spray, but as one perseveres deeper into the mainland on public transport the situation becomes more and more uncomfortable.

The only exception is the white bus between Ullapool and Inverness driven by Maggie's friend. I don't know his name (best not to know too much) but this driver must be one of the last true Highland Gentlemen.

He helps both young and old with cases and, more important, he asks from time to time if his passengers are too hot or too cold and regulates accordingly. I noticed Maggie gets special attention, which I thought seemed reasonable, as she travels fortnightly, but now I understand there is more to it.

She sits behind him and they chat. 'No smoke from such and such's house today,' says she. He slows down and they study a house well off the main road. 'She cannot be going to Inverness this morning,' he says. Clearly this driver and herself are very close. But I don't mind.

It is all very reassuring and reminiscent of Bus a' Leadaidh to South Lochs (the way things were) or Docherty's buses in Donegal (the way things still are). I'm just a little worried about his concern for her body temperature.

I realise heating control is impossible on the *Suilven* because, as you all know, a certain valve has been stuck for years at melting point. There is apparently only one man in the company with the strength to turn this valve and he works two weeks on and two off. He must turn it on when he goes on leave and back off when he's on duty. The result is, whatever the season, travellers have a fortnight's roasting and a fortnight's blast-freezing. This might work very well for regulars like my wife and the crew but we occasional sailors always seem to travel at boiling point.

There is scarcely time to cool down in Inverness when I found myself on a Skyeways bus driven, naturally, by a Skyeman. I knew he was a Skyeman because he asked us before we set off to 'use the bags provided' for our rubbish. Who else but a Skyeman would have the impertinence to assume Lewis folk would be carrying rubbish. A bag of herring, perhaps, and chickens for the wedding; but certainly not rubbish.

The Skyeman also likes to keep his bus at boiling point. Desperately uncomfortable, but nothing like as bad as the Lowland branch of Citylink. It is a great pity all those green chaps, who managed to stop the transportation of livestock from Prestwick, don't turn their attention to the way Citylink treat their livestock. Would you believe this gang of highwaymen do not allow passengers to carry food or drink onto their metal-fatigued buses in case they have to employ some poor woman to clean their scrap vehicles at their various terminals. Luckily, it shouldn't cost much to nationalise that lot when the time comes – very soon.

Perhaps you think I protest too much about these mobile furnaces, but I should point out I am no stranger to heat. It doesn't seem that long ago since I spent a day on a bus in Java squashed among 90 fat women with the temperature over 100 in the shade – if you could find any. This seemed quite natural. You sweated and drank water, but when you have to strip down to the jockstrap while travelling through the snow-covered hills of Perthshire it is far from natural.

Still, it is not in my nature to complain – although there are no taxis available in Glasgow at this time of year unless you book in advance, and they won't take your booking if your journey is too short. Take a note, North, to put them also on the nationalisation list.

The purpose of the journey, you may remember from last week, was to get to Duddingston Kirk in Edinburgh at 12.30 Saturday. At 10 o'clock in Maryhill in Glasgow it was discovered she hadn't packed my shoes. This is how it came to pass that at 10.45 I am haring down Buchanan Street with a bag of 'rubbish' on my back wearing my Sunday suit over a pair of tattered yellowish walking boots. People in the city don't notice much, but later, in the church, sitting in Sir Walter Scott's old pew, I felt quite conspicuous. What with trying to hide my spags while at the same time keeping a lookout for Calum Rifkind, it was a very uneasy service.

Last week's readers will be pleased to hear the devil did not appear. We got Catriona married to a proper Dutchman and not to a Van Der Merwe. Although the guests came from Holland, Germany, South Africa, Canada, Lewis and even several more distant parts, the gathering was not so international as it sounds. When you stripped them of their present nationalities they were all basically Dutch or Scottish. A volatile mixture. Any offspring will almost certainly go forth to conquer and to build empires.

I hadn't realised in my dreadful ignorance how much Scottish history is attached to the old stones of Duddingston Kirk and Prestonfield

House. Both date back to the 12th century.

When I said I sat in Scott's pew I cannot be absolutely certain, but it is likely, for he was an Elder of that kirk. What I do know for sure is that I tread in the footsteps of Jock Thompson. The Rev Thompson, who called the congregation 'ma bairns', was the minister in 1805. And all these years I thought he was the first manager of Falkirk FC.

I would guess Duddingston was a Protestant church at that time, although it seemed to swing from one foot to the other over the centuries. What it is at the moment is hard to say. The 'minister' wore a frock and it all seemed very High Anglican to me if not a wee bit Romish. The service seemed a little light and airy, and they had a Christmas Tree behind the pulpit. Make of that what you will. But I must assume, despite the lack of brimstone, the young couple are indeed truly married.

When the Kirk business was done we all rowed across Duddingston Loch to Prestonfield House, in keeping with the romantic mood of the day. This, I understand, was the route usually taken by the Rev Menteith when he was doing an illicit line with Lady Hamilton in 1603. So overwhelmed was I by the historical atmosphere I forgot to take my usual quota of drink, which was as well, considering the heat I had to endure on the return journey.

1995

Friday, 6 January 1995

The third day of the year is without any doubt the worst day of the year for people who imagine they know how to enjoy themselves.

The brain, having been shrunk by alcohol, has far too much space in the skull. It floats about like the last small pickled onion in a jar. It is fair to say that under normal circumstances a man or woman with a big head will also have a big brain to go with the head. (Whether this affects the efficiency we don't know; we are merely talking about size.) On the third day, however, the size of the skull may have no bearing on the size of the brain.

There is no more peculiar sensation than the feeling given out by a brain lolling about in a skull that is too big for it. For some reason a fierce heat is generated when the cerebrum is allowed to move about in its own bloody bath, causing the owner of the new small brain to imagine he needs cold water.

Regular sufferers often misinterpret this message, thinking the brain is crying out for more alcohol. Naturally, they oblige, thus postponing the painful day of sobriety, by which time the brain will have shrunk even further. That is, if it hasn't died altogether.

Cold water is what the brain wants and what it should get. Unfortunately, this necessitates getting out of bed and descending to the kitchen – a dangerous manouevre even if you put the lights on. It is safer to have these things to hand before you go to bed, but if you remember to take precautions the chances are you haven't yet reached the stage where the brain has shrunk. Also remember if you try to get up you risk a nosebleed. Better to stay on your back for as long as possible, even if you have to resort to the cold water in the hot-water bottle.

Although staying in bed is safer, it is by no means comfortable. I assume you have the usual wet towels to cool the brow and the back of the neck, but this only buys a little time, for soon all the water will have turned to steam and the fever comes back with a terrible vengeance.

Yet, these are only the physical symptoms of a shrunken and dehydrated brain and are nothing at all when compared with the mental torment. When I say sleep is impossible, I mean sleep for any length of time. There will be short tortured moments of semi-conscious *bruaillean*. These may last only seconds in reality but what is reality? Your reality, as you suffer, can be a year-long nightmare or it can last for ten years. This is why you sometimes see a relatively young man with a head of curly hair on a Friday and then on Monday the hair on his half-empty skull has turned completely white.

Only those who have gone halfway down this road can begin to imagine what this man has suffered. In one second of *your* reality he has possibly been chased for ten years by fire-breathing dragons. For year after year, summer and winter, he has very likely been no more than ten yards ahead of the fire. At the same time he would, as like as not, while running from the dragon, have to guard his head from encircling vultures with bloody talons that threatened to tear his eyes out.

All this time, you must remember, he is running along a narrow path through deep jungle containing serpents and poisonous reptiles of every description. One false step and he has had it. It is possible at some stage of terror-stricken flight the path will become suddenly very steep and almost impossible to climb although it is no bother to the dragon. With a cavernous chasm on both sides, he is now faced with death at the jaws of the animal or a drop off the cliff into certain eternity. With a scream of terror he awakens himself and the wife. The wife screams even more loudly when she sees an 'old' haggard man beside her with a head of pure white hair.

For the first few days of the New Year take a close look at people you meet who appear at first glance to be about age 75. Look to see if they have their own teeth, for teeth will not generally go in one night of horror. If the main signs of ageing are a few lines and a head of white hair, the chances are you are looking at one of these boys who knows how to enjoy himself.

For several reasons, this year, I went to bed early on the night the youngsters gathered downstairs. The noise and roars of laughter hardly disturbed me at all. I had my own mind-altering substance in the form of a large hardbacked book by Joseph Heller called *Closing Time*. Several times since I took down my Christmas stocking I've looked at the book. That is, I've looked at the cover – dark figures dancing towards the Grim Reaper – afraid to open it, expecting to be disappointed.

Yossarian and Milo Mindbinder from *Catch 22* are now in their late sixties and coming to terms with death. Although not as serious as *Catch 22*, *Closing Time* is wonderfully depressing and an ideal present for men or women who have reached an age at which they would rather go to bed with a book than join a party downstairs. There is no guarantee, though, *Closing Time* will not cause bad dreams, especially on this terrible 3rd day, when we find it so difficult to rise at all.

FRIDAY, 13 JANUARY 1995

This Sunday, Sunday the 8th, is the first Sunday proper of the New Year. We can hardly count last Sunday because so few remember it. So, with this one, we'll make a new beginning.

We will shed the corrupt baggage accumulated in our wasted lives and start afresh. Each must do this in his or her own way, and we must all, as they say, speak for ourselves.

On this cold breezy morning of the first Sunday proper I was torn between an eerie and unusual notion to go to church and a long walk on the moor. Notice how already a new cleanliness has crept into my life and my bedroom.

While in the past I would have settled for a cup of tea and a smoke and back to bed with the weekend comics, I am now contemplating a walk. Perhaps, if you are too lazy even to contemplate exercise, you would like to come along and join me on the moor. Imagine you have already climbed into your wellington boots and your foul weather gear and that you too have a spaniel called Smut.

The dog is a wee bit confused. His Sundays do not usually start until mid-afternoon, but he is very intelligent and quickly catches on when he sees the wellies. It has to be a walk because he knows I wouldn't be going fishing on a Sunday.

A lot of people think he is stupid because he is excitable, but they are wrong. He is bilingual and a very smart boy indeed. He understands looks. Not only those directed at him but looks exchanged between humans in his company. I realise this is difficult to believe unless you've had a Smut, but it's true.

Anyway, forget Smut for the time being, and let us get on with our new clean way of life.

The first obstacle on this path of righteousness is the wellie stocking. Hard to find nowadays, at any price, they are even harder to maintain. They are not knitted to withstand the violence of the washing machine. After two goes in the hot spinner they are tightened and reduced to the size of a finger stall.

Still, at the risk of a hernia, I persevere, for the dog is going crazy.

Already I am beginning to suspect my new clean way of life will be the death of me. Out in the open, past the shelter of house and tall trees, the WSW'ly is fresh and cold (would it not, I wonder in a weak moment, be as well to let the pancreas expand). I keep the wind on my left hip, slightly behind, and it is very comfortable.

When I gain the top of the ridge called Beann an Leig I turn and lean on the wind looking down on North Lochs and across the spray towards Cromore and Skye. As far as I can judge, Smut and I are the only people alive in the entire archipelago. There is no movement of man, cow or sheep. A stranger alighting from a spaceship would conclude that our villages had been overtaken by some unfathomable catastrophe that left buildings intact yet destroyed all life. Of course, I know what they're up to, but I'm not telling.

I turn my back on them and head NE. If that is how they choose to spend their Sunday mornings, then so be it. A day of reckoning awaits.

Approaching Loch Oichean, I accept that sooner or later I have to walk against the wind unless I carry on to Stornoway; but I don't want to do that, for I feel I've seen enough of that place for a lifetime. A quagmire of depravity if ever there was one.

Loch Oichean, the loch we get our drinking water from, looks fine to me, but not to the water inspectors of Brussels. Perhaps they're right and it is not good to drink water full of dead sheep and gulls' droppings, but surely it would do for washing. We could always buy mineral water for drinking, and no matter how thirsty it would still cost less than the water element in our Council Tax.

If someone had the spyglass on me they would assume I was soliloquising, but I'm not, for I have Smut. He nods agreement and leads me up the river to Loch Crogabhat, where the Arctic char used to be. Smut doesn't like this stream. He often stops and growls into it, obviously seeing something I cannot. Very likely it's an otter, another animal crapping in our costly water; but that is all right, because the otter is Green.

Taking advantage of the way the ice shaped the low ridges, I work my way back in semi-circles, sheltered from the wind by the steep slopes. This is the sort of walking you cannot do if you're driving sheep, and it's why I have a spaniel and not a collie.

As I re-enter the township behind the Council scheme called Campbell Place (some of us were never happy with that name), it strikes me that roads are a very good idea. When you've been walking on slippery moss, in deep heather and trembling *sùil-chruthaich (Sorry, Ed: cannot think of the English for that one; I hope people aren't offended)*, roads are easy. We have a lot to thank the Romans for. Smut looks at me askance but I remind him the Romans were pagans then, and he seems happy with that.

There is still very little evidence of human presence in the village. Campbell Place would make the *Marie Celeste* seem noisy. It is too early for church. I wonder if the few people who go to church stopped going would anyone get up at all on Sunday? This is beyond Smut and, just like us, what he doesn't understand he hates. He goes into a barking frenzy, yet even that disturbs nobody. There is not even a single movement of a nosey curtain. It is possible they have all died in their sleep and is this what Smut is barking at?

At last Eachainn Flòraidh's granddaughter appears with another barking dog. Although I still feel fat and a little flatulent, I'm sure this is going to be a peaceful year. Smut and I and the little girl with a whole long village to ourselves – on Sundays at least.

11 MARCH 95

Kenneth Street in Stornoway on a Sunday morning is not an arena I have often entered, but this last Sunday was an exception.

At about ten to eleven, when called out on an errand of necessity and mercy, I must have slipped into a dwam. Perhaps thinking I was heading for the Lodge, I made a subliminal turn up Kenneth Street when I should have by that time have been progressing along Sandwick Road, past the Boma (my preoccupation was possibly not unconnected with the Big House, but we'll come to that later).

What first caught my attention was the number of long Volvos being parked by clean-cut young men and not a few women. They stretched for as far as the eye could see in all directions, parked bumper-to-tail, polished and gleaming in the bright spring sunshine. From each enormous car one or two persons, rarely three, would disembark and head for the largest Free Church in the world.

They have perfected a strolling style all of their own – moving quickly with noble purpose, head slightly bent, eyes focused on the street 10 yards ahead, perfectly blinkered from the secular world. They each carry a Bible curled under the left arm (the way they have all adopted this identifying posture reminded me of how employees of the Chartered Bank used to stand at parties with their pints curled into their left armpits). The suits are immaculate and the collars Persil-white, exuding an air of great prosperity and at the same time an undeniable holiness.

It occurred to me that for these people church on a Sunday morning is a fine idea. They have dragged themselves out of bed, showered, shaved and shampooed and possibly cut their toe-nails. Were it not for the Kirk, they might have been tempted to lie in bed and get fat. But it occurred to me how much healthier it would be for them to walk to church instead of adding dangerously to atmospheric pollution with their large cars. In any case, it is bad PR to show how God is good to them in this world with material blessings while the others are also out strolling on a Sunday morning.

It would be easy to assume there is no good work left to be done in Stornoway. But while the Volvos were being parked another segment of society began to appear on corners leading to Kenneth Street. In groups of two or three, they also walk with a purpose. Some of them still have their stabilisers out from last night's drinking and they are as different in appearance to the first lot as it is possible to be.

These are desperate men heading for the County Bar. A stranger might make the mistake of thinking they too are heading for a church because Martin's Memorial is so close, but we know better. We see the signs. Thin men with thin blood, shoulders hunched against the cold, they have a walking style of their own caused by tender alcoholic ankles.

Perhaps it is as well they have the County to go to, for the alternative would be No 2 Pier and cans of super lager. On the other hand, if the pub was not open they would be well out of sight of the holy people on their way to church. Yet I wonder if the first lot ever notice the desperadoes, and if they do what do they think. Do they have Elders' discussion sessions and do they say to themselves: as soon as we get out of church today we must do something for these people. Or do they hurry back to their Volvos with eyes still blinkered.

There is evidently much good work left to be done in Stornoway after all, but we must leave the spiritual for the moment and concentrate on other forms of social work.

The reason I was hurrying along to the Boma on a Sunday was to check the entries for the North Lochs election. According to a notice in the papers, the closing time for nominations was 4 o'clock Sunday. I thought perhaps this was a misprint, but one never knows: they'll do anything to keep me out.

The election date is advertised as 14th April. Undue haste, I would say. How is one supposed to find time to organise fundraising events, and would it make much difference if we didn't have a councillor for three months when there is no money left in the kitty to be spent in North Lochs (is there ever).

There are very few people in the parish in a position to embark on even the shortest of campaigns with their own money. But Coinneach is one of them. He feels the time has come to take the Boma by the scruff of the neck – in a quiet and reasonable way, of course.

Politically he is in the same mould as Alec Allan of Carloway. They would probably be on the left flank of the old-fashioned Tory Party. Iain Macleod would possibly have been their man.

They have both invested wisely and are clearly the sort who could be trusted not to do any wild gambling with *our* cash.

Now that the Tory Party has been hijacked by crooks and barrow-boys, it is obviously not a home for Coinneach. Luckily Tony Blair came along and fashioned a party for the middle-classes to which Coinneach and Alec Allan clearly belong. Anyone who has more than 300 sheep can no longer be classed among the workers, but they feel quite comfortable in the modern Labour Party.

A few other names have been mentioned in connection with the North Lochs ward, but I feel sure they can be discounted. Now that a Labour government is an odds-on bet, it would make sense to have a Labour Council. Every day will be the first day of spring, Cunninghame North tells me, and I have to believe him. The question is: will the first day come in time to save what is left of public service? Let us pray.

FRIDAY, 31 MARCH 1995

COMMUNION CULTURE

Monday morning early, and the house is destroyed about my head. Three men with hammers are going crazy in the living room, obviously enjoying themselves ripping apart the ceiling I built with my own two hands. A ceiling, I might add, of which Michaelangelo himself would have been proud.

The reason for the upheaval is, as you would guess, herself. A small crack appeared some time ago, soon after the hot water tank burst, and gradually spread the full width of the room. It wasn't really much of a crack; more like a hairline fracture. Nobody noticed, or if they did they never mentioned it. It certainly didn't bother me; why should it? What sort of person studies ceilings anyway. What sort of mind is so empty it has to fill the vacuum with contemplation of imperfections in ceilings.

No need to answer, for I know the type. There is no point in telling it to read a book. If a new ceiling is what makes for contentment, by all means let her have one.

This business came to a head, as it were, two weeks ago with the Communions nearly upon us. The crack was the cause of my shattered peace, but, although she doesn't realise it, Holy Communion is the reason it is happening today. Communion Culture needs some explaining, and we'll do that in a minute when the noise abates.

When she first told me she had approached Geordie MacArthur, last week, about 'patching' the ceiling, I smiled a knowing smile. I knew the man, or thought I did. I estimated I had at least six months or perhaps a year's grace. The last thing I expected was a call at seven o'clock this morning telling me to 'Empty the room, I'll be over at nine'. Still, I thought, what is a little plastering.

After his first coffee your man stood in the middle of the floor looking up, shaking his head and making disgruntled noises. After much restless pacing, he stopped and made an announcement. 'This,' he said 'will have to come down.' I didn't wait to hear what had to come down, but judging from the hammering and ripping it sounds like most of the house. Suddenly there is a lull and I'm called in for interrogation. 'Who the %$** did this? Look, no dwangs! What kind of idiot did you hire? Was he a joiner or a blacksmith?'

A gloating woman behind me was about to say something but I elbowed her in the stomach and quickly thought of a name well known in the building trade. They might have known it, they said. 'Everywhere we go we have to sort things out after him.' It probably wouldn't have mattered whose name I'd given, for plasterers and joiners are worse than writers and doctors when it comes to the doing-down of their eminent colleagues. In any case, I wasn't going to give my own name. I looked suitably apologetic as I watched my Sistine ceiling being torn to the floor.

'*Robh tòrr agaibh aig na h-Òrduighean?*' used to be a common question on the Monday after. What they meant in long-gone days was: 'Did you have many strangers staying overnight?' Then the question came to mean: 'Did you have many for Sunday dinner?' Now it can only mean did you see anyone at all, or even, did you see many passing in their cars?

For the benefit of Anglicans and others to whom the drinking of the blessed wine is a weekly habit of no more consequence than the smoking of a cigarette, I should like to explain its significance in the Free Churches. To go forward for the wine is a decision of the greatest importance. It is the first rung on the ladder to Heaven and a step to be taken only after many months, or years, of anguished deliberation. Little wonder that few consider themselves worthy and that the occasion is treated with the utmost reverence. The self-torment associated with the taking of Communion is the reason it is offered only twice a year in each parish. To increase the frequency would diminish its significance and possibly allow some through the net who were not ready. A sensible precaution, although without Biblical foundation.

I hope that will help the infidel to understand our Communion Sunday's awesome cultural *cudthromachness*, if I may use a word that is overused in the new '*cultar*'. This twice-a-year festival is obviously not as *cudthromach* as it once was, yet it has left its mark in the genes of daughters of religious households. With *the* date on the Holyday Calendar drawing nigh, a crack in the ceiling soon becomes a chasm. Hence, Geordie MacArthur and his men with hammers.

But perhaps I'm going too fast. The hammering is bad, but worse, Geordie occasionally comes through to talk to me about Chung. To get back to the days when people on the Communion circuit had no cars, it wasn't uncommon for certain housholders to have to lay mattresses on the floor for those who had walked from perhaps as far away as Ness. You can bet your Bible they didn't notice cracks in the ceiling.

Yet, in expectation of a good crowd, hopeful hostesses did their best to make themselves and their homes attractive. There was no greater disappointment than to see a holy celebrity and his groupies troop into a neighbour's when you had bought a new hat and painted your front door. Sniggering youngsters used to maintain the long nights were not spent entirely in prayer. But whatever went on, it is all in the past.

You may wonder what all this has to do with my ceiling, and I have to confess I am not sure. Either my wife is thinking of going forward or else she is preparing for an even grander occasion. Whichever it is, I am happy to be kept in ignorance.

The hammering, I am glad to report, has given way to scraping noises. I would go through for a look, but I'm scared.

Friday, 14 April 1995

Having just spent a couple of days darkening doorsteps with a Labour candidate, I am, to say the least, a little bit confused. In my own village, where I thought it would be polite to introduce Coinneach, it often turned out they already knew him well but, as we were leaving, they would ask him: 'And who is this fellow with you?'

Quite clearly, the only passport to society in North Lochs is Bo Peepaireachd. Before I make my bid for stardom it is now painfully obvious to me I must buy a few sheep. In the middle of the longest village in the Long Island, at least half a dozen times I had to remind the candidate that time was of the essence and that Thursday's election had nothing to do with how many lambs had dropped, and even less with the breed. I realise, a little late, these matters are of greater importance than is generally understood among the under-forties. But there is no way you can canvass an entire parish if the pedigree of every lamb needs to be discussed in every house.

Putting sheep to one side for a moment, while we can, I learned a whole lot about ourselves as a people.

We have, for a start, a grand conceit of ourselves. Politics, they all agree, are fine for Mainlanders and people like that, but *we* have no need of such nonsense. (I would hope Coinneach's opponent in this contest would have come across even more of the same.)

It is generally accepted that the nation as a whole, of which we are a part, needs government, and that government is only possible if a single body of like-minded governors, good or bad, are in control. It is clear to the meanest intelligence that 648 'Independents' would result in total chaos. Yet somehow, mysteriously, this does not apply if the governors are reduced to 30 and the governed are *us*, in the islands. We can only infer that we are different to the rest of humanity. Despite our sad recent history, we retain a childish trust in our Independents.

The notion is pleasing to contemplate, but the satisfaction can only last for any length of time in a mind that is permanently self-satisfied. In any other it will soon lead to self-abhorrence, and ultimate rejection of tribalism. 'Wha's like us an' they're a deid' is fine for the Saturday afternoon terracing but a frightening philosophy for those who would hope to shape a world, or even a small community, for their grandchildren.

Grandchildren immediately spring to mind because we don't hold much hope for the generation in between us and them. These poor souls, except for a favoured few, are sentenced to a lifetime's enslavement because we were governed for the first long spell in modern times by Independents, or one Independent Governess and her few sycophant lieutenants. Those who didn't learn the lesson in that sad spell – that we can never be Independent – will probably never do so. I think it was Aristotle who first noted that those who are above politics, the Independents, think they don't need other people.

The signs on the mainland are that the majority have at least seen through the fraud. Among those who imagined they had security of tenure were senior civil servants. In fact, apart from those who signed up for the Army or worked for Bain & Morrison, I cannot think of another group that felt more secure than our public servants. Those at the top, the so called first division, hacked away at the lower rungs with great glee. Bribed by incentives, they wielded the axe with such enthusiasm they didn't notice the blade at their own feet. Now that they too are beginning to fall, there is much laughter in the land.

But these were, and those that remain still are, powerful people. They have turned to bite the hand that bribed them, so that hardly a day goes by without a damaging leak to the *Guardian*. They will do anything to save their own miserable skins. In their desperation they are prepared to join the dreaded Labour Party, but it is probably too late. With perhaps two years to go, the devastation will be complete.

But the word 'perhaps' is very important to the man on Death Row. Perhaps they won't last two years, which could mean many thousands of jobs might still be saved (quite a few in the Post Office alone).

You may well ask what a vote for Coinneach in a backwater like North Lochs could do to hasten their end, and the answer is quite a lot. His not inconsiderable weight on top of last week's mainland avalanche could topple the entire rotten edifice.

These and many other *cudthromach* thoughts passed through my mind as I listened, on draughty doorsteps, to Coinneach promising the moon, the stars and everlasting sunshine to anyone who would listen. It is astonishing what people expect or would like from their elected respresentatives in, dare I say it, politics. They might possibly have felt Bosnia too heavy a load to lay on a local politician, but you would expect, with half the planet in flames, street lighting to be low on a list of priorities. With government funding being reduced by the minute, I'm afraid all Coinneach could promise them was a bright torch each, and that he'd try to ensure they wouldn't get two torches in South Lochs (an eavesdropping stranger would likely have concluded ours was a village of highwaymen and rapists).

By 10 o'clock tonight we will, of course, know the exact measure of their fear of the dark. I would guess, if most of the responses we got were honest, about 70 per cent will vote Labour. Three different lifelong Tories (recent incomers) said they'd had enough and would never vote Tory again. Whether they can bring themselves to vote Labour doesn't matter much.

On the other hand, it is very difficult to know what to make of the silences. A long Gaelic silence, like a Gaelic smile, can never be accurately assessed.

FRIDAY, 5 MAY 1995

Warning: This column contains material of a highly explicit nature. If you are easily offended, turn back to page three.

'Have you been inducted yet?' has recently been a frequent cry in the Town. When I first heard this strange question it was from one woman to another. Naturally I assumed the ordination of women priests, now commonplace in southern Britain, had spread as far north and west as Stornoway. Probably, I guessed, among the Episcopalians or in Martin's Memorial, where they like to be fashionable. My guess couldn't have been further off the mark.

As I edged closer, the better to eavesdrop, I soon learned their type of induction had nothing at all to do with the simplifying of the Gospel and everything to do with the base earthly body. A fine couple of bodies they were, I might add, ample with the promise of warmth and comfort. Yet, although these two desirable ladies of the Town seemed perfectly formed to us, they were evidently not built to their own satisfaction. This is why they had subjected themselves to induction.

The latest craze to get a grip, if that isn't too earthy a word, is a particularly strenuous programme of physical exercises necessitating costly machinery and a human slavemaster. Before one is allowed to enter the torture chamber one must be inducted. Full details of the ritual are, of course, only known to those who have been inducted, but we can guess it must be similar to initiation to the Craft. The essential difference, because all sexes frolic together, is that there is no baring of breasts – left or right. Once you have sworn to worship the body and paid your ten quid you're in.

And once you're in, boy, are you for it. They have rowing machines, cycling machines, peat-cutting machines, running machines, walking machines, climbing machines, sex machines and machines of every description on which you can simulate all the pleasurable activities known to man or woman. There is also a person at the ready to monitor your bodily functions should you become over-stimulated and to give you the kiss of life when you pass out. Great fun.

It is easy to understand why young men should want to have flat bellies and muscular necks, but the first obvious question is why they should want to bond with machinery rather than the real thing. We have a superabundance of water and an unlimited supply of rowing boats. If you want to stretch the sinews, our hills and moors are still free to all (although there are some who would like to stop that). Even if all you want to do is walk on the level, we have roads of a sort, and you can get a pair of sturdy boots from the Millionaire Cobbler for twenty pounds. If you want to simulate walking on a rough pebble shore, there is a suitable stretch on the Lochs road only three miles from Stornoway. At least you'd be going somewhere.

It's the not going anywhere that makes the torture chamber so unappealing. Rowing, as it happens, was one of the few exertions young men of my time never minded until laziness forced them to give up all sport. Possibly the attraction of rowing was that it could be done sitting down. Many's the boy from as young as 12 who would spend the day rowing back and fore marvelling at the agility of a seal ripping fish out of a net. Even when one was slowly trolling along the coast going nowhere in particular, the scenery would change from cliff to cave. Not that it was always so leisurely. There were boys in Bernera who could leave a 40-horse outboard in their wake when the need arose, as it often did.

Sitting in a gym, no matter how sophisticated the technology, sounds a poor substitute for proper rowing and cycling. Cycling in Lewis would need a long book to do it justice (and I have that very thing in mind). With the villages being so far apart, the bicycle was a necessary prelude to the more important carnal gymnastic to follow. It was hardly surprising that the men of the West Side became notoriously proficient in all three sports, and that is all I'm saying for the moment.

Given that women's chief purpose is to please men, one of the great mysteries in life is why they would wish to be thin. They spend a great deal of time and money, painting their faces and doing their hair, so that they should appear desirable in the eyes of men. We must presume they subject themselves to the torture chamber for the same reason. Evidently they haven't the faintest notion of what appeals to men.

Man, throughout the ages, has fantasised about the likes of Roseanne (a well-rounded woman in a slick American TV comedy). If women would look at the works of the great artists from the time they first started slapping paint on canvas, they would know what fuels the beast in man. There is no reason to suppose the average man on the croft in 1995 is any different to Rubens in 1620.

There is nothing wrong with plenty of flesh, as long as the waist is still discernible. The exact proportion of the ideal woman varies from lecher to lecher but the one that doesn't rate is the thin woman. Apart from anything else, the thin woman is useless on the *tairsgear* when she hits a tough stretch of peat. A well-built woman when she stands beside you at a fence that must be crossed will offer the ample pad on her hip for you to step on while climbing over.

On the other hand, perhaps I have it all wrong. Perhaps they do not want to fuel the beast in man, and this is why they want to look like Twiggy. Perhaps, who knows, a size 12 is cheaper than a size 16. Very practical people, women, usually.

But they should think of the long winter months and the cost of running an electric blanket. I can provide statistics, if anyone wants, because my first wife was thin and could never get warmed up. With the present round and jolly wife we can sleep out under trees without a blanket.

And now she talks of going to get inducted. Let us have an end to this nonsense. Lie back and grow fat.

FRIDAY, 12 MAY 1995

'Fifty years ago today' is how they all started their columns this week. This put me in the notion to go back and have a look at my own early diaries.

Well, 50 years ago today was not a good day for me. It was a bright sunny day but the north-easterly was fierce and cold. Being carried to the peats in the nanny's creel was a dashed uncomfortable way to travel, although I didn't complain much at the time. A powerful woman, the nanny; she could leap the bogs with me on her back while knitting a stocking for victory, but she wasn't the sort to put up with girning.

I should also add that I rattled about quite a bit in the creel wrapped up in an old bit of Harris Tweed. This was because I was extremely small, thin and fragile. So poorly that I wasn't expected to live for very long. But I surprised them all and thrived because, although I remained very thin and still do till this day, I wasn't prone to the common illnesses of that time. Yet, all in all, I had a pretty raw deal.

It wasn't much of a life propped up against a heather turf watching women at work. The old one, the Granny, was clearly the boss, and a tyrant to boot who gave the other women a hard time. I wasn't sure, then, which of the many spare women was the mother and which were nannies – Seonag Rob, Màiri Mhòr Chaluim Iain, Curly and I don't know how many more – because none of them had any milk in those lean times and I had to make do with National Dried Milk occasionally laced with a spoonful of rum to pull me through as if I were an orphaned lamb. The Dried Milk tins turned out to be very useful a bit later on for making boats and the taste for rum never left me.

Perhaps it wasn't all that bad with so many nannies about, but it would have been nice to have had some young men around. Except for a few very old men of 50, survivors of the First War, and a couple with flat feet, there wasn't a male on the scene with whom one could bond. I was cheesed off with all these women, although I didn't realise this until my psychiatrist explained 40 years later.

There was yet another type of person, I see from my early scribbling, that I couldn't class as men at all because they were so old it didn't make sense. As old as the hills, I often heard. They had long white beards and sat at the gable-ends receiving messages through their accumulators and passing the information to those who moved about. I supposed they were the secret agents who first learned the war had ended. Only it hadn't, of course. Not for me.

The old man had been posted to the Far East near the end. This was rough luck. You would have thought having spent years in the North Atlantic on a crowded corvette, dropping depth charges and firing torpedoes at U-boats, they would have told these guys they'd done enough and sent them home to help the women with the peats. But no, they sent them east for another chance to be killed by suicidal Japanese.

By strange coincidence the old fellow was in Jakarta the day the war started and ended back near the same spot 50 years ago today. I shouldn't have written ended because he survived, but you know what I meant. My grasp of English, 50 years ago today, was slight, as will quickly be seen by anyone who buys the 'Early Diaries' for twelve million; but for all that, the serious historian will find them every bit as useful as the notes of Churchill, who was all the time as a newt.

I was the one who suffered, but not, I must admit, as much as Alasdair Beag Alasdair Thormoid, who was still, 50 years ago today, being tortured by the Japanese in some hellish camp in South-East Asia. Although, like the rest of them, he never spoke much about the nightmare, we read and heard about it and I'm not sure I have forgiven them yet. Hiroshima was bad but it was all over in a second and couldn't compare with one many of you knew being systematically tortured for years.

My chief complaint, 50 years ago today, was how I missed out on a fancy name. Because of the uncertainty of the old man's whereabouts, and the grave suspicion that he might not come home, I was given his name. Had he returned a little earlier, instead of waiting until I was nine months old, I might have been given a fancy name like Marmaduke or Jeremy and my life would have been much easier. Perhaps I would have gotten a job with the BBC if I had not been saddled with this name that no one can spell or pronounce. Thank you, Mr Churchill, as if you hadn't done enough damage at the Dardenelles.

But to get back to the diaries: I see an entry here on the occasion of my reaching the age of six months. Half a year old today and what do I get! More

National Dried Milk and a dose of syrup of fix. I guess I spelled it that way because it was supposed to fix anything, especially blockages. At the hint of a blockage each nanny in turn fed me syrup of fix until it was coming through me like paraffin. I was pretty fed up with that war and women in general.

Occasionally among the women a certain man of undetermined age would appear and pass on a few words of advice on the rearing of young boys. Words like 'You should always bathe him in cold water' or 'Throw him in the sea so he'll learn to swim'. Luckily, they never took his advice because he was alleged to be an atheist who read novels on Sunday. This old fellow wanted to teach me to play the chanter, but this was discouraged because the instrument could only play the idle music of the Devil. Nobody can tell how things might have developed had my war really ended 50 years ago today.

There will be some of you ready to cast doubt on a six-month-old child's ability to write a diary, but you must remember I was very advanced. Aye, very advanced indeed.

FRIDAY, 19 MAY 1995

'AT DAWN THE RIDGE EMERGES MASSED AND DUN...'

Seldom have I seen such a morning as this Sunday. There is not the merest whisper of a breeze and Loch Erisort at high tide is as still as death. The only wisp of cloud is high and far away over Gairloch, there is a little warmth in the white morning sun, peat smoke mirrored on the calm surface of the sea spirals lazily from a chimney in Cromore and the only sound on the land is the singing of the lark.

When I sit straight up and prop up the pillows behind me, I can see the cattle in Crossbost and frolicking young lambs. Johann Sebastian Bach is making music suitable for the Sabbath on the radio by my bedside, and in the bed itself a warm woman slumbers. Any second now this woman will awaken to minister to my needs. She will stretch contentedly and ask me if it is time she went down to crispen some bacon, butter some oatcakes or anything else I can think of.

You would think, then, a man in these circumstances would register a measure of contentment if not outright happiness, would you not?

Alas, this is not the case. Despite nature's unlimited bounty, I am consumed with bad humours and bile. My mind is poisoned by venomous thoughts and I am totally preoccupied by murderous intention towards Sandy Matheson. Unless I let them spill out onto the page I'm afraid I might explode.

Matheson, you might remember, was once a famous man in the town of Stornoway. Perhaps you saw his photograph in the *Gazette*. Youngest Mayor, youngest Convener, youngest Grand Master, Fellow of the Royal College of Alchemists, goalkeeper for School 'A', wealthy businessman and the son of a famous man to boot. You would think that was enough. You would expect a man like that to say to himself, I've done my share, I'll take it easy now; but he won't. He will not rest until he has me destroyed.

About a year ago I had to create a terrible scene on the premises of the newsagent Roddy Smith (proprietor S Matheson) over the disgraceful business of selling incomplete newspapers. Angry letters were exchanged and the case went within a whisker of landing in the laps of m' learned friends. Eventually the matter was resolved when British Airways accepted the blame. Apparently they were in the habit of ditching the most convenient bundles of print whenever they were overloaded with passengers. I accepted their apologies and an appropriate sum of cash by way of compensation, and all unpleasantness was forgotten for a time.

Then, two weeks ago on a very busy Saturday afternoon, I rushed into the same paper shop, collected my paper and only noticed Zia Mahmood was missing when I sat down to my chops. Incandescent with rage, I phoned the shop and demanded my money, only to be told this couldn't, alas, be done. Finders keepers, or something to that effect, was what the woman said. I resolved to go in there and wipe the floor with them as soon as they opened on Monday morning, but by then I had started smoking again and couldn't have cared less about anything.

On this otherwise glorious Sunday morning I am once again without my comic. Yes, they did it to me again, only this time I was on my guard.

I opened the paper apprehensively, hoping I wouldn't have to create a fuss, but sure enough it was half a pound light. Unluckily I was served by a young part-time girl, otherwise I would have said a bad word. In the event I merely tore a Royal Bank of Scotland pound note in two and offered her half, to which she replied: 'I couldn't take that.' Well, what do you think of that? The child was prepared to take the full price for half a paper. But never mind . . . it's the big fellow I'm after.

After this traumatic encounter I wandered about for 10 minutes, shocked and dazed, looking for my car in the Coffee Pot car park but couldn't find it. Eventually I did find it in the main car park on the pier, but by this time I was soaked to the semmit and my shoes were ruined. In my condition of extreme agitation I arrived home without the Saturday night steak or the wife's medicinal brandy, as a result of which we had to eat some cholesterol-laden crab claws washed down with tea.

My poor mental and physical condition this morning cannot this time be blamed on British Airways. Unlikely as it might seem, we have suspected for a long time BA staff at Glasgow Airport like to read. Being very poorly paid, they cannot afford to buy their own papers and were thought, wrongly as it happens, to lift the occasional bundle for Stornoway. This has now been disproved. Word reaches me from the bush that the Monk in Back received his complete paper yesterday, which clearly shows I am the victim of a vendetta. Someone in Roddy Smith's is deliberately trying to drive me crazy.

When I took my troubles to the Lawyer, he thought, as lawyers would, it was all about money. Money is of course the least of it. Fifty pee means little to Sandy Matheson, although considerably more, no doubt, than it does to me. It is injury to the psyche that will make the damages worthwhile. If m' learned friend refuses to take my case seriously, I have no alternative but to lie in wait for Matheson when the nights lengthen again and mug him. One way or another justice will be done.

The measurement of a jury's award could be based on a distraught man's inability to appreciate a morning such as described three hours ago. Now a cold wind has arisen and a large cumulus is threatening to unload its cargo and I feel much better. Such is my sense of bitterness and injustice.

Friday, 2 June 1995

Anyone who has driven through North Lochs in recent weeks will have realised it is only a matter of very short time until a tragic accident happens.

The Comhairle, in their wisdom, have undertaken to improve the scenery in Leurbost, perhaps to make it look more like Ranish with deep ravines and artificial hills. This generous but mistaken venture has resulted in the most wanton act of vandalism ever perpetrated by governors on the governed. And all this for the sake of speed.

Motorway madness is something we tend to associate with mainland Britain and Tory governments, but now we have it on our doorsteps. By motorway madness I don't mean the behaviour of crazed drivers; I mean the laying of costly concrete and tarmacadam where it is neither needed nor wanted. In Leurbost the concept has been taken to an unprecedented extreme.

The road through the old village was considered inadequate for present-day traffic loads and the expectations of people in a hurry, and perhaps there was some truth in this. So what do they do? The road is not good enough, so let's destroy the village. Where will it all end, is what people who live on the edge of the precipice are asking. There is nothing left for us to do, say others, but to emigrate as our forefathers were forced to do before us.

Let us look at the problem sensibly, as sensible people should have done. We had a narrow stretch of pot-holed road that did not permit of overtaking or even allow for a moment to admire the Loch. At very little cost the dangerous stretch could have been resurfaced and frequent passing places could have been provided for those who cannot get up in time for work.

But this would not do. We had to have a motorway like Point, Back, Uig and South Lochs. The politics of envy have carried us to the stage where families have to evacuate their houses in the cause of speed. The cost to the ratepayer of rehousing those whose foundations are being undermined will be astronomical – possibly amounting to the sort of money that would build a new school – but that is not the worst of it.

It happens that the new motorway has to pass through several of the few mature gardens in an island where trees are lamentably scarce. Middle Leurbost was one of the rare areas in the entire archipelago that somehow could afford to spare a little space, time and soil for decoration. Half a generation after two hungry children were imprisoned for taking shellfish at low tide without the consent of the landlord, their grandchildren, miraculously, had become so unimaginably affluent they could take the time to plant trees instead of potatoes. (What could they have done with set-aside?)

Now the bulldozers are bulldozing through, creating a concrete desert, so we can get to Stornoway five minutes early. Deep caverns have been hacked out of the hillside, and old familiar landmarks have been sliced in half, desecrating the grand design of the moving ice. Whether you believe the outlines were shaped by God or by the weight of ice, you have to admit they were pleasing, and they were. The Supreme Architect must be writhing in his grave.

But what does this matter to the latter-day architects of a philistine Tory age whose only mission in life is to complete the Thatcherite dream of a tarred nation. (You shouldn't be seen in a hard-hat near the scene, Malcolm, in case people think it is all your fault.)

On a more down-to-this-earth note, we should also remember it is the time of year for young students to come home. They like speed, will borrow their mothers' XR4s, and either fall into the temporary gully or else, when the high-speed highway is complete, they will mow down some slow-moving church-bound cailleach.

Never mind the cailleachs, because unlike us they are ready to go. The sad thing is that all this is happening at a time when even the filling-in of potholes is unnecessary because more and more poor crofters seem to be driving vehicles we wished we could have had in distant underdeveloped continents. Four-be-fours, they call them, and they don't mean rafters. Eventually, when these become cheaper, with their balloon tyres, they will replace the tractor on the croft.

As far as I am concerned, this will not come soon enough. Much as I like to have visitors. I have terrible trouble getting them out to the main road late at night. I'm not sure who to blame for this because I cannot remember who was responsible for the original cattle grid and the squint walls on either side that set people off reversing in the wrong direction. Maybe it was Roddy J, but then maybe I helped him when we were both young and foolish and neither able to help the other very much.

The end result is my bad back. Inevitably nowadays when the wee wife is saying goodnight I automatically go and put on the seaboots, because it is only a matter of minutes until I have to lift a car out of a drain.

I have noticed over the years that the more intelligent they are the more difficulty they have with reversing.

By far the worst cases are ceilidhers from a certain ward of Ospadal nan Eilean – and here I am talking about the staff. Whether they have too much on their minds . . . who can say. I guess reversing is a bit like golf. Eminent colleagues often ask me how an intelligent man like the Lawyer can play golf and all I can say is: 'Watch his backswing.' Only an empty mind can complete the turn, with perhaps the exception of Tom Watson.

The turn out of my *staran* has often been taken like the Lawyer's backswing. The obvious thinking is the sooner we get out of here the better. It would be hard to judge the worst but Sheila, the cuddliest of the nurses, must be the star. With one and a half glasses of wine she found the stream between me and Charlie next door – a full 20 yards short of the road.

Or perhaps it's a tie between her and Iain Kennedy on holiday from Canada. This is an athlete of mature years who has done some intricate work in the intestines of human beings, yet it took him a full 20 minutes to negotiate that infamous stretch. Cunninghame North, who is not at one with machinery, is realistic enough not to attempt it: he walks down and lets his wife drive.

What worries me now is what might happen when they reach the Comhairle canyon out the road. I hope my anxiety, as is often the case, is all over nothing. Wait till I get my five-be-five.

FRIDAY, 9 JUNE 1995

SPORT

Those who stayed up late at the weekend to watch Brazil play Sweden would not have been disappointed. Even Jimmy Hill had to concede this was what football should be about, and whatever the Scots will say about Jimmy Hill, he knows the game better than most. I suspect Jimmy, like most of us, thought football had reached its zenith with the Brazil team of 1970; but there are signs the fresh crop of wee boys from Rio could be almost as good.

After several days of exposure to the brutal, loutish game of rugby, it was a marvellous treat to relax and be entertained by the exquisite skill of the fresh crop of wee boys from Rio. What I have never understood is how referees don't seem to notice Brazil always have about 15 players on the field; against Sweden there appeared to be even more of them. I dare say this wasn't a great Swedish team, yet although they were twice the size of the little men they seemed to be outnumbered by about two-to-one.

Ronaldo, I understand, is only 18, and the tiny Juninho we haven't seen the likes of since Jimmy Johnstone was the same age. The name Dunga sounds as if it should belong to Point but, although that parish produced good footballers, I don't believe there is any connection.

The cardinal rule of football is that you must keep your eye on the ball. When wise old coaches gave out this advice presumably they meant both eyes. This is where Brazil have a great advantage. They must have practised the basic skills so much they are free to use their eyes to keep tabs all the time on their team-mates. Either that or they have eyes in the backs of their heads. Or perhaps they just pass into any open space knowing they have so many men to spare that one will soon appear to cushion the ball and carry it as if it were a natural extension to the body.

There was a time when people were relegated to full-back if they were short on skill, heavy-limbed or past their best and perhaps good at scything. Brazilian full-backs, if such a title still exists, have more ability than the best of our inside-forwards. It is like playing with 10 sober George Bests in a team. We will look forward with interest to see if they will be allowed to play football against England, or whether they will be hacked down and crippled early in the game.

The only other game I saw recently, by way of stark contrast, was Lochs against Point in Leurbost. Lochs, I'm afraid, have a traditional full-back in every position, but this suited them on the night. The ground was of the sort cattle used to get bogged down in and only the strongest could plough their way through. Point, although not short of skill, were mostly lightly built and had little chance in the mud.

I couldn't help noticing many of the Lochs team are built in the shape of Angus Beattie, and I wonder if the manager Eddie Richardson has them on some sort of body-building course. Or is he feeding them too much of his own renowned cooking? With three exceptions who can carry the ball for a few yards, Eddie has to rely mainly on strength; but he's doing a grand job with what he's got. I see no reason why Angie Hogg should not be given a game once he has the varicose veins sorted.

Still on the subject of sport of sorts, my wife had a strange and disturbing encounter the other day.

After I had spent a great deal of money I couldn't afford in Bain and Morrison, she patiently awaited delivery by lorry (believe me, if you need a lorry to deliver from that quarter you can forget about foreign holidays for a while).

In due course word reached her that the lorry was in the village. Naturally, she set about preparing a table fit for a king. Delicacies of the most exotic nature were laid out. Tea of exactly the right strength was drawn and kept warm in red-white-and-blue cosy. Costly Belgian chocolates were unwrapped and a fine cognac was uncorked in case your man should feel like breaking his golden rule. When everything was exactly as she judged would please him, she slipped into 'something more comfortable' and waited.

Alas, the driver was not Kelso. Much to her dismay, there was a stranger on your man's beat. No sooner had the new boy (who need not be named) disembarked than he started trying to attract her attention with what seemed a desperate urgency.

'Duncan Ferguson's got the jail,' he yelled. This alarmed the wife, who has some cousins called Ferguson. She racked her wee brain but couldn't recall any of the Ferguson clan called Duncan and she told him so.

If the man was distressed when he arrived, he was doubly so now. He didn't wait for tea. He didn't speak again. He hurriedly shed his load, casting suspicious glances in the woman's direction, and left as soon as he could, driving quickly but erratically through the village.

The good Lord only knows what damage was done to this boy's psyche. Several days later when he was able to speak, they tell me, all he could say was: 'There is a woman in North Lochs who doesn't know who Duncan Ferguson is.' Only similarly afflicted fanatics can understand the depths of the man's traumatic experience. Still, he has the consolation of being surrounded by sensitive, understanding colleagues who will no doubt, in their own caring way, soon nurse him back to health.

Saturday night sport in the Narrows has taken a turn towards the nasty.

If nothing much else, I have learned one thing in a long life, and that is to treat with extreme caution 'factual' reports by young men after the pubs shut. Yet I have little reason to doubt the latest story.

Last Saturday night one youngster was set upon by another and kicked for no apparent reason. Nothing new there, you might think; but this time the attacker was of the skinhead variety and, according to witnesses, sporting Nazi insignia. Perhaps this is a lone sad idiot, but on the other hand it would be wise to keep an eye on him to see if he has any friends.

Even better sport. On Monday last Prince Andrew, the second-in-command of the grandest quango of all, dropped into Stornoway for a game of golf. While many loyal Rangers supporters lined the fairways waving their royal blue knickers, Mr K's reaction, when told of the Arch Parasite's visit was: 'Did he pay his green fees?' Apparently not!

FRIDAY, 16 JUNE 1995

After 10 rest days I return to my place of work, and it looks very much as if it isn't a day too soon. The walls and the ceilings are clean enough and the scientific utensils are gleaming. The refrigerator, although entirely lacking in the small comforts of life, is spotless. The white coats are freshly laundered.

However, I am not very long at my desk until it becomes all too obvious advantage has been taken of my absence. The first abomination to catch my eye was a furrow in the carpet of the main 'waiting room'. This gross infringement of office rules could have been perpetrated by a burrowing animal, such as a rabbit, but this doesn't seem likely because there is nothing in the place to eat for man nor rabbit. During my 10 days of recuperation I have been reading detective stories, and I think I've learned a thing or two.

I suspect the injury to the carpet was caused by a person, as yet unknown, swinging some sort of club. But we'll let that pass for the time being because further evidence of negligent, nay, criminal, activity leaps out at me from every page of the most important document in ours or any other office.

As every patient knows who has ever been kept waiting for a prescription or whatever, case notes have to be written by hand in old-fashioned ink. Phenomena of great rarity are entered in red ink. There is a good reason for this, and getting gooder all the time as the risk of legal action increases every year (I blame all these films they see from the United States of America). You can understand my horror when I uncover irregularities.

On the sixth day of June in this most legal of documents an entry that might possibly have been of the greatest import is partly smudged by what looks very much like blood. At this stage I decide to take the sensible precaution of inviting a sceond opinion, because you never know when or what you might find yourself accused of in these days of letters from ministers.

As good fortune would have it, Rodney was passing by. Rodney, a keen local aviator, is familiar not only with the law, he also comes of Lochs crofting stock and is therefore not without medical expertise. I was more than happy to have him in on the case. Before we came to the bloodstains he discovered an important entry made on the second day of June that was completely obscured by what we were in agreement could only be a tuft of sheep's wool.

'I thought as much,' *ars esan*. 'I have long been of the opinion crofters with coarse hobbies should be prohibited from part-time work in surgeries and similar medical laboratories.' On page 12 of the sacred ledger a dirty, rusty smudge had me puzzled for a while, but Rodney had it sussed. 'The same man,' he thought. 'He is very likely still castrating lambs in the old way and possibly into the modern technique of sewing prolapsed wombs back into ewes with his sailmaker's needle.'

The further we dug into the good book, the more inevitable it became the accusing finger could only point in one direction – and one direction only. 'What do you think of that one?' I asked him, pointing to a thumb print the size of Mac an t-Srònaich's big toe. 'All circumstantial,' he ventured. 'We must make sure.'

On the 12th we found two pages stuck together by what could be nothing else but the crisply-fried fin of an oily herring. All that remained for us to detect was where herring had been caught recently and prepared for eating by a man who has no time to sterilise his fingers. The case is almost ready to be presented to Debbie, the Proc, but that leaves us far from the solving of my problem.

What do I do with the important statistics that may one day be used for research if they are congealed in wool, scales, flesh and blood? In a very short time this supreme document of the thermodynamic dynamic history of our age will give off a bad smell. In the interests of posterity it cannot be destroyed. There is nothing for it now but to preserve a full month of detailed scientific notes in an oaken barrel of Cailean Neillie's coarse salt.

Time has been called by the great ref in the sky.

The heir to my estate has come charging into the ancestral home – mob-handed. Murray MacInnes on his own with his temper, and his Maradona hand up, can be said to amount to a mob. They demand I follow them to watch Lochs play Ness. Ness, no less – the strongest Lewis football team of recent years. At the same time they claimed I understood nothing of 1995 football.

Naturally, I declined, because I'd heard the club and the manager were unhappy with my comments on the Point game and were threatening to sort me out. Nevertheless, I sneaked up the West Side route, with my spyglass, and now I have to concede their accusations are (partly) justified by results.

Ah, but! Who was right about Brazil? Didn't skill, despite the drizzle, beat English thuggery on the day? Nothing personal, dear Eddie, but I made the mistake of assuming because many of your Lochs players are as big as rugby players they would be equally clumsy. I offer humblest apologies for my hasty assessment on that night in heavy ground.

Iain Murdo and Gary have a wee touch of class, and the boy they call Stoon is not all defender. Eachainn, who is named after the same South Lochs Eachainn as myself, tends to be what English commentators call over-exuberant as he gathers oncoming sweepers on his scythe, yet his ability is not in question.

Having beaten Aths 6–1, and now Ness, perhaps there is more to the modern Lochs game than an old crofter can grasp, dear Ed. Remember the cake.

FRIDAY, 23 JUNE 1995

For the last few weeks I've had both eyes out for a suitable moter car for the wee wife, but so far my search has yielded nothing that fits her requirements. People who know tell me Glasgow is the place. They say the further north you come the more you have to pay. Whether or not there is any truth in this piece of pub philosophy I couldn't say, yet, like most people in search of a bargain, I'm ready to swallow any story if it is told by someone whose hands are covered in grease and whose knuckles are bleeding.

This is why, despite dreadful past experience, I have been perusing the Glasgow paper. However, I am easily distracted, so that long before I reach the adverts I have become engrossed in a long letter from a conservative gentleman from the town called Kilmarnock. This man is disturbed by the threat of a national minimum wage – and who can blame him, for unless there is a change of government sooner rather than later we will all be on it.

But I suspect this is not a concern of our man in Kilmarnock. For a blootering stick he uses an 'apprentice hairdresser'. 'Take the apprentice hairdresser at £2.35 an hour,' he says. 'Would you like to throw her on the scrap heap?' Forget for a moment that he makes the crass assumption she has to be a woman; his point is that if her wage is forced up to £4 an hour we will all stop having our hair permed. The 'apprentice hairdresser' was an unfortunate occupational illustration.

Whatever else we might stop, we will never stop having our hair done, even when we're nearly bald – or especially when we're nearly bald. If you look at ancient sculpture you will see the Greeks spent a great deal of time on their hair. Two thousand years ago the Romans, when they weren't building roads, thought of little else (my friend Gus once dreamt he lived in these times and that his job was a public hairdresser). Do you suppose all this is going to stop if some poor 'girl' gets paid £4 an hour? I think not. My own meagre purse is protected from this particular drain because my wife goes to Mamie's, but I have heard, from unfortunate colleagues, there are wives who pay as much as twenty pounds for a 'clup'.

To get back to the man in Kilmarnock . . . His letter is so long that towards the end of it his apprentice hairdresser has become a 'hairdresser', and guess what! He still has her on £2.35 an hour. No slip of the pen, methinks.

I fear there are many more like him – and not just in Kilmarnock. When speaking for those who live by the sweat of the poor girl's brow, he should have said what he meant – and that is, we cannot give them a penny more, for there will be less for us.

He is wrong, though, as are all his cronies in crime. They are fairly skilled at this type of propaganda but the truth is a minimum wage would have no effect on employment. Those who have made exploitation their profession would simply pass the cost on to the customer and invent new gimmicks (perhaps hire Gus).

As a matter of fact, the minimum wage, if applied to apprentices, would bring immediate and lasting benefit to the great majority of struggling households and therefore society as a whole. We cannot all be doctors, so the chances are you have an apprentice electrician, a nurse or similarly useful tradesperson in the house. You know what happens to them. The day they are old enough to warrant the going rate, they are down the road to make way for cheap labour.

The follow-on effect is one we are all too sadly aware of. The apprentice's car is repossessed. Plans for a wedding have to be shelved and perhaps he has the engagement ring thrown in his face. The girl has no choice but to bring the child up on her own, much to the disgust of the tax-paying employer who engineered the disaster in the first place. And all for the sake of £1.65 an hour.

Sorry about that little diversion, but the stupidity of the Tory press makes me frightfully angry.

Now, where were we? Ah, yes, looking for a car. Some of the adverts in the Glasgow paper are entertaining but extremely puzzling.

'Sixty thousand cherished miles' is a common one. What do you make of that, then? Do you suppose all the mileage was done around Loch Lomondside or is this some pervert who really liked driving?

Here is another one that is difficult to figure: 'Must sell due to immigration'. Is this someone from Bangladesh who needs a bigger car because he expects the extended family to join him? Or could it be that

Immigration Officers have caught up with him and unless he sells the car and gives them the money they'll strangle him to death?

But the best of them all is: 'One lady owner from new.' This is a bit like trying to sell a horse and claiming you've flogged it severely every day for its own good.

Still, the search must go on.

Morain taing, a Mharisa, a ghràidh, airson do chuireadh gu trì latha fada còmhla ri Tormod Tioram air Tìr ann an Uibhist. Ach tha eagal orm. Thug Maggie suil air, agus labhair i le guth làidir: 'Too dangerous'.

I hear Lochs won again on Monday night by six goals to nil. Although this was only against West Side, it seems early season critics will have to revise their assessment. What a team, Eddie; don't forget the cake.

FRIDAY, 14 JULY 1995

Coming over the breast of a hill in the Castle Grounds the other day with my old friend Norman Macgregor, we spotted at a distance the unmistakable figures of Bronco and Fred MacLennan. They were at the game of golf and one or both of them had a young boy working as a caddie.

'I sincerely hope,' said Norman, 'that boy is not from a Christian home.' I knew what he meant. Any young man should strive to increase the range and depth of his vocabulary through mixing with Elders, but in this case it was a very poor choice of Elders.

As it turned, out the boy, we were later told, was the son of Dr Gray Mhurchaidh 'An Sheoc. On behalf of the club I would like to apologise to the good Doctor, for I am sure he would have had to spend the weekend washing the boy's mouth out with carbolic soap.

While we relaxed after our exertions, discussing the mysteries of the Universe, it came to light that many members of the Golf Club, like Doctor Glas, are of a religious bent and strict adherents to one or other of the Free Churches. A very cosmopolitan corner of the Castle Grounds is the Golf Club nowadays. We have hillbillies from Uig, Shawbost and Ness as well as the aforementioned churchgoers.

They are all, of course, very welcome. Now that people no longer do physical toil, golf is an invaluable form of exercise and the only sensible game for the older person. Very welcome, I said, but I have one or two serious complaints. It has been noticed that an unhealthily large number of members, for one reason or another, do not frequent the clubhouse. They come and they use the facilities, often changing into their golf shoes in the car park, and then they go.

This is not good enough. It costs a great deal of money to run a golf course and the annual subs go only a small part of the way towards meeting this cost. The yearly subscription of about one hundred pounds is by far the lowest in the Kingdom. It should be remembered, by those who change in the car park, that the subs are low only because of the money taken at the bar from poor crofters like me and Dixie.

Not for a moment do I suggest that all members should be forced to drink. Those who can tolerate sobriety and reality all the time should be allowed to do so, but that does not mean they shouldn't buy for those who cannot. They should come in and talk to people like Kelso. Although he doesn't spend any money himself, he is a wonderful catalyst. He makes people happy and encourages generosity in others. So much so that they often don't realise until the following day how much they've spent on him.

If, despite our pleading, the holy men still refuse to come to the bar, I am pleased to say someone has come up with an excellent suggestion whereby the burden of upkeep will be shared by all. An additional and very reasonable extra fee of fifty pounds per month will be paid by those who do not use the clubhouse. It is a small price to pay for external peace.

Because of the nature of the game of golf, eternity and the meaning of life are subjects that are endlessly discussed in the Club. Although followers of the old-style religion are dwindling in number, there are still a few guys around who would like to live forever.

Personally, I cannot think of anything more frightening than eternal bliss. After about a million years I would expect to be pretty fed up with the lush green fairways of heaven. Or perhaps, if one were really bad, eternity in a bunker would be the sentence. Imagine the calluses on the left hand after even such a short time as one thousand years.

I'm afraid I have a terrible problem with the business of the soul. If I suspected it were about to escape the body, I would have someone standing by to swat it like a cleg. On the other hand, those of us who are good and try to spread happiness have a right to expect some reward. We certainly should expect something better than people like the Rev Angus Smith, who spends a lifetime spreading misery. The man doesn't even play golf.

And yet the people who live in hope of winning what they think will be the greatest prize of all are perhaps less to be pitied than whose who are obsessed with the National Lottery.

I warned about the dangers long ago, but already matters are a great deal worse than even I feared. Although the great essayist Orwell wasn't much good at writing novels, he wasn't far wrong with 1984. The following is a scene from that depressing book I had forgotten until I saw it quoted the other day. We should all take heed. It was written, remember, in 1948.

' "I tell you no number ending in seven ain't won for over fourteen months!"

"Yes, it 'as then!"

' "No, it 'as not. Back 'ome I got the whole lot of 'em for over two years wrote down on a piece of paper. I takes 'em down regular as the clock. An I tell you, no number ending in seven . . ."

'They were talking about the Lottery. Winston looked back when he had gone thirty metres. They were still arguing, with vivid, passionate faces. The Lottery, with its weekly pay-out of enormous prizes, was the one public event to which the proles paid serious attention. It was probable that there were millions of proles from whom the Lottery was the principal if not the only reason for remaining alive. It was their delight, their folly, their anodyne, their intellectual stimulant. Where the Lottery was concerned, even people who could barely read and write seemed capable of intricate calculations and staggering feats of memory. There was a whole tribe of men who made a living simply by selling systems, forecasts and lucky amulets.'

What can we say except that we hope this system of taxation, or theft, will be abolished or reformed by Mr Blair, who will surely now follow Major into No 10. Poor John – one of the few men who will go down in history as having tried to fall on his sword and missed.

FRIDAY, 3 JULY 1995

I have just finished and enjoyed a wee book of essays written by Torcuil MacRath, who lives down in the village of Grimsiadar. Now that the sun has gone down for the year, you could do worse than start the reading season with Torcuil's stories set around Loch Urnabhaigh (the booklet is published by the *Gasait* but is fine for all that).

Torcuil's detective work is of special interest to those of us who lived near Loch Urnabhaigh, and there can be no doubt that the loch should be called Urnabhaigh and not Loch Grimsiadar. My only regret is that he didn't add a final modern chapter on why those of us who lived on the south side of the loch called Grimsiadar Belgium. It was just one of those things we accepted and didn't question in our youth. Unlike Torcuil, we were not terribly inquisitive.

But what I would really like to know is what happened to the ghosts. Not that Torcuil dwells on ghosts: he merely mentions a few in passing. But you can take my word for it they existed. There can be few glens or lochs that harboured more ghosts than Urnabhaigh.

My one theory is that they are lying low or have moved away since the introduction of street lighting. It is possible they have an aversion to unnatural phenomena like electricity and other strange things invented since they were of this earth. And who could blame them.

On the other hand, they may still be out there in the dark and nobody would know because people don't go out at night any more. You will often hear some young person of the electrical age question the existence of ghosts because they have yet to encounter them in person. The fools! Where would they be likely to see ghosts unless they materialised on *Coronation Street.*

Please, my children, do not doubt, for I have seen them with my own two eyes. Bad ghosts and good ghosts. And so have all my friends.

The first man of roughly my own generation to fall foul of a bad ghost was the late Councillor Alasdair Neileag. On a dark winter's night he was negotiating the perilous bend near the Teampall when the 'thing' got him by the throat. He didn't see it. He didn't have time to run. It got him by the neck and gave him a fierce shaking that left him nervous for the rest of his days.

As for strange lights, we were so accustomed to those we considered them hardly worthy of mention. Sometimes they would turn out to be another earthly being with a torch, but not always. At about the age of six I was going through an early phase of scepticism, despite frequent sessions of frightening stories around the fire. It had occurred to me even then that it was always someone else who saw strange apparitions. And then it happened.

While making my way home from Coinneach's, down by the cold dark north side of Feannag na Gaoithe, I saw up above me against a faint skyline, travelling in the same direction, the unmistakable figure of a squat man. Although I was at that time as hardy as the night was black (only much later did I become the nervous wreck I am today), I started whistling to let 'him' know I was real and nothing to be afraid of.

Keeping one eye on the potholes in my path, I reserved the other eye for the figure up above that drew ever closer as we continued on our bearings that should inevitably have converged above the well. He certainly did not turn back, for I had my eye on him all the time. He did not cross my path, and yet when I reached the point where we had to meet he was not there.

Nothing untoward has occurred at that spot yet, except that Ivor cleared a lot of the soil away with a JCB while building a road to his new house. Yet there is still time, unless this squat evil 'man' has been frightened away by the noise of modern machinery and electricity.

That he was evil there can be no doubt, otherwise he would have spoken. This gave me strength in the following year, believing as I did that I had met a force of darkness and had stared it out. It didn't dawn on me until much later it had probably adopted me and is my protector until this day. It is clear to me now that they only manifest themselves in the presence of the sort of innocence and purity that can only exist in childhood.

Towards the end of that year electricity arrived, to the accompaniment of loud destructive blasting. Several boats were destroyed through the use of too much powder and this upheaval caused the ghosts to seek quieter moorland pastures.

However, once again, I was making my way down Feannag na Gaoithe, on a night of black darkness that can only be compared with Archangel Tar, when a woman – or a slender willowy figure one had to assume was a woman – undulated out of the side of the hill threatening to envelop me in the billowing folds of her white, flowing, dare I say it, shroud. This time I did not stand my ground because I recognised her. I ran home.

Two hours later, that same evening, the dreaded electrons were allowed to flow through the wires, and not long afterwards the connection was made official and the woman on the hill died. This is hardly proof that electricity has alienated ghosts, but you must agree it is odd they have kept their distance since that night.

And, ever since, nothing has surprised me. Although a glimpse of my shadow can scare me, it never surprises me because I live in expectation of ghosts. Sadly, not one creature from the other side has manifested itself since these early days, which is in some way a terrible disappointment.

From the age of 12, when we were old enough to borrow boats for the crossing of Urnabhaigh to visit the beautiful young girls that surrounded Torcuil, the only ghostly claws we felt about our necks were the horny hands of the owners of the boats and the Daddies of the girls.

The Urnabhaigh girls of glorious memory were, of course, younger than Torcuil, and perhaps there was a shortage in *his* green days, which might explain how his passion lay dormant until he met Angela from

Eriskay. Or do we read too much into his one careless mention of a woman of recent times?

28 JULY 95

Six weeks if it's a day since I put the word out I'm looking for a suitable car for the wee wife, and not a word out of anyone. Admittedly, she is as difficult to fit for a car as my old friend Daniel B is for a shoe.

Daniel, one of nature's gentlemen, needed a special shoe even before the gout got a grip because of the unique width of the feet at the bow. From the stem of the shoe, at the heel, until you reached the fallen arch, he was neither here nor there, and not much different from the rest of us; but after that he was as wide as the St Kildans were long. After 70 years' constant walking after sheep on the same feet, the for'ard section of both feet cannot be contained even by specialists such as the Millionaire Cobbler.

The situation is much the same with his cousin, my wife. Her requirements sound simple until you add them together; when you do the sums, they are impossible. I will not bore here with a list of her disabilities. Her one great terrifying fear is the black frost. On more than one occasion she has watched a nurse's car in front of her slither off the road and into the peat, and that was in the winter days when they started as late as quarter to eight. Now that they start at quarter to seven, I doubt if even John Alec will be up out of his four-poster to spread the necessary drop of salt to keep these old women out of the ditches.

The upshot of it all is that she wants a four-be-four. Now that I'm retiring to concentrate on The Novel, and she is going to be the breadwinner, she desperately needs some mode of transport that will ensure she brings in a few pennies while I do the housework.

Having considered all the possibilities, I have come to the conclusion the only safe way of getting to Stornoway at 6am in winter is by boat. Any old boat will not do. Although we are well sheltered from the prevailing south-westerly, the occasional north-easterly can raise quite a swell around the mouth of Loch Urnabhaigh. A fast boat would not be suitable, which is why I'm going for a sturdy traditional clinker-built job. This will mean getting up out of bed very early in the morning, but what does that matter as long as our women are protected from the perils of the road.

I see exactly what I want advertised in Ranish this week, with creels and all. Unless someone beats me to it, that is the boat for me. I'm not sure what a PRM box and 23.6 VCU means, but I think it would carry a few fat nurses. It promises to be a very interesting winter, for we could have some fun on these voyages.

Another very good reason to opt for a sea-going vessel is that I am pretty fed up with cars. A spot of bother with the MOT – actually, quite a few spots – left me as sick as the proverbial parrot last week (why parrot, I wonder), not to mention a few pennies down. Once again I had reason to be grateful I married into money, but it is not without limit.

People who know tell me the 'test' is going to become much stricter in the near future. Very soon we will reach the stage where all cars over three years of age will have to be sent to Barra. In some ways the folk down there are very lucky. Not only can they whistle on a Sunday, they don't need an MOT. In other ways that matter a lot more, they are, of course, not so fortunate. May the Protestant Angels of St Peter look down on them with compassion.

In the short term, while waiting for the boat, I'm afraid one must have a car of some sorts. So, the search must go on.

There can be nothing on this earth more depressing than a read through used car adverts. Yet, as I mentioned a couple of weeks ago, there are a few laughs to be had with the Glasgow folk. The smart boys down there – you know, the ones who say 'I can do that one for two nen nen fev' – must have all gone to the same school.

The best one I've come across recently said: 'Rover 820, great condition. Lucrative car.' I puzzled over this one for some time but cannot begin to imagine what he meant, unless maybe it was stolen. Another good one was for some fancy class of Toyota. 'Supra. What a looker; what will your neighbours think?' I can hear quite clearly what my neighbours would think. Doilidh Cluaisean would say: 'That guy's off his head; bad enough when he got the goat.'

My search has taken me to some strange places, but I fear it will eventually end on the West Side of Lewis. On the East side our only garage is a rather high-class establishment and out of my range. Hence my journey this very day to see what Dennis has on offer. If not Dennis, perhaps Sgadan or some other Siarach master of the banger.

We on the East Coast have often wondered what it is with these guys in the West and how so many of them came to be interested in old metal. It could very well be that they were originally a wandering tribe of Gypsies. In the days before the old banger they very likely went around mending pots and pans and stealing hens.

They provided a very useful service then and they still do. It doesn't matter that the front half of a car doesn't match the back end; the important thing is the price. And welding, they say, is stronger than the original steel. Without further delay I must go now and see if there is a rust-coloured Escort van to be found in Bragar. Age doesn't matter because it only has to last until I get the boat.

I worry about going amongst the Siarachs on my own, which is why I make it quite clear where I am going. If I'm not back next week you will know where to find my parts.

4 AUGUST 95

In another paper earlier this week, while writing about the new boat, the *Isle of Lewis*, I regret I let emotion flood the decks. Grown men should not be ashamed to cry but I'm afraid my sentimental attachment to the old manifested itself in extreme bitterness towards the new. My only excuse is that we are all poorly equipped to deal with grief.

When I learned they were about to take the *Suilven* away I was distraught to say the least. The natural reaction was to lash out against the usurper. Of course, there is nothing wrong with the *Isle of Lewis*, as long as she has the right crew, for the crew makes the boat.

Compare my situation with a man who has taken on a second younger wife. For whatever reason, he has sacked the old bird, yet he finds the second doesn't match the first in the kitchen – never mind her performance in heavy seas. Very often he doesn't give her a chance to prove herself. Such was the case with myself and the *Isle of Lewis*. I lashed out in my grief without having given the 'new one' a fair trial.

For 20 years or so the *Suilven* has been like a wife to me. Most of that time she was very good, but when she was bad she was very bad. In the kitchen/galley department her attitude was 'You can take it or leave it, for as like as not, it is going over the side anyway', yet most of the time she got us there and back.

Last week Torcuil said she was not at all loved. I have to disagree with him this time. Torcuil is young and not long enough married to understand that love is not all passion; an affair that has lasted as long as mine and the *Suilven*'s is based on an understanding that goes deeper than the keel. She was . . . dash it all . . . I must not weep . . . she was more than a wife. She was like a mother to me. And now they tell me she is going to New Zealand.

There is some consolation in the knowledge that she is destined for service in the colonies and not doomed to the knackers' yard, but nevertheless it is a terrible wrench. What is to become of old hands like Cromarty, who could turn his hand to the soup when Roddy-who-called-him-a-cook was on leave? And don't let us forget Ùisdean the Skipper, who turned back for my wife's handbag. His likes will never be here again.

Perhaps all these guys are looking forward to a new life in New Zealand, but I wonder and worry, how are they going to get there?

New Zealand is a long way away and in between us there is an awful lot of turbulent water. New Zealand is not Ullapool, and the raging oceans of the southern hemisphere are not at all like the gentle eddies that surround the Summer Isles. It is all very well saying she is going to New Zealand, but how, may we who cared for her ask, is she going to get there? Short of dismantling her and sending the bits on a 747, I see no obvious answer to this problem.

Still we must assume she has been sold cash on delivery and we have a duty to deliver her, one way or another. My friend the Barvas Navigator is in semi-retirement but is still available for consultation. He thinks the voyage is impossible and said the mission reminded him of the time we set out to tow fish cages to South Uist. I had to remind him that the South Uist mission was accomplished against terrible odds and against the advice of consultants (who jumped ship in Harris). Give us men and skippers with the drive of Angus MacMillan and New Zealand can be reached, even if it takes the rest of this century.

Success will depend on meticulous planning. I'm afraid Archie's idea of taking the entire complement of Lewis sheep for ballast – later to be unloaded for the poor people of Bosnia – is not on. We may have to wait in the shelter of Ireland for many a long day for a weather window to cross the Bay of Biscay. Biscay is unavoidable whichever canal we set a course for, and the sheep would starve faster than we could eat them even with old stalwarts like Gandy the Chief Steward on board.

Even at this early stage of the expedition the would-be crew are not at one. Some suggest we should head west through the equatorial Atlantic doldrums and through the Panama Canal, but then we are faced with the endless rolling Pacific where spare parts for the old engine are few and very far between (remember how it seldom lasted the half-mile between No 1 and the lighthouse without a new elastic band).

The relative quiet of the Med and the Suez Canal is probably the only realistic route. Yet even with the use of makeshift sails I can foresee that '96 would be quite old before we saw Port Said. If we should make it down to the Horn of Africa and aimed to pass south of the Maldives with Jakarta as our first port of call, I can see more than Cromarty threatening to mutiny in early 1997. The alternative of hugging the southern coast of the Asian continent and letting the North-westerly monsoon drive us down from Madras towards Sumatra would leave us at the mercy of pirates, who would no doubt take advantage when we lowered sails on the Sabbath (we have to assume that by this time the engine was mere ballast).

If, against all odds, in the summer of '98 we have left the south coast of Java, we will meet such a raging sea as the Ullapool boys have never seen. Any further south-east and we have dropped off the map of my personal experience. I suspect the crew would be tempted to jump ship at Bali and spend the rest of their days in grass skirts chewing beetlenut.

Torcuil said something last week about the *Suilven* heading for the quieter waters of New Zealand. Quieter these waters might be – I wouldn't know – but I sincerely hope someone was pulling his leg and mine, otherwise we may have genuine reason to grieve. New Zealand, did you say? We are surrounded by humorous rogues who will tell you anything.

FRIDAY, 11 AUGUST 1995

LITERALLY SPEAKING

Between myself and yourself the red lights have put the fear of my life on me. I was making my way in, from the outside of the town, with an idea in mind I would carry on down towards South Beach where I usually park if Matilda the traffic warden lets me. I was going at the red bullet of my life. All of a sudden the car before me pulled up as if she had reached the end of her tether.

It wasn't long after that until people coming down the hill from Matheson Road stopped also, and before you could blink an eye every man jack was stopped and out of the car taking a great interest in what was going on ahead. And little wonder.

For, as Colin MacIver the man who is highest at Lewis Offshore said, I have been coming down that very same road for 40 years and light red nor green never came into it until this day. With the confusion that was in everything, I put her into reverse and went back to the place I came from in the hope I would make better progress down the other side where there were no lights of any colour at all. A poor day has fallen on us all to be sure. He is one dozy Hebridean, that one.

A cailleach from Shabost, who only comes into Murdo MacLean's to buy a corset before every Communion, has been at halt at Mitchell's

Garage since last Thursday and refuses to take a step this way or that until the lights stop flashing. Who can blame her. It is the idiot in the Council who never ever heard of a filter that is the cause of everything that's in it. Because of this man every other man who only wanted to go to Woolies now has to wait until the people going to Point get there ahead of them. The poor people of Back aren't in it at all because they are still stuck at the roundabout that was sprung on them so heartlessly in 1985.

Co-dhiù, as I said, I am trying to make my way into the town on a Thursday morning in the new car I bought from the Pooka for a very extraordinary price, but I cannot get past the lights because I am so dozy, not to come on colour blindness. This is neither here nor there but had I not been colour blind and dyslexic I would have been the master mariner the Barvas Navigator is today.

But never mind about that, I have come round the roundabout, yet I cannot get any further ahead with my journey because there is a stretch of cars as far as the eye can see and further. It is a very analytic language, the Gaelic, when you come to think of it, and that is a part of the problem. It makes people very polite and considerate even when they can tell red from green.

Anyway, to pass the time, I came out of the car and left it on my two feet, putting one in front of the other up the place where every one was at stop. And do you know what I'm going to tell you: the man at the front holding us back was not the Shabost cailleach at all at all but a man from the *Glasgow Herald* called Simpson Cameron or Cameron Simpson. It doesn't matter what you call these Glasgow boys without a Christian name, for they will always answer to Jimmy.

'Hey, Jimmy,' I yelled in what they think is English. 'What is going ahead here anyway?'

'A good story,' said he. The poor boy thought the men and women at the wheel-drive were puzzled by the traffic lights. If he had taken a step back or two, he would have seen they were at a different game altogether. They were at the game of Jess. Ever since they discovered the Lewis Jessmen and took them away to the British Museum, the native tribes had lost interest, thinking the game was not for them but for other quick-thinking boys like Jimmy Cameron Simpson.

However, suddenly out of the blue heavens above, the masters came to the town of Stornoway to put their brains on display.

Next to golf, cricket, rugby and watching paint dry, the Jess must be the most boring game ever invented by the Indians. The Indians, we are understanding now, invented Algebra, which is why I am so determined to beat Vishu at something. My chances have never been better now that he is held up at the traffic lights and will be penalised two strokes for every minute he cannot tell red from green. A typically dozy Hebridean.

Sorry, I seem to have made a long diversion, but that is the way we are. Coming back from where I had gone forward I nosed into every car that was stopped and sure enough they had the Jessboards out and playing between the two front seats of every Volvo. The Jess seems to have got a terrible grip on the boys ever since the masters came to Town.

For the boys of Stornoway, like Bronco and Kelso, it is very difficult to put a measure on the importance of the names who came to Town to play Jess. It is more or less as if Jack Nicklaus, Tom Watson and Daley had fallen into one's pub for a pint. If that doesn't shake them out of their torpidity, I don't know what will. *(Torpidity – I'm not sure if I have the right English for that, but look up Loath for him, Bronco, in Dwelly's.)*

Now, where were we? Where else but trying, in our dozy way, to get past Mitchell's Garash. I don't think I've spelled Garash properly but I'm chust trying to fall in with Mainland Folk's singular attempt at a foreign language. Don't put an accent on the second 'a', for that may confuse them and drive them back to garage. Very easily confused are the people who have only Beurla.

On my way back from where I have been, it was easy to see that things were not as they should. When the lights turned to green nobody moved. The cailleach from Shabost wound down her window, stuck out her head and shouted in the direction of Matheson Road: 'Go on yourself, you're older.' Good manners again, but that is the cause of the traffic snarl-up. Their likes will never be here again.

FRIDAY, 18 AUGUST 1995

This morning I caught the reflection of my own face in the shaving mirror and it occurred to me something was amiss. Accustomed as I am to the steady, steel-blue gaze that reassures me I am in command of the Universe, I was disturbed to be confronted with two haunted red-rimmed eyes that betrayed uncertainty and emotion.

Slowly, the dreadful realisation dawned. I have drunk the dowry, and all that remains of my useful working life is to give my eldest child away to a Rangers supporter from Dunblane. Earlier in the week I had hoped for an invitation to the stag night, but apparently the father of the bride is not welcome at these hooleys. There was nothing for it but to pawn the dowry and console myself with the most destructive of medicines available to the lonely and abandoned – the bottle of Grouse.

In a matter of very few hours now I have to hand the child over to a Lowlander, without Gaelic, who happens to be a Rangers supporter. Too often have I asked the Saints to look down on me with compassion, so I guess that is too late.

What should I do at the stroke of noon, when the padre asks if anyone has any objection? Has objection ever been voiced from so near the pulpit? Will I be able to hold my tongue and let my child be led down the road to Ibrox? Probably I will, because herself has bought an 'outfit' and to cancel now would be too costly. Money has always weighed more than faith.

Anyway, we are far too busy this week to worry about the future consequences of a mixed marriage. Herself has varnished everything in North Lochs that doesn't move, and even things that don't move a lot have a splash of fresh paint about their person. I guessed when Geordie Macarthur was hired to do the ceiling, at the costliest rate this side of Las Vegas, there was more spending than mere Communion. I was led to believe she was going forward herself: only these several months later did I learn what it was all about.

Naturally, the garden has to look good for the daughter's future mother-in-law. I missed a day's sailing with Archie over the cutting of grass that was doing no harm to anyone. I don't mind that too much because I have worked hard over the years to give her a nice garden. Unfortunately, we are not at one when it comes to colour.

'Forty shades of green' has always been my ambition, although I don't mind a little primrose or yellow when the yellow's on the broom, but anything too gaudy reminds me of wrinkly old colonial women. Blue, in particular, is an abomination in the eyes of God and anyone else with taste.

We had more or less confined her flirtation with blue to a few shrubs behind the shed where only the dog and a few traditionals go to pee late at night. No one would notice. Everything in the garden looked fine for the sacrifice of the daughter. Lo and behold, didn't we wake up yesterday morning to an apparition that defies description. Murdie next door had taken a notion to brighten up our end of the village for the wedding.

Now, when Murdie takes a notion, as old patrons of the Park Bar can testify, anything can happen. When he first painted his weaving shed pink, we put it down to a particularly bad dose of New Year. In any case, pink rusts quite nicely and very quickly, so that very soon the shed blended in fairly well with my scheme of browns and greens. In no time at all it was possible to look over towards Cromore and not notice the pink.

I had half a leg into my trousers the other morning when Maggie drew the curtains and called me to the window. She sounded so alarmed I thought perhaps the Church of Scotland minister was naked in *his* garden, but it was only Murdie at it again.

'At it' are the two most devastating short words in the English language. Usually they are followed by 'again', and all too often they need no qualifier. Your man is at houghmagandie or at the drink. Sadly, in Murdie's case it means he's been painting.

The colour he chose this time would be fine on the top of a distant hill because it would be unnoticeable against a clear sky when the sun is high. Looking down, or even across, at a sky blue is painful in the extreme.

Yet I am grateful, for it will give shy strangers something to talk about when their glasses are low. The particular shade of blue Murdie has chosen is not without a drip of history. Unless you've been to Turkey, it is difficult to visualise the striking blue blueness of this blue.

Maggie, who is often wide awake when we travel abroad, asked on a tour to Ephesus what the odd blue door on farm cottages meant. The simple answer was that members of that household had saved enough, and this was their way of showing it, to have sent one of the family on a pilgrimage to Mecca.

All these years, I thought Murdie's only pilgrimage had been to Copland Road, but it seems I may have underestimated his deep commitment to spiritual matters. Or could he already have fermented some sinister conspiracy to do a deal with the Rangers supporter who will one day inherit my croft?

Let us not dwell on my paranoia, for we must get on with the speech I must make as a father. Never before, at whatever occasion, have I attempted to make a joke. 'Please do not attempt it,' pleaded Maggie. 'You will forget the punchline.'

Nevertheless, let me try this one out, I said, because I had been reading Milan Kundera. In Prague, it seems they have a joke against the English that goes: 'English Lord, to his Lady on the morning after the wedding: "I do hope you're pregnant, my dear. I shouldn't want to go through these ridiculous motions again".'

She looked at me, unsmiling, with the mixture of pity and hatred normally reserved for elderly senile relatives. 'The Reverend Alasdair Macfarlane told that one in 1932 and now you tell me it's reached Prague.'

She is probably right. I will leave the jokes to the best man and go back to the Grouse.

FRIDAY, 25 AUGUST 1995

A few of the boys gathered outside my place of work yesterday to admire the new car I bought from the Pooka at MacRae and Dick's, and, to tell the truth, they were not terribly impressed. When I say 'new' car, I mean new to me. The registration book looks like something out of the Old Testament without the 'begats'.

But I don't care much how many people owned it before me, although naturally one cannot help wondering why they all got rid of it so quickly. Life is too short to worry about these things and there is nothing else that costs so much that has such a short life as a car.

Before the Pooka let me loose on the road, he showed me how to double de-clutch – or is it de-cludge? I am not very knowledgeable about mechanical things. When I mentioned this to the boys they exchanged meaningful glances and suppressed smirks that didn't go entirely unnoticed. 'It shouldn't be necessary in 1995,' said one expert, 'to double de-clutch; that went out with the Baby Austin. You'll probably find the syncromesh is gone.'

Later on in the day, when I was lying back on the psychiatrist's couch unloading my burden, the man I pay seventy pounds an hour to listen to me came to the surprisingly quick conclusion that I am one of life's victims and that I probably thrive on my mental disability. 'Why else,' he said, 'would you deliberately go to the Pooka for a car when you know his reputation.'

I confessed then I hadn't actually been dealing 'head to head' with the Pooka but with his second-in-command, Alex, who happens to be a missionary's son and an old friend from school. 'You are in worse shape than I thought,' said Dr Clarke. 'No sane person would have anything to do with a missionary, let alone the son of one of them who has probably no scruples at all.'

I felt terribly depressed leaving the shed where your man does his private 'homers' at the cheap rate, but I am much too busy to worry about cars this week. I had to give my eldest child away to a Lowlander with no Gaelic who also happens to be a Rangers supporter. Is it any wonder I find myself on the couch?

The Rangers part is not of great importance, for after all what is faith compared with hard cash, but language and the lack of the main major tool of argument is something I cannot handle. My own wee Partick wife, who naturally had no control over her early upbringing, was only half a person when I rescued her from the tenements. In darkest Africa she taught herself to read and write the Gaelic language while I was learning Bemba, and now she feels she has completed herself and it shows in the self-confidence that oozes through when she has to talk to other medical people who have only the Latin.

But to get back to the child I had to give 'away': I worry about the crisis that will inevitably occur in later life. No matter how well-suited the couple, and nothing makes two people more compatible than plenty of money, there will nevertheless be fierce disagreements. If they happen to be thinking people, these disagreements will have to be thrashed out in some language that is common to both.

Milan Kundera, Kafka, Mary Beith and Jaroslav Hasek – all Celtic cousins – would have me believe you have to belong to Prague before you can begin to express feeling. Poor fools. Unless you have the Gaelic, you might as well be deaf and dumb.

In the course of the average lifespan a man and wife will fall out over many things, but given the right common language they will fall back in again. But only if they choose the right words. On a romantic night out in Paris, in the Notre Dame Cafe, looking over at the scaffolding that has been holding the famous church up for many years, the waiter brings you two coffees and two Cointreau and asks you for ten pounds. This is fine if you're very young, but if you have been married for a quarter of a century economy outweighs romance. You start to argue, but it is impossible to deal with the French, who have no Gaelic. I mention the French experience merely to emphasise the dangers of mixing with people who haven't got the language.

Naturally, I didn't mention any of this on the daughter's big day. What to say was a tough question. It is always easy for a best man, who can make jokes, but a bride's father should have some words of wisdom. I didn't feel old enough to be a bride's father, although the bride, as a child, used to ask me: 'What were things like in the old days, Da?' If I had tried to tell people without Gaelic what things were like in the old days, they wouldn't believe.

Still, Gaelic or no Gaelic, I like the boy who is one day going to inherit my estate. I notice he has mastered the art of listening to MacKinnon women. For 90 per cent of the time he seems totally deaf, yet he is alert for the 10 per cent during which they may require an answer.

And he has his priorities right. On the day after the wedding he wanted us to play golf. I told him I thought this was ridiculous and on the first day of married life his duty was to be by his wife's side. The second day is a different matter.

Your man the Gollan Uigeach did us proud. Despite his lack of Gaelic he can cook and knows his way about booze. For a traditional wedding there was surprisingly little fighting – only the Paisley cousins, who don't feel they have enjoyed themselves unless they waken up with black eyes. It was as well I employed the Barney Blues Brothers as chuckerouts, but goodness knows what the gentle folk of Dunblane made of it all.

For some reason I feel all the better for having gone to church and I think I'll make a habit of it. I particularly liked the idea of the Biblical instruction that the wife should submit to the master. I had forgotten that one and so evidently had my wife. I will remind her every day until the next wedding.

FRIDAY, 1ST SEPTEMBER 1995

Picture, if you can, peat-cutting day in North Lochs in the spring of 1946. The men who survived are more than happy to be back at spade and *tairsgear*. Their women are preparing food for the day, but there is a scarcity of delicacies fit for heroes.

Rationing was its tightest and meat in particular was in short supply. We can easily imagine the men in the Kennedy household, who were all nearly seven feet tall, and their neighbours Tormod Mòr, Oididh and Aonghas Man, thinking how much better a day it would be for a slice of beef.

John Angus a' Cheanadaich, according to his wife Màiri Anna, was hardly ready for concentrated protein, or for hard labour. She thought it wise to take him away to Callanish for the day. By way of consolation she left those at the peat a tin of corned beef.

This was no ordinary tin of corned beef. It was Màiri Anna's salvation. A symbol of self-denial that had served its purpose. For three years that same five-pound tin of corned beef had helped her retain her sanity. Pol's wife made a huge pie out of the contents of that historic can, and Màiri Anna never saw it being eaten.

After Pearl Harbour the British contingent in Shanghai knew it was only a matter of days until their already uncomfortable situation became much worse. Màiri Anna spoke last week, in this paper, of the irony of being kept alive by the Jews who had fled Europe, who bought the trinkets for a pittance, that allowed them the money to buy food: but she never got round to the tin of corned beef.

Calum Morrison, who had a hard time later, presented the tin on the night before he was taken away to an adjacent camp and Màiri Anna nursed it in the desperate years. With two young children and a sick husband, the temptation to open the tin was often hard to resist (to quote what must be the understatement of all time), yet she didn't. She was always aware that things could get worse.

So the tin of corned beef was still intact at liberation and survived miraculously until peat-cutting day in that spring of '46.

I have been trusted with Mairi Anna's notes, although she knows I am a sharer and an exhibitionist. Perhaps 'The Spring of '46' should be the title of the film – the first powerful Gaelic movie – we plan to make of her adventure that started in the Twenties. Who knows? Of time there is no shortage.

On the other hand, do people who have never lived any kind of life deserve to know?

The Stornoway Communions have once again come to an end and we are pleased to report there were hardly any disturbances. A police spokesman said the crowds dispersed in as peaceful a manner as you could wish for. 'It was no worse than any Mod,' he said.

This was no mean achievement when you come to consider the crowds that gathered in the Narrows, yea, even on a Saturday night so close to the Sabbath. Despite the vengeful tone of ye Old Testament text, there was scarcely an eye taken nor a nose bloodied.

'This proves my point,' said a youthful and progressive Elder who had left the church for the good life. 'That a heavy hand is not called for at these raves. Let those who call for adherents to be chained up on Saturdays be assured such extreme measures are not necessary.'

'Human existence,' he went on, 'being an hallucination containing in itself the secondary hallucinations of day and night (the latter an insanitary condition of the atmosphere due to accretions of black air), it ill becomes a man of sense to be concerned at the illusory approach of the supreme hallucination known as death.'

We see here that our man had got the philosophy of Marcus Aurelius, De Selby and Masonic Magic all mixed up. Nevertheless, he makes a good point. All men and sheep should be left free to roam the range, unfenced, no matter how fast or how heavy the traffic.

Still, the search for a cure for grief goes on, and culminates in the locking-up of children's swings. 'But is the invention of a Supreme Architect merely a consequence of man's need for meaning?' asked an ordinary man in one's club (it might have been Hogle). 'Or is it a manifestation of his reluctance to relinquish his lost youth? I mean,' he went on, 'does he grieve for lost loved ones or does he despair at having lost forever the early marks by which he navigated good times?'

'A good point,' said another through the froth. 'But I'll be damned if I see the need to drive nails through children's chutes in the playpark. If that is the best we can do for ritual, give me the Goat's Pen any day.'

An extraordinary meeting was called during which it was agreed that a puzzle of such depth and weight could only be solved by people wiser than ourselves. Much as the drainage problem was cured through the hiring of consultants from the Mainland, so the big question of God's private attitude to locked gates could only be gleaned by insights into the minds of men like Young John MacLeod and Cardinal Winning.

The Captain suggested that instead of music nights with Peggy Sue, Eddie Cochrane and similar Satan's children of the Fifties we should invite the aforementioned to lead us in debate.

We look forward to an interesting and uplifting winter league. If any mysteries are solved I hope and pray the first will be what Dr Taylor's four no-trumps meant.

FRIDAY, 8 SEPTEMBER 1995

There is no such thing as plain sailing. In the same way as any realistic person never allows for the perfect shot in golf, the sailor never expects the ideal wind, yet sometimes they both happen.

When we left Loch Eynort in South Uist at 2300 last Friday, my Skipper Archie made several complicated calculations involving wind, tide and, for all I know, the curvature of the earth. 'Given the prevailing conditions – little or no wind – we should be approaching MacLeod's Maidens at dawn. Set a course of 276,' he said, before he tied me to the tiller and disappeared down below to cuddle his wife.

Even with my limited knowledge of the planet I thought 276 a strange course to set if you're going east, but then I remembered that the Skipper used to be a weather man and thinks in reciprocals. He was trying to make things easy for me.

I defy anybody under 80 to steer a boat by a rough compass at the stern. Two cables out of Loch Eynort I suspected I was meandering more than a little. It seemed a sensible idea to fix on a star by the mainmast and stick to it. Such a night few people have been privileged to enjoy. The sliver of moon had sunk below the horizon and the Milky Way never seemed so milky. Unfortunately, as one became accustomed to the dark, a great many stars I had never seen before began to appear, and soon I became uncertain of the one I had chosen to follow.

Now and again I risked a quick flash of the torch on the compass but I soon gave that up because every time I created a little artificial light I couldn't see anything at all for five minutes – not even the Milky Way.

About five cables from the mouth of Eynort, before the Huisnish light was fully visible, a slight north-westerly wind, not mentioned on the forecast, arose and drove us along at a steady pace. By this time the night was Bible-black and getting blacker. Several dolphins came to keep me company at the stern, so close and friendly I would have called the two down below, but I was afraid they might still be playing at young love.

Temporarily distracted by the dolphins, I forgot my star for a minute or two. When I started to search for it, not only was it gone for good, so also was the entire celestial dome. A thick layer of stratocumulus had spread in with the westerly wind, darkening the night that was already darker than any you have ever seen or could imagine. Not only that, the favourable westerly wind had become too friendly altogether and was pushing us along at seven knots instead of the three planned for by the Skipper.

Very soon though, out in the open, I had Neist Point Light in sight and another bright light to the south-east. If I aimed somewhere in between, I reasoned, although a poor mathematician, I would eventually find Skye. There was a third bright steady light slightly south of east and getting brighter. This one was no help at all, for it soon became three lights. A white one on the masthead, and lower down at the base of the triangle two more lights, one green and the other red.

The alarming aspect of the red and green was that they seemed to remain a steady fixed distance apart, which could only mean the vessel was bearing directly down on me. From the deep recesses of the mind an instruction from the distant past told me to shine a light on the white sail. In the empty pitch-black ocean, this must have put the fear of God into the incoming vessel, for suddenly I could only see the red light.

Preoccupied with impending collision, I had momentarily lost my bearing. We could be slightly further north than planned and heading for the treacherous Dubh Sgeir, or we could be further south and heading for some islands marked on the Skipper's chart. A daylight examination of the chart showed the islands to be coffee stains but I wasn't to know that at the moment that mattered.

In the meantime it was obvious we were sailing faster than ever and the black night had attained a depth of blackness unimagined even by Welsh poets. The famous Skyline of Skye, itself black enough at any time of the day, began to appear in my imagination as clear as a picture by Tommy Mackenzie. Although I'm not a nervous person *(What? – Ed)*, I decided to call the Skipper – second honeymoon or no.

He reluctantly agreed to get an accurate fix on our position with a shaky hand-held compass and after some time at work with dividers he made the contemptuous announcement we were still 10 miles west of Skye. This is where we are, he said, stabbing at the chart, give or take half a mile, before disappearing once again into the lee of bum island.

When he put the light out after his calculations, the inky blackness of the night was like the deepest valley of hell itself. The coastline of Skye began to manifest itself on all sides and behind. On a direct course to MacLeod's Maidens the Skipper's 'give or take half a mile' was weighing heavily on my mind. I desperately wanted to see the Maidens but not through the hull of the boat. I could only conclude the presence of your man's wife on board had blunted his normal sense of safety.

Lo and behold, out of the darkest hour of the black night, a light appeared that could only be some bodach's house in Portnalong. The power of Protestant prayer had directed me to the correct spot – halfway between the Dubh Sgeir and the coffee stains.

At half past two in the morning the Portnalong bodach's visitor must have left and the old fellow put the light out, leaving me once again at the mercy of a hostile coast. Swallowing my pride and forcing the Skipper to abandon his pride and his carnal gymnastics, I made him turn round and head out into the open ocean where it was safe to wait until the dawn.

When the first glow of the morning sun illuminated MacLeod's Maidens I wished I'd had a camera, but I didn't, so I must try to describe them. *(Then you must do it next week, for space must be left for other people's stuff: Ed.)*

FRIDAY, 15 SEPTEMBER 1995

**EACHAINN'S NOTES FOR THE LAST VIEW FROM NORTH
LOCHS WERE COMPLETED BY ARCHIE MACDONALD,
HIS SKIPPER ON HIS FINAL VOYAGE...**

Last week I was about to describe our arrival at MacLeod's Maidens
when time and space ran out and I was cut down in full flow.

But that was last week on this brief voyage and those of us still aboard
must make the best we can. The Maidens are a group of statuesque rock
pinnacles guarding the north entrance to Loch Bracadale. Evocative of as
many a theme as the mind can conjure up, they just stand there and endure,
cold and aloof as death itself. Whoever called them maidens needs a shrink.

The Skipper's wife is frying sausages down below and soon we're
hooked into the mud below Carbost Inn. The armada of Uist yachts
around us is rousing itself as the crews get ready for the distillery tour. We
take to our bunks and the cook heads for the shore to return immediately
saying, 'The tour starts now'. A tuneful snore was one response.

Later, like all good cooks, she brings something back and by nightfall
the whole fleet has entered into the spirit of the location, including George
MacAulay, who had worked his passage over to do some spraying; he
can't be a proper yottie. *Barents*, the Uist jeweller's handcrafted steel sloop,
arrived late with more friends and soon everyone was doing eightsome
reels aboard *Oigh na Seilge*, the fleet's handsome flagship from Lochmaddy.

Next morning, fortunately after breakfast, our cook jumps ship back
to Uist aboard *Barents*. Much later we discover that the bottle of Talisker
went with her.

'We'll sail out,' *ars an Sgiobair*, feeling very superior since the rest
were motoring into the headwind. 'With an engine like ours they would
probably also sail,' *arsa mise*.

At the headland we bear away south and east between the Cuillins of Skye
and Rum, and off Soay the wind dies and our single-cylinder thumper has to
be fired up. The evening shipping forecast finds us still on the wrong side of
Sleat. At Armadale we pick up a mooring in the dark and boil the potatoes

to go with the cooked chicken Angie left instead of the malt. In the hotel an Oriental gentleman was on his way to Ostaig to learn Gaelic. I must remind the Skipper to speak it when he issues orders before it's too late.

We're early off on Monday to catch the tide at Kylerhea and turn back half a mile out when the absent-minded Skipper realises he's left his mooring sling still tied to the buoy. Normally a generous person, he can be oddly possessive about little things. I think he's forgotten how to splice a new one. Throughout the morning we tack against a moderate north-easter, past crabbers and clammers and a heavily-laden Norwegian coaster. Past Gavin Maxwell's old house at Sandaig and the playful otters dodging the rings of whirlpools in Kylerhea's tide rip. Under the ribbon of the bridge (no tolls for yotties below) and into Broadford, well reefed against an increasing force 6 howling down the Inner Sound.

And there we cowered behind the pier for the next day and a half. Copy deadline was met early and in person, and as a reward for this and for not messing up their nice office too much, the esteemed Editor took us out for dinner, which was cut short when a friendly fisherman casually warned us we'd soon be aground if we didn't shift the boat down a bit.

Tuesday and the rain and wind from the north keep us hemmed in for more R and R in Broadford; beachcombing together for a fender lost in the night, buying mince etc to make the dinner (we'd forgotten the leftover half-chicken) and discussing John MacLeod's latest chequered outpourings in one of that day's dailies (of which we bought a few). That boy might make something of himself yet.

In the evening the Skipper lit the Tilley. He said it was to drown out the snoring but I don't believe him. He's getting soft and I don't know how he's going to survive our trip to the Faroes next year, but maybe *Barents* with her big stove will take us if she goes again. I finish Faulkner's 'Sound and Fury' and give it to Archie with instructions to pass it on to the Barra literati. Can't remember now who I got it from, but maybe it will find its own way home.

Wednesday is fine with little wind and we motor north through Caol Rona where a sea eagle overhead is taken as a friendly omen. This is strange because the Skipper is a crofter from Uist and Uist crofters are threatening to shoot these magnificent birds. We remember the leftover chicken and he dishes or rather hands it up for breakfast.

We fly into Uig to a cosy berth beside the *Bonnie Lass,* whose crew also offer us a mooring in Scadabay if we find ourselves there next night. Stepping ashore and here's Mairi's bus arriving and also who should be stranded here but Angie Mhop, Scotland's prime sea-angler. This would be my last night aboard, so I treated everyone to a final big supper ashore. We were down to tins of bully beef on the ship, and earlier in the day while the Skipper was trying to relax the appropriate muscle up in the heaving heads, I had taken the precaution of tossing the mince leftovers to the eagle; and not just for its benefit as a wee change from lamb.

Later in the evening, replete with the delights of Uig, Angie announces that any time we meet the *Sweet Promise* on the high seas he will throw us as many clams as we can eat.

Next day is perfect for sailing – force 3–4 – but too far into the north to make Leurbost. Tarbert is as high as she will point and there will be no more tacking. Off Gaelvore an unusually friendly skua gives us the once-over, then leaves us in peace, and we are into Tarbert by early afternoon, tie up, make a quick phone-call to Maggie and then stretch out on the cockpit seats in the warm sunshine to share a last bottle of red wine. Already we're reminiscing about the pleasures and pains of the past week and looking forward to the next trip.

SOON we hear Smut's bark and climb up the ladder to meet them. 'How do I smell after a week at sea, a ghràidh?' ars esan as they embrace. 'Well, I always said I'd take you as you are,' ars ise, 'except that beard.' And they went away north together and Mairi and I sailed south for Uist.

And that was his last stepping ashore on this voyage. Eachainn died of a sudden heart attack a day and a half later.

Bon voyage, a Charaid.